TumbleWords

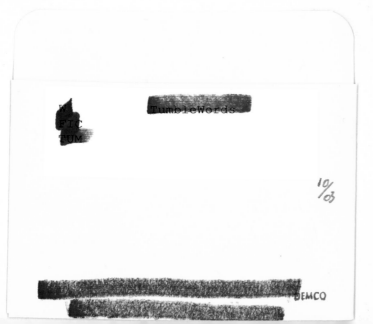

Tumble

WESTERN LITERATURE SERIES

TumbleWords

WRITERS READING THE WEST

EDITED BY WILLIAM L. FOX

FOREWORD BY DONALD MEYER

UNIVERSITY OF NEVADA PRESS

RENO   LAS VEGAS   LONDON

Western Literature Series

A list of books in the series appears at the end of this volume.

The paper used in this book meets the requirements of American National
Standard for Information Sciences — Permanence of Paper for Printed Library
Materials, ANSI Z39.48–1984. Binding materials were selected for strength and
durability.

Library of Congress Cataloging-in-Publication Data

TumbleWords: writers reading the West / edited by William L. Fox;
  foreword by Donald Meyer.
        p.   cm. — (Western literature series)
     "TumbleWords . . . was conceived as a community-based project which
  would bring writers to read their works for local audiences" — P. xv.
     Developed by the Western States Arts Federation (WESTAF) in 1991.
     Includes index.
     ISBN 0–87417–271–3 (alk. paper)
     1. American literature — West (U.S.) 2. West (U.S.) — Literary
  collections.   I. Fox, William L., 1949–   .   II. Western States
  Arts Federation.   III. Series.
  PS561.T86 1995
  810.8'0978 — dc20   95-17115
                                                                          CIP

University of Nevada Press, Reno, Nevada 89557 USA
Copyright © 1995 by University of Nevada Press
All rights reserved
Book and cover design by Erin Kirk New
Printed in the United States of America

9   8   7   6   5   4   3   2   1

This book is dedicated to those writers of the West who constantly do battle with the elements in order to reach their audiences: the weather, the distance, the many languages of the region, and the vagaries of for-profit publishing and public arts patronage.

Contents

Foreword

The writer in the twentieth century has been described as being involved in a solitary discipline sometimes removed from his family, the community in which she lives, the audience he is trying to reach. Living in the interior states of western America (Utah, Wyoming, Idaho, New Mexico, Arizona, Colorado, Nevada, and Montana), which are culturally underserved, and geographically for the most part rural, can be described similarly. Therefore in 1991 it was entirely appropriate for the Western States Arts Federation (WESTAF), the only regional arts organization in the United States to administer a literature program, to develop a project that would touch in real ways both western writers and western audiences.

TumbleWords: Writers Rolling Around the West was conceived as a community-based project that would bring writers to local venues to read their works for local audiences. Developed initially in partnership with the National Endowment for the Arts' State and Regional Program, the project was begun in 1991 with an "underserved community" grant in three states: Idaho, Utah, and Wyoming. In 1993 with additional funds from the Lila Wallace–Reader's Digest Fund, TumbleWords was expanded to include five more WESTAF states: Arizona, Colorado, Montana, Nevada, and New Mexico.

The goals of TumbleWords are to create new audiences for literature; to introduce audiences in traditionally underexposed communities to literature through the presentation of literary readings; to provide opportunities for writers to present their work to audiences in their own states; and to encourage and develop connections between writers and communities within the larger arts community. TumbleWords has met these goals by going into inner-city neighborhoods, small towns, Native American reservations, and communities where thousand-acre ranches are the equivalent of city blocks — and the project has had significant impact.

Both writers and presenters, emerging or experienced, worked together to bring forward vital literature of today's West. In the past year, I submit, WESTAF has built new audiences for literature in profound ways. For proof I have only to point to the letters from troubled teens, from a rancher's wife who for over twenty years had always wanted to write but didn't know how to start until she attended a TumbleWords reading, from kids in an inner-city neighborhood who had never imagined meeting and talking with a living author. It was hoped that this project would lay the groundwork for ongoing literature programming in the western states, and I truly believe we are well on our way to bringing literature to more people, while also honoring the commitment authors have to their work by offering them opportunities to present it.

The achievements of the TumbleWords project have been described as "extraordinary." WESTAF is committed to building on these achievements by working to develop a western presenting network for literature, to increase the audience for literature, to enhance educational opportunities throughout western communities by providing the greatest access possible to these poems, essays, and works of fiction, and to inspire westerners to adopt writing as an exciting and meaningful profession.

WESTAF offers special thanks to Bill Fox for his commitment to this organization and this project, as well as to the University of Nevada Press for its support.

DONALD MEYER, EXECUTIVE DIRECTOR
WESTERN STATES ARTS FEDERATION

Acknowledgments

My association with the Western States Arts Federation has lasted through fifteen years, three executive directors, and numerous staff people. Part of why it has been not only possible, but rewarding to work with a regional arts bureaucracy is that its people have made a lasting commitment to writers and publishers in the West. Bill Jamison, Terry Melton, and Donald Meyer have each dedicated their leadership, as those three executive directors, to creating new avenues of support for literature in our region. Without them TumbleWords would not have been possible. Among the many staff people who have kept literature alive and well through times rich and poor at WESTAF are Cheryl Alters Jamison, Richard Balthazar, Gina Briefs-Elgin, and Sandy Bigley.

Literature Projects Director Robert Sheldon came to WESTAF with a strength of purpose and vision almost unequalled in the history of the organization. His faith that WESTAF could actually increase the role of literature in our communities by involving writers should be an inspiration to public arts agencies across the country. Not only did he shape TumbleWords; he has also been a weekly sounding board as this book has progressed.

TumbleWords is above all else, of course, a "local" program in the sense that the regional organization has worked with state and community partners to help design and implement programs. Each of the participating eight states has had a TumbleWords coordinator and/or state arts agency person who has acted as an administrative bridge between WESTAF and the communities writers have visited. Not only have these coordinators helped make the readings happen; they have also assisted me in tracking down the writers in their states. My thanks to each of them: Tonda Gorton in Arizona, Tom Auer in Colorado, Diane Josephy Peavey in Idaho, Corby Skinner in Montana, Sharon Rosse in Nevada, Dolly Sloan in New Mexico, G. Barnes in Utah, Guy Lebeda in Wyoming, and Mark Preiss, who worked in both Nevada and Utah.

Tom Radko, the director of the University of Nevada Press, cannot be thanked enough for his support, enthusiasm, and valuable advice. Neither can my wife, Beth Bradley Fox, the director of programs and service at WESTAF. From the two of them I seem to have inherited more wisdom and kindness than a writer could expect out of life.

The TumbleWords Communities

Introduction

Editing a book on the basis of geography is a difficult idea.

For one thing, writers tend to follow ideas in their work, regardless of artificial boundaries, whether they're between different media or states. You can — and will — find avant-garde poets in Reno whose work looks like it belongs in New York City; there are natural history essayists in New York who write as if they live in Bozeman. And oftentimes those people did, in fact, move from the intermountain West to New York, and vice versa, following teaching jobs, or spouses, or the notion that their personal or aesthetic turf would be greener on the other side of the Continental Divide. You're on easier ground if you edit around a shared concern, such as the environment, or if you trace a factual development, such as playwriting in the West in the last twenty years.

In the Intermountain West — roughly that region between the western coastal states and the Great Plains — this editorial difficulty is compounded by the lack of a singular shared history. Most of us moved here from somewhere else, from California to Montana, or from Utah to New Mexico, not to mention from Boston to Las Vegas. None of our cities and precious few of our towns have stayed anywhere near close to the same during the last century, or two decades, or even ten years. There are remnants of a shared culture preserved with difficulty here and there, mostly Native American and Hispanic ones, but the majority of us in the region have had our cultural roots so hybridized that we're constantly reinventing ourselves, our society, even our use of English.

Nor do our states even look remotely the same. Take the overwhelming, shared physical characteristic of the region, the lack of water. Aridity manifests itself here in so many variations that it's not even a single climate. Imagine a drive from the sagebrush drylands of southern Idaho to the salt playas in central Nevada, through the sandstone of Four Corners and into the surrealistic cacti gardens of Arizona and you'll see what I mean. About the only other thing most people would agree these states have in common is distance, a theme that underpins almost every introduction to every anthology about anything western, including this one.

At least since Siberians migrated over the land bridge, distance and access to water have been major governing factors of human survival in the region, as both Spanish and Anglo explorers have pointed out for centuries. The writer Wallace Stegner possessed an historical wisdom and vision large enough to encompass the region within a series of statements so accurate they might almost be mathematical hypotheses. They are compelling bedrock observations and, as such, are relevant to the literature of the region, no matter who wrote it or when: from N. Scott Momaday to William Kittredge, Edward Abbey to Terry Tempest Williams, Owen Wister to Barbara Kingsolver. As Stegner notes early on in his seminal book *The American West as Living Space* (U of Michigan P, 1987),

> The West is defined, that is, by inadequate rainfall, which means a general deficiency of water. . . . The West that we are talking about comprises a dry core of eight public lands states — Arizona, Colorado, Idaho, Montana, Nevada, New Mexico, Utah, and Wyoming. . . . Aridity, and aridity alone, makes the various Wests one.

After describing how that central fact governs "the look and location of western towns, the empty spaces that separate them," he goes on to state a corollary:

> In the West it is impossible to be unconscious of or indifferent to space. At every city's edge it confronts us as federal lands kept open by aridity and the custodial bureaus; out in the boondocks it engulfs us.

My paraphrase of this is that our part of the country has had distance defined for us by its physical size and intensity. For instance, communities might be spaced an hour apart by car in the Great Basin because that's how often water occurs there. In some parts of the region, mountains rise and fall so rapidly, so steeply, that valley communities still have trouble receiving broadcast signals. One is not only cut off from vehicle traffic by winter snows but blocked from hearing the news by a mountain shadow. It's this combination of factors defining distance that has kept us, the audiences of the Intermountain West, from experiencing the arts as much as we might like. Shortening these distances was the reason why the Western States Arts Federation (WESTAF) was created almost thirty years ago — and it's the reason for TumbleWords. (It's ironic, though entirely logical, that the meeting of the West's state arts agency directors, which resulted in the chartering of WESTAF in 1974, was held in conjunction with a gathering of their states' governors to discuss the management of water issues on a regional basis. Even the West's arts bureaucracy owes some of its nature to aridity!)

Over 150 years ago there was an opera scene in Virginia City, Nevada, to rival that of San Francisco, a city that was built with the silver extracted from underneath that mining camp in the western Nevada mountains. How remarkable that in the most desolate part of all the country, international opera stars were singing. The reasons were simple: distance and money. To get to San Francisco before the advent of trains, people travelled by stagecoach, and Virginia City was a stop along the way. Performers made a living by picking up gigs wherever town theaters could afford them en route. There was enough money — and newly found civic pride — for San Franciscan theaters to hire famous performers to entertain and enlighten the newly rich. And there was likewise enough money and pride in Virginia City for the citizens to build an opera house and pay performers to stop for a night and sing.

Today as one drives through the remnants of mining camps in the West, precious few of them surviving as viable towns, one finds old opera houses, often restored as tourist attractions, and sometimes still functioning as performing arts spaces. They're a cultural parallel to the pony express stations, relay points for the arts as they propagated across the West to reach the coast. But just as the mining camps had their cycles of boom and bust, so too did arts programs throughout the region. As the gold and silver money faded so did the ability of many towns to afford the arts. Only money could overcome the costs of travelling great distances — money available only on the coast, or fitfully in the larger interior towns where there were new land grant universities.

Imagine, if you will, the difference for a performer on tour even today. Let's say you're a musician in the New England region booked for five performances in as many nights and towns; it's a trip you can undertake by car, driving leisurely from city to city with plenty of time for sightseeing, lunch, a nap before curtain. In some states it's only fifty miles by freeway from one major venue to another. The same tour in the Intermountain West couldn't be done easily in five days, much less by car; venues run up to four hundred miles apart. It means paying for airplane fares and extra days on the road. The fare for a flight from New York to Los Angeles in 1994 was $250; the fare from Flagstaff, Arizona, to Cheyenne, Wyoming, not an atypical stretch for an artist on tour in the western region, was $678.

It is simply more expensive to move around from audience to audience in the West. The money to help overcome the cost of bridging the distance wasn't often available until public funds were dedicated to that purpose almost thirty years ago with the establishment of the National Endowment for the Arts (NEA) and their partners, the state arts agencies. Even then, the NEA tended to fund mostly tours for big companies performing in big cities (of which the West had fewer than the East), and the states were pretty much limited by law to funding only their own resident artists touring within state boundaries. WESTAF was created by the western state arts agencies in order to overcome distance and circumvent state boundaries, and it started a movement that gave rise to seven regional arts agencies serving all of the United States and its territories. The state arts people figured that, one, they could save money if they could arrange logical tours for artists, tours that followed from town to town along an interstate, for instance; and, two, that a private, regional arts organization wouldn't have to battle with state legislators over funding artists from out of state.

Now what, you may ask, does all this have to do with writers and readers? It's all part of the same picture: the pattern of cultural distribution throughout America. Without getting into the differences between how books, paintings, and operas are produced, distributed, and consumed by audiences, let's just say that authors have had just as hard a time getting around the West as have cellists. If you were interested in seeing a live author — just as you might have been in hearing a live symphony performance or seeing a painting in a museum — and if you lived in the West, especially in a city with less than 250,000 people, you were mostly out of luck.

It's no accident that WESTAF was the first — and remains the only — regional arts organization with a literature program. Distance and money, again. While the NEA and the state arts agencies were helping support tours of the performing and visual arts, their total expenditure of public funds on literature was less than 3 percent of their program budgets (music, for example, took over 50 percent). So even as the various public art agencies were beginning to address the very American problem of cultural distribution across a huge geography, literature was still a stepchild within its own professional community. And that was just the national picture; it was worse in the West, given the exaggerated problems of terrain. As a result, not only did the West have to overcome its own size, like some prodigious child; it didn't even have access to its own voice. Writers in the region couldn't get together, couldn't reach publishers, couldn't get their books reviewed; and audiences couldn't find out who the writers were, couldn't afford to bring them to town, didn't have places for them to read. And there wasn't enough money available from the NEA and the state arts agencies to address the problem. Not even close.

Many people at all levels within the arts community knew something was wrong, but it wasn't until WESTAF hired David Fraher, the young executive director of the Wyoming Arts Council — and a writer who had graduated from the Iowa Writers' Workshop — that things changed. Fraher was contracted in the early 1980s to travel around the western region and talk to writers, editors, publishers, bookstore owners, and state arts agency people to find out exactly what their needs were, and to devise ways WESTAF could help. The result was WESTAF's first, and very successful, literature program, the Western States Book Awards. Its primary purpose, though, was to help the writers and their publishers: to get writers into print with western small presses, to help those presses become more professional and stable, and to draw national media attention to the voices of the West. Now in its tenth year, Western States Book Awards have played an important part in improving the access of writers in our region to national publishers, and in providing technical assistance to publishers in the region, helping ensure their growth and survival.

As valuable as the awards are, however, the needs of most writers and their potential audiences in the West, especially the intermountain ones, have gone largely unmet. You'd have had more luck hearing an award winner read in Minneapolis than in Flagstaff or Cheyenne. When WESTAF hired Robert Sheldon as Literature Projects Director in 1991 that, too, finally began to change. Sheldon had been in the book trade for twenty-three years; a bookseller, distributor, editor, he wasn't an arts administrator but a book person, and he brought a fresh vision of what was needed to connect writers with their audiences throughout the region. While expanding the book awards from a biennial to an annual event, he began at the same time to explore the idea of a regionwide reading program with the states arts agency staff people, with colleagues at WESTAF, and with writers and publishers. What he heard was what he already suspected: if WESTAF really wanted to help literature in the region, highlighting the accomplishments of less than a dozen western writers and publishers every year wouldn't help nearly enough.

All this came to a head in August of 1991 at Sundance, Utah, where WESTAF had convened an "Idea Exchange" for literary professionals from around the region. During two days of intense discussions, a strong consensus developed about the touring of writers in the West. After all, there had been reading circuits, especially for poets, for years in the region, generally from city to city where there were university creative writing programs to host them. And WESTAF had been putting together promotional tours for the winners of the book awards, so why not expand on an existing practice? After further discussions with the WESTAF board and staff, Sheldon proceeded to design a touring program and to seek funding.

In 1992 TumbleWords was launched in three states with a grant from the NEA. Because WESTAF already had its hands full running existing programs, and because, in essence, all arts happen at the local level, the decision was made that each state would have its own TumbleWords coordinator to help select writers and participating communities, to arrange for the writers to meet with community representatives, and to encourage the communities to choose which writers would visit. Each TumbleWords event was thus unique, featuring different writers, towns, venues for readings, and other activities, such as community writing workshops.

TumbleWords, therefore, isn't edited solely according to geography or to showcase the writers who inhabit a politically designated territory. It's a documentation of how writers and communities have connected through the poems, stories, and essays that express the region. It's a core sample of a specific literary stratum, TumbleWords 1992–94, the beginning of what may become the largest literary presenting program in the history of the country.

If this anthology isn't about geography as much as it is about distance and our attempts to overcome it, are there other definitions at work in the selections? Of course. The funds from the NEA had an interesting caveat attached to them, a specialized piece of bureaucratic artspeak designed, in part, to help answer the concerns of Congress that public funding for the arts not be spent exclusively to subsidize attendance at operas by the upper middle class. As usual, the catchword is both genuine and ingenuous: "underserved."

I can recall the reaction of staff people at state arts agencies around the country when the word first surfaced: *Underserved.* People who had never been to an opera? People who could only afford to see ballet once a year? People who couldn't even afford to get to a town where live classical music was available? People who didn't know what an opera was? People who went to opera but never to an art museum? Let's just say that someone, somewhere, was wise enough to select a word that could be continually reinterpreted to meet a variety of needs, and we'll leave it at that. Needless to say, in terms of access to writers, the audiences of the West—whether they're in Austin, Nevada, and on the "loneliest highway in America," or in inner-city Denver — have been underserved. Or, in the words of some, just plain "unserved."

The attachment of that caveat to the NEA funds meant that the state Tumble-Words coordinators tended to favor selecting writers recognized in their states as relating well to audiences, which, in turn, often meant that the writers were already doing community work such as school residencies, or they had received a fellowship grant, or a Governor's Arts Award. The generous grant the following year from the Lila Wallace–Reader's Digest Fund to add five states to the project, while not specifically targeting the "underserved," was predicated on the goal of connecting artists to audiences, and the focus on underserved communities was maintained. You won't find, therefore, much of the avant-garde in this collection, simply because the project seeks to reach and build new audiences, not to puzzle or challenge them.

At a second level, community representatives had a chance to meet the writers, to hear them read samples of their works — to, in effect, audition them. These people chose writers who were likely to be of interest and accessible to the community. And finally, at a third level, the writers themselves selected works to read that new audiences would find meaningful. So in general, a cowboy poet might pick a verse that someone unfamiliar with working cattle could understand, and an urban Chicano poet, verses about pride of heritage.

As a result, this anthology isn't about examining the state of contemporary literature in the West, or attempting to trace the careers of each of the writers. It's a picture of how a partnership of public and private arts agencies is enabling writers to reach out and reconnect local audiences with their own memories and voices. All this history of presenting culture in the West boils down to the words of Kim Barnes in Idaho who, in the statement at the beginning of the Idaho section in this book, claims, "[T]he story of the individual is the story of the family, the community, the tribe."

There were ninety-one writers touring in TumbleWords during the slice of time that's been sampled here, and seventy-two of them were able to send work in response to the invitation to participate in the *TumbleWords* book. Every touring writer who submitted work is in this anthology. I asked each of them for three things: a story or chapter or essay from a prose writer/storyteller, or three to five poems from a poet, from works presented to TumbleWords audiences; a brief biographical sketch (for the "Contributors" section, which you'll find in the back of the book); and any anecdotes they'd care to share about their TumbleWords experiences, which I had hoped might illuminate what the WESTAF project was doing and how it was working. Excerpts from those anecdotes appear at the beginning of each state's section.

The book is organized alphabetically by state, the authors likewise within each state. It was suggested that I consider breaking the book into prose and poetry instead, but there's a trace of continuity, of artistic community, within each state that I thought it valuable to preserve. The Montana writers, for instance, seem to share a concern about weather that their colleagues in Denver tend not to mention; the poets of New Mexico often champion a cultural heritage that their peers in Idaho seldom voice. You can catch both a literal and a figurative example of such a community very clearly among the Utah writers, whether it's Merry Adams and her brother Tom Austin trading quips, as well as stories of their childhood, or from Austin's sense of dramatic vernacular monologue that bears kinship to the almost Homeric scale of comic despair in David Lee's poems. And you can find it between Abelardo "Lalo" Delgado and Richard La Foré, both from Denver, with La Foré referring to himself as "a great fan and friend of the 'papa' of Chicano poetry, Lalo Delgado."

What you will find in common throughout the book is the absolutely abiding concern of the writers not only to express their own stories, but in so doing to pick up the threads of our collective and cumulative intermountain existence and try to weave stories we can all understand. This is no small task in a region that paradoxically defines itself as a place of mind where the residents stubbornly retain the supreme right to the individual voice.

As always, any editing task is based on choices, which are in turn based on often unspoken cultural assumptions. I hope I've made clear that among such assumptions in this anthology are those of the federal, regional, and state public arts agencies in identifying "underserved" audiences, the choices of the state TumbleWords coordinators and the community representatives, the selections made by the writers in what to read and, then, what to send me for consideration — and finally, my own judgments about which pieces most clearly articulated their — our — voices. In choosing to present *TumbleWords* as documentation of a project, rather than yet another "Best of the West" book, I trust that future critics and editors will find the layers of assumption at least instructive. And, as WESTAF seeks to expand its support toward a regionwide literary presenting program touching all our audiences — telling all of our stories — I hope that its roots are re-membered.

WILLIAM L. FOX
SANTA FE, NEW MEXICO

Arizona

READING UNDER BRIDGES

Lake Havasu City, Arizona, is the home of the old London Bridge, brought over stone by stone. The Colorado River was split to run beneath it. Its easternmost span, extending over land, shelters a stage. This was where — at the invitation of Bertha Nyboer of Mohave Community College — I arrived to read in March 1994.

I found a sound man testing a mike, my name and face on posters, and many empty folding chairs. Bertha and her assistant, Stephanie Brewer, explained that our audience was now strolling the waterfront, peering into shops and licking ice-cream cones.

Sauntering under the bridge, they'd be seduced by language, captured by narrative: this was the plan. And they'd sit down to listen — maybe for a minute, maybe for ten. I was, after all, an accident in their afternoon. They'd leave as easily as they came. Freely as the pigeons that descended from the bridge to flutterstrut after hot dog crumbs and shards of potato chip.

So I began. And as I read, people did stop, curious, listening impassively before moving on. Riverfront joggers clopped across my field of vision, heads craned my way to pick up the odd phrase. They didn't slacken their pace. Neither did I.

The Colorado was full of boats, pleasure craft easing by with throbbing exhausts and oily auras. Spotting me, some pilots drew up to the embankment. Who was that gesticulating fellow on the platform, leaning forward so earnestly above a pile of wind-flapped pages?

Across the river, a fat tour boat left its pier with hoots of warning. Families of ducks swam by, quacking hungrily for handouts. On I read, my amplified voice *echoing from the vaulted ceiling. Water lapped on stone. Beyond our tunnel of shade, brilliant sunlight streamed.*

I've read in classrooms, auditoria, in private homes and bookstores, in coffee shops and bars. But bringing words to London Bridge was particularly joyous. Most of my listeners gave me easy licks and sips of attention, as gently as they consumed their cones and Cokes.

And as I offered one thread more to their contentment, we ceremonially assembled the experience of being human. I think the strollers and joggers and boaters felt that literature belonged in that moment of their lives — with the ducks and the blowing candy wrappers — echoing off the stone — in the shape of the old bridge.

JONATHAN PENNER

James Cervantes

Temporary Meaning

Things sit around, decompose, or get thrown out.
This is what I think of the broken hoe
and a blackened orange while neighbors hammer
and grackles drop and stab into the watered lawn.
Now, at this moment, the universe clicks into place,
admits quite openly that all is pointless and gives
temporary meaning to several philosophies.
At what point, I wonder, will it dawn on everyone?
Should I run to the fence and ask, "Have you gotten it yet?"
Instead, I yell: "Your repairs are useless!"
The mindless hammering stops and it occurs to me
that I am the chance generator of a silent wave
that rolls in all directions, sucks everyone
into its undertow and never spits them out.
Or that I'm the last to catch on and the first one
tossed naked onto the long-awaited Mohave beach.
This would explain a sign that says "Psychic Dump."
It would also explain how easily birds
have learned the ring of a cordless phone,
and why every time they sing, I run to answer.

James Cervantes

Signal Deaths

Victor Power

The crow in a graveyard
looks up at me like an old man
charged with the census
of his village,
but iridescent blackness
goes back to hunting
in the grass of the dead.

I wouldn't have noticed it
but for my friends,
who, on the day of Victor's death,
claimed to see or speak
with doubles of their long-dead friends.

Nor would I have stayed
to become the crow's business
if its pecking in the grass
had not reminded me
of those who turn their backs
and never face us again,

or those who see us drinking
but never hear the toast.

Vera

Print, print: the sound of a file
that diminishes nothing. Yesterday,

time fell back. It is darker
when I wake up. Too often,
I see the heron turn whiter
as it rises from the bayou
beside the funeral home.

She may have died
a few days before, this aunt of mine,
but here she is, her face
supplanting each face
in the viewing room, coming round
until I too accept it.

It was after that
the heron rose,
unnoticed at first, then yawing
above willow and cottonwood,
going away
above the odd neighborhood,
a few homes and the gray docks
that ship and receive.

Mr. and Mrs. Death

Mr. & Mrs. Death, driving an MG,
hit the tall, lanky fellow
I am helping across the street.
Upon which Mr. Death vaults
from the sporty weapon, though I don't realize
it's Mr. Death until I look at his lady,
who is beyond doubt Mrs. Death,
paler than albino, with the grin
of a dog that grins.

This could have been
El Día de los Muertos, except

I saw myself from within myself.
It was my usual body asleep
up to the skillful transition
at the neck, where, quite bonelike,
I held my skull. Ruthless equations,
rattling bone planks, this unfaithful bridge!

Jeanne Clark

Joe Spinner

Joe Spinner, whose face is a flat iron
Whose face is thick, yellow milk
Schoolroom paste hardened on a bristle brush
Whose walk is the strike down an alley
That makes a pinsetter jump
Whose walk is a schoolyard seesaw
Whose voice is the frozen lake breaking
Under December's first skaters
Joe Spinner, again, whose teeth are the rap of knuckles against a door
Whose teeth are pegs in the joints of fine furniture
Whose mouth is a locked closet
Lipper on the deck of a whaler
Whose words walk backward out a door
Whose words are grayed laundry
Whose thoughts are the felt of a chalkboard eraser
Whose thoughts are a rolled-up newspaper
Whose head is hard water under a speedboat
Joe Spinner, whose head is the egg of a Mute Swan
Whose hair is the sharp spine on a bluegill's back
Whose hair is the morning grass of the Governor's front lawn
Whose eyes are the blue tips of kitchen matches
Whose eyes are boiled onions
Whose eyes are the split galls of a felled oak
Whose hands are charged with powder
Whose hands are a bluegown's tin cup
Birds full of buckshot jerking in midair.

Jeanne Clark

The House Next Door

The woman called you stupid and stupid
Left the front porch door to her house

Open just a crack. The word *stupid* ran,
Bad child, in and out of that door.

The paperboy delivered the news
On the front lawn of the woman's house.

And with your fingers smeared black,
You pushed the paper,

Now burning, through the door
Because the woman called you stupid.

You set the morning on fire.
Bad child black hands morning woman next

Door crack stupid. You tried to tell them.
What happens next, you ask me

When I tell you the story of the house next door.
They move you, I say, to a new house.

Jeanne Clark

Prison School

I graded papers in the afternoons.
The table was 4 × 9, inmate built.
They only stayed through the morning.

Today the school ward door opened. Norm Henry,
The principal, talking to someone,
The sound of feet, fast and hard, down the hall,

My name backwards, NeeGee, not Jeanne E.,
Joe Spinner, breathless, at the top of the steps,
His fatboy arms full of lilacs, gray T-shirt,

Chinos, the wet blue sneakers closed with Velcro.
He had been fishing, he said, for the first time.
Joe Spinner threw the lilac branches down.

I asked him how he liked it. Joe Spinner said
The lilacs were for me. These lilacs were,
Joe said, the only living things he could catch.

Jeanne Clark

Reckoning

The Man said, he's dangerous, Miss.
And Joe smiled,
A yellow-toothed smile, chicken fat yellow.
The Man said if I take these cuffs off him.
And I said take them off.
When Joe put his two uncuffed hands on my shoulders,
He was laughing like something was really funny
With the Man saying he ain't like a human being.
And me saying what's wrong with him
And wondering what Joe — now dangerous
Because some woman the State paid
$200 a month to raise him
Kept him seven years in a chicken coop —
What was Joe going to do next?
He was going to put those cuffs back on,
The Man said, before we'd all live to regret it.

William Clipman

Perfect Time

The best drummer I ever heard
was a Guatemalan girl not more than four or five
on a street corner in Nogales, Sonora.
Her father played bass drum and trumpet
and she played snare
while her mother and siblings — two toddlers,
a third in a sling, and the fourth in the oven —
begged money from passersby.

Her backbeat was impeccable, her accents inspired
by heat, hunger, and the rhythms of traffic and feet.
I looked into her obsidian eyes
to find the secret of her perfect time
but her stare was opaque, her expression
ancient and changeless as Mayan stone.
Her hands had lives of their own
obeying only the song's unbroken pulse.

She knew in her blood, nerves, and bones
what shamans and fire walkers know:
how to be here and not here, self and other,
flesh and spirit simultaneously. She played
the immense and perfect signature of the universe
on and on to its natural conclusion,
finished with a dramatic roll —
the only moment her face showed a trace of effort —
then calmly sat down on the pavement to rest.

And I walked back across the border
carrying my changed life.

William Clipman

Winter of the Hawk

As farmers bring in sorghum and alfalfa
from the vast flat mosaic
between Cañada del Oro and the Gila River
and pack their winter cotton
into bales big as boxcars,
the other bumper crop is hawk:
they are everywhere this year,
sleek, fat, clear-eyed killers
perched in bare trees,
on fence posts, power poles, saguaros,
billboards — even on the tip
of the straw jutting skyward
from the giant soft drink
available for only 69¢
at the Toltec Road McDonald's —
warming puffed-up chests in horizontal sunlight,
scanning the fields
for any sign of carelessness.

Framed against low rugged mountains
sculpted out of mist by dawn
they soar, dive, mate, cavort, and hunt,
reclaiming the neatly mutilated desert
from pesticides and pellet guns.
They gaze over the ostrich ranch
at the foot of Picacho Peak
and dream big.
Once, mind clear, one cruised
just ahead of the windshield at seventy,
dropped its talons for a moment,
thought better of it,

and peeled off into the blur.
Now, out on the reservation
between Snaketown and San Tan,
new lambs cling to their ewes
while rams eye their fence-line horizon
with ungulate suspicion: beyond their vision
hawks patrol the mystical Superstitions
powdered with early snow.

Dennis Hickman

The Rez

We'd been living on the rez for five years, and I had the place figured out, I thought. At least as far as the white people who came to work on the rez were concerned. They were either colonists or panderers. The colonists were people who wanted the Navajos to be treated like regular American citizens, like equals. The panderers were needy people who wanted the Navajos to be beautiful and wise. For the panderers, whatever was wrong with the reservation was not the fault of the Navajos, and, in fact, nothing *could* be their fault. I was a colonist, and I'd decided I could deal with whatever craziness the rez had to deal out. But that was before the intruder took up residence in my brain.

I had driven the twelve hundred miles to my parents' home with our kids while Amanda stayed back on the rez to teach summer school. After we'd been gone a week I got a call from her at 2:00 A.M. She said the weirdest thing had happened. "I just took a bath," she said, "and went to bed, and then the dog came into the bedroom and started to growl. I didn't feel like getting up and letting the dog out. But I got up anyway and turned on the light, and this young guy crawled out from under the bed. He had a ridiculous grin on his face, and he just stood there. So I ran out the front door, and I guess he went out the back. I ran up to Joe's place and he called Security." Her voice seemed thin, but calm.

"Jesus," I said. "That must have been scary. I take it the guy was a Navajo," I said.

"Oh, sure," she said. "Nutty things happen on the rez, you know that." She was trying to have a sense of humor about it. "The Security guy went all through the house. They looked all over the compound, but they didn't find anyone."

"I was thinking of the kid who stole your bike, Mandy. Do you think it was him? The one named Benny something. Begay, Tsosie, Curley, Becenti. He'd be maybe fourteen or fifteen by now."

She said she didn't recognize the intruder. She guessed he was a teenager, but then she'd been so surprised, she hadn't paid much attention. She was staying with Gina, one of the single teachers, for the next couple nights, and I shouldn't worry. No, we shouldn't come home right away. I was planning to leave the next day for a conference in Seattle, and she thought I should go ahead. She and Gina had been planning a trip to Phoenix over the weekend anyway, and now she really felt like getting away from the rez for a while. She'd be all right.

There hadn't been that much craziness on the rez. Two years before there had been the Navajo foot fetishist who pretended he needed help fixing the clutch of his pickup. As it turned out, he'd talked four women, including Amanda, into sitting in his pickup while he'd fondled their feet and ankles. A couple of our kachinas had disappeared mysteriously. But there hadn't been that much craziness, not dangerous craziness. The rez had seemed to be a place where you could let your kids play outside without having to worry about someone driving up out of nowhere and stealing them away.

The kids and I drove up two weeks later, and I saw what the July monsoons had done to the yard. There were big hollyhocks, milkweed, and about a thousand of those rubbery green weeds I didn't know the name of. There were at least four of the huge Rocky Mountain bee plants with purple flowers and thick roots, like little trees. And all this growth in less than a month!

I had never pretended to care much for the yard. It was a sore point between Amanda and me. She was always talking about the yard, as though it could be transformed into a place to have barbecues, a place for people to sit outside and enjoy the sunset. But it was not really a yard at all. It was either a sea of mud or a mass of weeds. Amanda had to admit, even when she was mad about the yard, that it probably wasn't worth improving. Not unless we ended up spending the rest of our lives there, and we didn't plan to stay there any longer than we had to. We told each other we were people who loved Martians. We'd been in the Peace Corps, in the Orient and the Middle East, and we loved to see cultures mingle and clash. This was the reason, I told myself, that we'd stayed on the rez for five years, longer than we'd ever stayed anywhere else.

She came out to greet us with sunglasses on and a new summer outfit — white top, bare midriff, red shorts. She'd acquired more of a tan than she'd had when we left. For some reason I'd expected her to look different after her traumatic experience, and she did, although I couldn't exactly say how. She gave the kids a hug, and they ran inside.

"Everything's fine here," she said. She gave me a kiss.

"Are you O.K., Amanda? I mean, how are you really feeling?" She had finished her shrinking two years before, and it had seemed to be a success. She had seen the right therapist, and the anxiety had gone away.

"Sure, I'm fine. But I'm very careful now, and I make sure I know where the baseball bat is when I go to sleep."

I reached over very slowly and took off the sunglasses. I was hoping I could see more, but there was nothing unusual in her eyes. I gave her another kiss and went to get the luggage out of the car. Then I went to every one of the doors and windows, inside and out. I found a spot where the screen on the back storm door had been forced with a knife or a screwdriver. I yelled down the length of the trailer for Amanda to come and take a look. "Look at this. Do you see what that guy did?"

It had occurred to me at first that the whole episode could have been in her imagination, but here was physical proof. I knew, because I was in the habit of looking for intruders, just to be on the safe side. She seemed to be distracted, uninterested in the door.

"Gina and I had quite a good time in Phoenix. We went to a couple of parties, and there were plenty of guys who were interested in me." We were standing on the back porch of the trailer. She was staring off toward the red hills across the valley. I could hear Max and Julie wrestling with Mason the dog inside.

"Of course, they were interested. I'm always telling you you're a great beauty."

"But I always thought there had to be something a little weird or unusual about the men who liked me. Like they had to be bright or creative or something. With their heads in the stars. But these guys were just ordinary good-looking males, mostly divorced, and I could have slept with any of them." There was real anger in her voice, as though I had said something horrible to her. Her face was a bit flushed, and it was hard for me to see what she was thinking behind the sunglasses.

"Why are you telling me this now? I've just driven all this way with a couple screaming kids, and you want to start a fight? I always tell you you have a tendency to sell yourself short. Of course, they'd be attracted to you."

"Well, I didn't sleep with any of them, but I get the feeling you wouldn't care if I had. I mean, they were just jerks, but they sure were interested. They could see I was someone who had opinions about things. I don't think they're used to that."

"Of course, I'd care if you did such a thing, especially if you did it only out of spite for me." I could hear a kind of whine in my voice that I tended to get when we argued. And I had to think this was why she was hungry for fighting, because she needed to hear me whine or yell or smack my fist against the flimsy wall of the trailer.

"I don't know, Dana. Sometimes you seem so low-key about everything. I wonder if you really care."

She was always setting traps for you so that you couldn't go one way or the other without setting her off. If I said "I care," she's say it was only under duress that I said such things. If I said I didn't, she'd say, "You see, I've been right about you all along." The phone rang and she went inside to answer. I heard her yelling down the length of the trailer. "Dana, let's go. There's a suspicious-looking guy over at the trading post." She came out of fights quickly; she drew energy from them, and she was now in a state of excitement. I drove as quickly as I could, but when we got there it was just a young drunk who she could see was too tall and too old. "I think his face needs to be more round, too," she said.

When we got back to the house, Max, the ten-year-old, had crawled under the bed to see what it was like. He met us at the door. "That guy must have been crazy. How could he stand all the dust under there? And there's hardly any room, even for me."

"That's one thing I haven't mentioned," Amanda said. "Before I went to sleep, I noticed that the bed was sitting on a paperback book, but I really didn't think anything of it. I know, after the fact it seems like something I should have worried about."

I resisted the temptation to say, "Why couldn't you be a little more careful, Amanda?" Over the phone for the past two weeks I had kept saying to her, "You can take care of yourself. I'm sure of that."

Our trailer was in the northeast corner of the compound. There was a dirt road we could see out our front window, and it intersected with another dirt road that went out to the lake. From our window we could see everyone who was jogging, riding bikes, going for walks. For a few days I found myself looking a little harder than usual at the runners and walkers and cyclists. When someone looked strange, I would grab the binoculars and look him over, even though this spying on the population made me feel ridiculous.

So when I went out running myself, I imagined that in every little house and hogan I passed there was some nutcase watching me with binoculars, wondering what dark things I had to hide. I had found in the past that thinking about the Navajos and what drove me crazy about them helped me improve my times. Now I thought about the intruder every time I ran, and I felt my legs stretching out more and the blood pumping faster.

I could see Amanda getting undressed in the bathroom, and the kid is already there, peering around the corner of the bathroom door. She takes the bath slowly, not paying much attention to her surroundings. She gets out and he's back under the bed. She's naked for a while, drying herself and then trying to find a nightgown to put on, and he's watching all the time, sticking his head around the bed, thinking this is really great, seeing the red mark the water leaves on her back. He sees her white breasts, coral-colored nipples. And then when she's finally in bed and the light is off, what does he think? What does he think is next?

A week after we'd returned, about sunset, Amanda came back from her nightly journey around the compound, holding a piece of paper behind her back. She got more comfort from talking about her problems with her lady friends than she did from being around me. I accepted this as a fact of life. I was glad to see she wasn't afraid to walk around outside, and she was careful to return before dark. "I talked to Brenda — you know, the new art teacher at our school? The one you offended at the Robinson's party? I talked her into trying to play police artist." She continued to hold the picture behind her back. "I promised her you wouldn't try to kill the kid or anything if the picture helped us find him."

"Brenda is a real panderer," I said.

"I know she's needy. She doesn't trust you. But I told her the reason you act so angry about the Navajos is just that you really care a lot, and you hate to hear people tell happy-face lies about them. And it's true, you know, you feel guilty about them, just like the rest of us."

She showed me a drawing that wasn't quite as disconnected as the police artists' composite pictures you see on TV. I was surprised to see that the face in the drawing was almost pixielike and a bit chubby. Amanda kept the picture in the kitchen, made some Xerox copies, and showed them to our neighbors and friends. There were several more false alarms, one at the hospital, one at the post office, and another at the service station.

Then one Saturday I saw Farbee at the post office. The mail was usually late on Saturdays, and there were about thirty pickups parked around the building. Farbee was a kid I had in class. Like many of them, he had a peculiar name and a hatred for school. I had decided on an etymology for his name. He probably had a father named Farley and a mother named Beatrice. They had spliced the two names together and given him a one of a kind. I had heard he was living with his grandparents, and no one seemed to have any idea what had happened to his parents. He was apparently waiting for a ride. For the first time I made a connection between the drawing and a real human being. The nose was wrong.

Farbee's was flatter and more prominent than the one in the picture, but otherwise it was a match.

I stood there for a moment, trying to decide what I should do. I had thought about how I would like to murder the intruder and dump the body in a wash for the ravens and the coyotes to chew on. But I really doubted that I'd go through with it.

"What are you looking at, queer?" the kid said.

"I don't have to put up with that nonsense during the summertime. This might be a good time to put an end to all your problems, Farbee."

"Not even. Just try it, pervert. My grandma could kick the shit out of you."

"Stop sneering for a moment. I have an offer for you." I noticed that the kid was wearing his Denver Broncos T-shirt. He had a Celtics shirt too, and that and a couple pairs of jeans made up his entire wardrobe for school. "I need the weeds cleaned up in our yard. I'll give you twenty dollars if you do a good job. But I need it done today. You waiting for your girlfriend or what?"

"You bet. I don't need no twenty bucks. My women pay to be with me." He was like many of the Navajo kids I knew in his inability to talk with grown-ups.

"Well, I've got the tools there. I've even got gloves, so you won't have to ruin your delicate hands. You want to make some money, show up at my place this afternoon. You know which trailer we live in?" I watched closely for some sign of recognition, some admission of his guilt, but he didn't show any.

"Sure, it's the dump in the corner. Only a totally rezzed-out person could live in a place like that." He spat out Skoal on the ground a few inches from my feet.

"There's a basketball pole out front and a blue Subaru. Don't be too proud. I like to help out Siberian Americans. I really do. Just see that you show up before it gets too late."

When we had company — a new teacher or someone from Phoenix who was just visiting the school — Amanda was always afraid I would seem too negative, because I wouldn't give the usual noble savage party line that people like to hear. People wanted to hear that kids like Farbee had a great deal to be proud of, that there was some fine Navajo tradition that he could fall back on to solve all his problems. But there was no such tradition. There was a neurotic, paranoid witchcraft tradition, a tradition of sings for curing physical and psychological ailments, and some arts and crafts. But there was no identity in all this for Farbee. He was a lost soul for good reason.

Amanda didn't seem too thrilled to think that the real criminal might be

coming over. She didn't think it was likely he was the right one. "I'd almost rather forget the whole thing," she said. "I mean, they're not going to throw this creep in jail, even if we find the right one.'"

"It could scare him and make him more cautious. Look, I know the kid. He's a lost soul. His highest aspiration in life is to spit Skoal farther than anyone else. But, you know, if he is guilty, he'd love the idea of returning to the scene of the crime, pretending he knew nothing about it, and getting away with it." I looked out the kitchen window and saw Farbee coming down the road that led to our trailer. "Is that him, Amanda? Take a good look." I reached for the binoculars on the top of the microwave.

"Thanks, but I don't think I need those," she said. She looked at the kid, and then she picked up the picture that she kept next to the Mr. Coffee. Then she turned around and started crying. There wasn't anything I could say right then to validate the way she was feeling.

"I'll be back in a minute," I said. I showed Farbee the rake and gave him the gloves.

"I want to see my twenty bucks, Chetwood," he said. I took out my billfold and help up a crisp bill.

"You see," I said, "the real thing. This should take you about an hour and a half, I suppose, if you work hard. Let me know if you need anything. You can take the weeds down by the Dumpster when you're through." I pointed down to the end of the row of trailers. He started pulling the weeds, and he seemed to be working at a pretty good pace. "Someone going to pick you up?" I asked. I didn't relish the idea of taking this kid off through some god-awful dirt roads in the middle of the night, even if that would give me the perfect chance to murder him.

"Yeah, don't worry, you won't have to keep me overnight. Disappointed?" I didn't answer and went inside.

Amanda had stopped crying now, and she was still staring at the picture. "You know, the trouble is, I can't tell whether the picture is more real or my memory of what happened. I guess the two have kind of melted together."

"Is he the right height, do you think?"

"That part, yeah, he's about right. And I guess he's more or less the right age. I don't know. I have the feeling the original creep was pretty stupid. I mean, I could have killed him if I'd had a baseball bat. Not that that was the first thing I thought of when it happened. He took a long time coming out from under the bed. Is this one of the dull ones?"

"No, he's bright, but he hates school. He hates me, too, I guess." I had gotten so I could hear the monotony in my voice when I talked about my students. And Amanda hated it, too, hearing me talk about them. The kids she had to work with in the lower grades were cute and less malicious.

I looked out and saw the kid had managed to get the small Rocky Mountain bee plant all the way out of the ground. He had more strength in him than I had thought. I went to get the ax in the back bedroom. I had just bought it at the Kmart in Gallup two months before, and it had a wonderful fresh hardware-store smell about it. I went out and gave it to Farbee, and I could see the kid knew how to use an ax, sliding his one hand all the way down the handle and hitting the roots hard.

I went back inside, feeling a little better about the whole project, even if Farbee wasn't the guilty party. "You bring a little felon like that home and then you give him an ax?" Amanda said. Her eyes were red and puffy, but she was neither laughing nor crying.

"He needs to cut those monster plants down. I don't know how else to do it." I took out a can of Classic Coke and gave it to the kid. Farbee didn't say thanks. He drank some and then put the can down and started chopping again. The whole yard smelled like a salad of beeweed and milkweed. "You could say thanks, Farbee," I said.

"All right then, thanks so fucking much. Excuse me!" Then he said something in Navajo that I didn't understand. I came back and got the shotgun out of the bedroom. I put three shells in it and put the gun on the kitchen table. Mason the dog was lying on the kitchen floor waiting for his late-afternoon feeding. Amanda was sitting there thumbing through a women's magazine, thinking about something else. The kids were off at a friend's birthday party. I was glad about that, having them away from the house with Farbee around. I caught her eye and pointed at the shotgun. "Just in case," I said. "But don't shoot to kill unless you have to." In the past I had worried that she would shoot herself or even me, and I had made sure there were no shells in the house. But I had confidence in her sanity now, and the gun on the table said as much to her.

Farbee rapped on the door. He gave me back the ax. "I'm finished with this," he said. "Could I use the restroom please?" he asked Amanda. He didn't act as though he knew Amanda or had ever seen her before, clothed or unclothed.

"It's just down the hall by the washer and dryer," she said.

"You planning on shooting someone, Chetwood?" he asked.

"Dove season starts next week, Farbee." The truth was that I hadn't hunted for years. The shotgun was just for protection and for firing off a shot in celebration on New Year's Eve and the Fourth of July.

The kid went back out and pulled some more weeds. He had about an eighth of the yard left to go when I heard a pickup pull up. I looked out and saw an old Navajo woman in a velour blouse and a gathered skirt. She got out of the pickup to talk with Farbee. "Hey Chetwood," he yelled. "I gotta go. Where's my money?"

I figured it would take me about half an hour to finish the weeds that were left. The sun would still be up for an hour. "All right, Farbee, you did okay. I'll finish it off." I gave the kid the twenty and saw him pile in the back of the pickup where a couple old men were asleep.

It took me twenty minutes of pulling and dragging the weeds over to the road and another twenty of pushing them up to the Dumpster with the rake. The yard looked bare. There were still two stumps of the Rocky Mountain bee plants, but the rest was deserted by living things. It was just the last minutes of sunset. I could see a red sliver sitting on top of the mesa across the valley. When I came in, Amanda was setting the table for dinner. "You want to move the gun? I guess we're safe now. I don't think that was the right kid. I'm sorry."

"Don't be sorry. You got your yard cleaned up anyway." I went back out and stood on the porch. I could see the kids down by the Dumpster. They were coming home carrying some shiny party paraphernalia. I looked at the heavens and saw there was a storm headed in from the west that would be dumping water into the empty yard before the night was over.

I was tired of thinking about the Navajos, but I couldn't help myself. It was better than talking about them with Amanda, because she just got upset. The truth was that there were times when the Navajos had gotten hold of me and made me one of them, irresponsible, self-centered, and despairing. Or at least they'd gotten hold of me for a while. There was the time when the kids and I had been driving back from Gallup with our new car. It was one of those trips that you just want to get over, because you can't imagine anything worse than even a small dent in a new car. As we came down the hill into town, we saw a toddler, barefoot and in diapers and a T-shirt, running along the side of the road, at least forty yards from the nearest house. "Maybe we should stop and take that kid to his house," I said.

"No," Max and Julie said. "Let's just go home." And the kids had been right, because the toddler would just be back out by the road in another five minutes, and his mother or aunt or ten-year-old sister who was supposed to be taking care of him, would be sitting staring off into space or watching *Wheel of Fortune* on the tube. I drove on, and I didn't lose any sleep that night. But I did sit on our porch for a long time, staring at the shiny blue car and listening for the sirens. If I hear the sirens, I'll feel guilty, I said. I'll turn myself in to the Navajo Police.

I stuck my head back in the door and smelled dinner cooking. Amanda said it would be another half hour before it was ready. I went back out to the porch and looked at the bare yard, thinking about that toddler for the millionth time, and then I saw a runner out on the road, somebody I hadn't seen before. There was just enough light to see him, and he looked like a teenager. Skinny and shorter than me. For all I could see, he was the right one, more right than Farbee. I looked down and saw I had on my shorts and running shoes. I yelled to Amanda that I'd be back in a little bit, and took off right away without stretching. He was just loafing along, and even at my typical nine-minute-mile rate, I figured I could catch up with him in a couple of miles.

I didn't know what I would do to him or how I would know if it was him, the culprit. I was really rezzed out — very tired of thinking about the intruder and all the rest — but my legs felt great. Even if he confessed that he had lain in wait to see my wife naked, I was ready to forgive him. Maybe I would tell him the story of the kid in diapers along the highway. Maybe I would tell him about the foot fetishist, about the absurdity of fondling the feet of four strange women. Imagine making this the focus, the chief obsession of your life! It was worth a good laugh. And then maybe we'd just run alongside each other for several miles without talking at all. Until one of us felt stronger, took off with a few quick strides, and left the other one running alone.

Christopher McIlroy

All My Relations

When Jack Oldenburg first spoke to him, Milton Enos leaned over his paper plate, scooping beans into his mouth as if he didn't hear. Breaking through the murmur of O'odham conversation, the white man's speech was sharp and harsh. But Oldenburg stood over him, waiting.

Oldenburg had just lost his ranch hand, sick. If Milton reported to the Box-J sober in the morning, he could work for a couple of weeks until the cowboy returned or Oldenburg found a permanent hand.

"O.K.," Milton said, knowing he wouldn't go. Earlier in the day his wife and son had left for California, so he had several days' drinking to do. Following his meal at the convenience mart he would hitch to the Sundowner Lounge at the edge of the reservation.

After a sleepless night Milton saddled his horse for the ride to Oldenburg's, unable to bear his empty house. As he crossed the wide, dry bed of the Gila River, leaving the outskirts of Hashan, the house ceased to exist for him, and he thought he would never go back. Milton's stomach jogged over the pommel with the horse's easy gait. Two hours from Hashan, Oldenburg's Box-J was the only ranch in an area either left desert or irrigated for cotton and sorghum. Its twenty square miles included hills, arroyos, and the eastern tip of a mountain range — gray-pink granite knobs split by ravines. The sun burned the tops of the mountains red.

Oldenburg stood beside his corral, tall and thin as one of its mesquite logs. First, he said, sections of the barbed-wire fence had broken down, which meant chopping and trimming new posts.

Milton's first swings of the ax made him dizzy and sick. He flailed wildly, waiting with horror for the bite of the ax into his foot. But soon he gained control over his stroke. Though soft, his big arms were strong. Sweat and alcohol poured out of him until he stank.

In the afternoon Milton and Oldenburg rode the fence-line.

"Hasn't been repaired in years," Oldenburg said. "My hand Jenkins is old." Oldenburg himself was well over sixty, his crew cut white and his face dried up like a dead man's. He had bright eyes, though, and fine white teeth. Where the fence was flattened to the ground, Milton saw a swatch of red and white cowhide snagged on the barbed wire. He'd lost a few head in the mountains, Oldenburg said, and after the fence was secure they'd round them up.

"One thing I'll tell you," Oldenburg said. "You can't drink while you work for me. Alcohol is poison in a business."

Milton nodded. By reputation he knew Oldenburg had a tree stump up his ass. Milton's wife C. C. had said she'd bring their son Allen back when Milton stopped drinking. For good? he'd asked. How would she know when was for good? For all anybody knew tomorrow might be the first day of for good, or twenty-five thousand days later he might get drunk again. For a moment Milton remembered playing Monopoly with C. C. and Allen several weekends before. As usual, Milton and Allen were winning. Pretending not to be furious, C. C. smiled her big, sweet grins. Milton and the boy imitated her, stretching their mouths, until she couldn't help laughing. Milton clicked them off like a TV set and saw only mesquite, the rocky sand, sky, and the line of fence. After his two weeks, Milton thought, he'd throw a drunk like World War Ten.

At the end of the day he accepted Oldenburg's offer: $75 a week plus room and board, weekend off. Oldenburg winced apologetically proposing the wage; the ranch didn't make money, he explained.

They ate at a metal table in the dining room. Milton, whose pleasure in food went beyond filling his stomach, appreciated Oldenburg's meat loaf — laced with onion, the center concealing three hard-boiled eggs. Milton couldn't identify the seasonings except for chili. "What's in this?" he asked.

"Sage, chili, cumin, and Worcestershire sauce."

"Heyyy."

Inside his two-room adobe, Milton was so tired he couldn't feel his body, and lying down felt the same as standing up. He slept without dreaming until Oldenburg rattled the door at daybreak.

Milton dug holes and planted posts. By noon his sweat had lost its salt and tasted like pure spring water. Then he didn't sweat at all. Chilled and shaking at the end of the day, he felt as if he'd been thrown by a horse. The pain gave him a secret exultation, which he hoarded from Oldenburg, saying nothing. Yet he felt he was offering the man part of the ache as a secret gift. Slyly, he thumped his cup on the table and screeched his chair back with exaggerated vigor. Milton was afraid of liking Oldenburg too much. He liked people too easily, even those who were not O'odham — especially those, perhaps, because he wanted them to prove he needn't hate them.

Milton worked ten-, eleven-hour days. The soreness left his muscles, though he was as tired the fourth evening as he had been the first. Thursday night Oldenburg baked a chicken.

"You're steady," Oldenburg said. "I've seen you Pimas work hard before. What's your regular job?"

"I've worked for the government." Milton had ridden rodeo, sold wild horses he captured in the mountains, broken horses. Most often there was welfare. Recently he had completed two CETA training programs, one as a hospital orderly and the other baking cakes. But the reservation hospital wasn't hiring, and the town of Hashan had no bakeries. For centuries, Milton had heard, when the Gila flowed, the O'odham had been farmers. Settlements and overgrazing upstream had choked off the river only a few generations past. Sometimes he tried to envision green plots of squash, beans, and ripening grains, watered by earthen ditches, spreading from the banks. He imagined his back flexing easily in the heat as he bent to the rows, foliage swishing his legs, finally the villagers diving into the cool river, splashing delightedly.

"I don't think Jenkins is coming out of the hospital," Oldenburg said. "This job is yours if you want it." Milton was stunned. He had never held a permanent position.

In just a week of hard work, good eating, and no drinking, Milton had lost weight. Waking Friday morning, he pounded his belly with his hand; it answered him like a drum. He danced in front of the bathroom mirror, swiveling his hips, urging himself against the sink as if it were a partner. At lunch he told Oldenburg he would spend the weekend with friends in Hashan.

When he tossed the posthole digger into the shed, he felt light and strong, as if instead of sinking fence posts he'd spent the afternoon in a deep, satisfying nap. On the way to the guesthouse, his bowels turned over and a sharp pain set into his head. He saw the battered station wagon rolling out the drive, C. C. at the wheel, Allen's tight face in the window.

Milton threw his work clothes against the wall. After a stinging shower, he changed and mounted his horse for the ride to Vigiliano Lopez's.

Five hours later the Sundowner was closing. Instead of his customary beer, Milton had been drinking highball glasses of straight vodka. He felt paler and paler, like water, until he was water. His image peeled off him like a wet decal, and he was only water in the shape of a man. He flowed onto the bar, hooking his water elbows onto the wooden ridge for support. Then he was lifted from the stool, tilted backward, floating on the pickup bed like vapor.

Milton woke feeling the pong, pong of a basketball bouncing outside. The vibration traveled along the dirt floor of Lopez's living room, up the couch he lay on. The sun was dazzling. Looking out the window, he saw six-foot-five, three-hundred-pound Bosque dribbling the ball with both hands, knocking the other players aside. As he jammed the ball into the low hoop, it hit the back of the rim, caroming high over the makeshift plywood backboard. A boy and two dogs chased it.

Seeing beer cans in the dirt, Milton went outside. He took his shirt off and sat against the house with a warm Bud. The lean young boys fired in jump shots, or when they missed, their fathers and older brothers pushed and wrestled for the rebound. Lopez grabbed a loose ball and ran with it, whirling for a turnaround fadeaway that traveled three feet. He laughed, and said to Milton, "When we took you home you started fighting us. Bosque had to pick you up and squeeze you, and when he did, everything came out like toothpaste."

"Try our new puke-flavored toothpaste," someone said, laughing.

"Looks like pizza."

"So we brought you here."

Milton said nothing. He watched the arms and broad backs collide. The young boys on the sidelines practiced lassoing the players' feet, the dogs, the ball. When he finished a beer, Milton started another. Later in the afternoon he sent boys to his house for the rest of his clothes and important belongings.

When the game broke up, some of the men joined the women in the shade of a mesquite. Saddling a half-broke wild colt, the boys took turns careening across the field. Lopez drove a truckload to the rodeo arena, where a bronc rider from Bapchule was practicing. Compact and muscular, with silver spurs and collar tabs, he rode out the horse's bucks, smoothing the animal to a canter. Two of Milton's drunk friends tried and were thrown immediately. For a third, the horse didn't buck but instead circled the arena at a dead run, dodging the lassos and open gates. From the announcer's booth Lopez called an imaginary race as horse and rider passed the grandstand again and again — "coming down the back-stretch now, whoops, there he goes for another lap, this horse is not a quitter, ladies and gentlemen."

"Go ahead, Milton," Lopez said. "You used to ride."

Milton shook his head. Allen, thirteen, recently had graduated from steers to bulls. In both classes he had finished first or second in every start, earning as much money the past months as his father and mother combined. Would there be rodeo in California? Milton wondered. In school, too, Allen was a prodigy, an eighth grader learning high-school geometry. If he studied hard, the school counselor said, he could finish high school in three years and win a college scholarship. Milton didn't know where the boy's talent came from.

Tears filled Milton's eyes.

"Aaaah," Bosque said. His big hand gripped Milton's arm. They walked back to Lopez's house and split a couple of sixes under the mesquite until the men returned. Audrey Lopez and the other wives prepared chili and *cemait* dough while the men played horseshoes and drank in the dusk.

By the end of dinner everyone was drunk. Milton, face sweating, was explaining to Audrey Lopez, "Just a few weeks ago, Allen wins some kind of puzzle contest for the whole state, O.K.? And he's on TV. And C. C. and I have got our faces up to the screen so we can hear every word he's saying. And we can't believe it. He's talking on TV, and his hair's sticking up on the side like that, just like it always does.

"I can see them so real," Milton said. "When C. C. plays volleyball she's like a rubber ball, she's so little and round. She *dives* for those spikes, and her hair goes flying back."

Lopez slid his leg along Audrey's shoulder. "Good song," he said. "Let's dance." The radio was playing Top 40.

"Wait. I'm listening to this man."

"Milton talks you into tomorrow afternoon. Come on." Lopez pulled her shoulder.

Audrey shrugged him off and laid her hand on Milton's arm. "His wife and son are gone."

"Dried up old bitch," Lopez said. "C. C.'s too old for you, man, she's way older than he is. You lost nothing."

Grabbing a barbecue fork, ramming Lopez against the wall, Milton chopped the fork into Lopez's shoulder. A woman screamed, Milton heard his own grunts as the glistening tines rose and stabbed. Lopez ducked and his knife came up. Milton deflected the lunge with his fork, the knife blade springing down its long shank. Milton shouted as the knife thudded into the wall. His little finger had bounded into the air and lay on the floor, looking like a brown pebble.

Bosque drove both men to the hospital. The doctor cauterized, stitched, and bandaged the wound, and gave Milton a tetanus shot. If Milton had brought the severed finger — the top two joints — the doctor said, he might have sewed it on. The men refused to stay overnight. When they returned to the party, couples were dancing the *chotis* and *bolero* to a Mexican radio station. Gulps of vodka deadened the pain in Milton's finger. He and Lopez kept opposite corners of the living room until dawn, when Lopez pushed Audrey into Milton's arms and said, "Get some dancing, man."

Sunday Milton slept under the mesquite until evening, when he rode to the Box-J.

"That's your mistake, Milton," Oldenburg said. "Everyone's entitled to one mistake. Next time you drink you're gone. You believe me?"

Milton did. He felt like weeping. The next day he roamed the fence-line, his chest and neck clotted with the frustration of being unable to work. The horse's jouncing spurted blood through the white bandage on his finger. Finally he rode out a back gate and into the midst of the granite mountains. Past a sparkling dome broken by a slump of shattered rock, Milton trotted into a narrow cut choked with mesquite. As a boy, he would hunt wild horses for days in these ravines, alone, with only a canvas food bag tied to the saddle. He remembered sleeping on the ground without a blanket, beneath a lone sycamore that had survived years of drought. Waking as dawn lit the mountain crests, he would force through the brush, gnawing a medallion of jerked beef. Most often when he startled a horse the animal would clatter into a side gully, boxing itself in. Then roping was easy. Once when Milton flushed a stringy gray mustang, the horse charged him instead; he had no time to uncoil the rope before the gray was past. Milton wheeled, pursuing at full gallop out the canyon and onto the bajada. Twig-matted tail streaming behind, the mustang was outrunning him, and he had one chance with the rope. He dropped the loop around the gray's neck, jarring the animal to its haunches. It was so long ago. Today, Milton reflected, the headlong chase would have pinned him and the horse to Oldenburg's barbed-wire fence.

The sycamore held its place, older and larger. Though encountering no horses, Milton returned three stray cattle to Oldenburg's ranch. For a month, while the slightest jolt could rupture the wound, he hunted down mavericks in the miles of ravine, painted the ranch buildings, and repaired the roofs, one-handed. Even as the finger healed, the missing segment unbalanced his grip. Swinging the pick or ax, shoveling, he would clench his right hand so tightly the entire arm would tremble. By the second month a new hand had evolved, with the musculature of the other fingers, the palm, and the wrist more pronounced. The pinky stub acted as a stabilizer against pick shaft or rope. Milton had rebuilt the fence and combed the granite mountains, rounding up another two dozen head. Oldenburg's herd had increased to 120.

In late August Milton rode beyond the granite range to the Ka kai Mountains, a low, twisted ridge of volcanic rock that he had avoided because he once saw the Devil there. Needing to piss, he had stumbled away from a beer party and followed a trail rising between the boulders. Watching the ground for snakes, he had almost collided with a man standing in the path. The stranger was a very big, ugly Indian, but Milton knew it was the Devil because his eyes were black, not human, and he spoke in a booming voice that rolled echoes off the cliff. Milton shuddered uncontrollably and shrivelled to the size of a spider. Afterwards he found he had fallen and cut himself. Cholla spines were embedded in his leg. The Devil had said only: "Beware of Satan within you."

The meeting enhanced Milton's prestige, and Allen was impressed, though not C.C. "You see?" she said. "What did I always tell you?"

In daylight the mountains looked like no more than a pile of cinders. Milton chose an arroyo that cut through the scorched black rubble into red slabs, canyon walls that rose over his head, then above the mesquite. Chasing a calf until it disappeared in a side draw, Milton left the animal for later. The canyon twisted deeper into the mountains, the red cliffs now three hundred feet high. The polished rock glowed. Milton was twelve years old and his brothers were fighting.

"You took my car," Steven said.

"So what," Lee said. Milton's favorite brother, he was slim and handsome, with small ears and thick, glossy hair that fell almost into his eyes. Weekends he took Milton into Phoenix to play pool and pinball, sometimes to the shopping mall for Cokes. He always had girls, even Mexicans and whites.

"I told you if you took my car I was going to kill you." Steven always said crazy things. At breakfast, if Milton didn't pass him the milk right away — "How'd you like this knife in your eye?" About their mother — "Bitch wouldn't give me a dime. I'm going to shit on her bed." He wore a white rag around his head and hung out with gangs. Now they would call him a *cholo*.

"So what," Lee said. "Kill me." Cocking his leg, he wiped the dusty boot heel carefully against the couch. Milton was sitting on the couch.

Steven ran down the hall and came back with a .22. He pointed it at Lee's head, there was a shocking noise, a red spot appeared in Lee's forehead, and he collapsed on the rug.

"Oh my God," Steven said. Fingers clawed against his temples, he rushed out the door. Milton snatched the gun and chased him, firing on the run. Steven, bigger and faster, outdistanced him in the desert. Milton didn't come home for three days. Steven wasn't prosecuted and he moved to Denver. If he returned, Milton would kill him, even twenty years later.

Milton's horse ambled down the white sand, the dry bed curving around a red outcropping. Trapped by the canyon walls, the late summer air was hot and close. The weight of Milton's family fell on his back like a landslide — his father, driving home drunk from Casa Grande, slewing across the divider, head-on into another pickup. The four children had flown like crickets from the back, landing unhurt in the dirt bank. The driver of the other truck died, and Milton's mother lost the shape of her face.

Milton felt himself turning to water. He circled his horse, routed the calf from the slit in the wall, and drove it miles to the ranch. At dinner he told Oldenburg he needed a trip to town.

"You'll lose your job," Oldenburg said.

Milton ate with his water fingers, spilling food and the orange juice that Oldenburg always served. "The lives of O'odham is a soap opera," he cried, trying to dispel his shame by insulting himself. "I love my boy, O.K.? But it's him who has to hold me when I go for C.C. He doesn't hold me with his strength. He holds me because I see him, and I stop. Sometimes I don't stop."

Oldenburg served Milton cake for dessert and told him to take the next day off if he wanted.

The following morning Milton lay on his bed, sweating. In his mind were no thoughts or images save the swirls of chill, unpleasant water that washed over him. He could transform the water, making it a cold lake that pumped his heart loudly and shrank his genitals, or a clear stream immersing him in swift currents and veins of sunlight, but he could not change the water into thoughts. The green carpeting and blue-striped drapes in his room sickened him. He could have finished a pint of vodka before he knew he was drinking.

He could not imagine losing his work.

Abruptly Milton rose. In the corral he fitted a rope bridle over the horse's head. As he rode past Oldenburg, the man looked up from a bench of tack he was fussing with, then quickly lowered his head.

"I'm going to the mountains," Milton said.

He let the horse carry him into the charred crust of the canyon. The scarlet walls rose high and sheer, closing off the black peaks beyond. Tethering the horse to a mesquite, Milton sat in the sand. The cliffs seemed almost to meet above him. Heat gathered over his head and forced down on him. A lizard skittered by his ear, up the wall. A tortoise lumbered across the wash. The water rippling through him became a shimmering on the far wall, scenes of his life. Milton racing after Steven, aiming at the zigzagging blue shirt, the crack of the gun, a paloverde trunk catching the rifle barrel and spinning Milton to his knees. His father's empty boots beside the couch where he slept. His mother in baggy gray slacks, growing fatter. C.C.'s head snapping back from Milton's open palm. The pictures flickered over the cliff. Milton sat while shadow climbed the rock, and a cool breeze funneled through the canyon, and night fell. Scooping a hole in the sand, he lay face to the stone while the canyon rustled and sighed. The wind rushed around a stone spur, scattering sand grains on his face. Several times in the night footsteps passed so near that the ground yielded beneath his head. Huddled, shivering, he thought his heart had stopped and fell asleep from terror. He dreamed of the cliffs, an unbroken glassy red.

Early in the morning Milton woke and stretched, refreshed by the cool air. The only prints beside him were his own. That evening he wrote to C.C. in care of her California aunt, telling her he'd quit drinking.

When C.C. didn't respond, Milton wrote again, asking at least for word of Allen, who would have entered high school. C.C. replied, "When I got here the doctor said I had a broken nose. Allen says he has no father."

Milton knew he must hide to avoid drinking. When he asked Oldenburg's permission to spend a day in the granite mountains, Oldenburg said he would go, too. They camped against a rock turret. The light in the sky faded, and the fire leaped up. In the weeks since the former hand Jenkins's death, Oldenburg had become, if possible, more silent. Milton, meanwhile, admitted he had been a chatterbox, recalling high-school field trips to Phoenix fifteen years before, and rodeos in Tucson, Prescott, Sells, and Whiteriver. Oldenburg, fingertips joined at his chin, occasionally nodded or smiled. Tonight Milton squatted, arms around his knees, staring into the fire. About to share his most insistent emotions with the white man, he felt a giddy excitement, as if he were showing himself naked to a woman for the first time.

Milton told Oldenburg what C.C. had said.

"Your drinking has scarred them like acid. It will be time before they heal," Oldenburg said.

"There shouldn't be O'odham families," Milton exclaimed. "We should stop having children."

Oldenburg shook his head. After a while he said, "Milton, I hope you're not bitter because I won't let you drink. Drawing the line helps you. It's not easy living right. I've tried all my life and gained nothing — I lost both my sons in war and my wife divorced me to marry a piece of human trash. And still, in my own poor way, I try to live right." Oldenburg relaxed his shoulders and settled on his haunches.

Milton laid another mesquite limb across the fire. As the black of the sky intensified, the stars appeared as a glinting powder. Milton sipped two cups of coffee against the chill. Oldenburg, firelight sparkling off his silver tooth, wool cap pulled low over his stretched face, looked like an old grandmother. Laughing, Milton told him so. Oldenburg laughed too, rocking on his heels.

Soon after Oldenburg went to bed, Milton's mood changed. He hated the embers of the fire, the wind sweeping the rock knoll, the whirring of bats. He hated each stone and twig littering the campsite. His own fingers, spread across his knees, were like dumb, sleeping snakes. Poisonous things. He was glad one of them had been chopped off. Unrolling his blanket, he lay on his back, fists clenched. He dug hands and heels into the ground as if staked to it. After lying stiffly, eyes open, for an hour, he got up, slung his coiled rope over his shoulder, and walked down the hillside.

Brush and cactus were lit by a rising moon. Reaching a sheer drop, Milton jammed boot toes into rock fissures, seized tufts of saltbush, to let himself down. In the streambed he walked quickly until he joined the main river course. After a few miles' meandering through arroyos and over ridges, he arrived at the big sycamore and went to sleep.

Waking before dawn, Milton padded along the wash, hugging the granite. The cold morning silence was audible, a high, pure ringing. He heard the horse's snort before he saw it tearing clumps of grass from the gully bank, head tossing, lips drawn back over its yellow teeth. Rope at his hip, Milton stalked from boulder to boulder. When he stepped forward, whirling the lariat once, the horse reared, but quieted instantly as the noose tightened around its neck. Milton tugged the rope; the animal neighed and skipped backward, but followed.

During the next two days Milton and Oldenburg captured three more spindly, wiry horses. Oldenburg would flush the mustangs toward Milton, who missed only once with the lasso. The stallions Milton kept in separate pens and later sold as rodeo broncs. Within a couple of weeks he had broken the mares.

Milton consumed himself in chores. Though the Box-J was a small ranch, labor was unremitting. In the fall, summer calves were rounded up and "worked" — branded with the Box-J, castrated, and dehorned. The previous winter's calves, now some four hundred to five hundred pounds each, were held in side pens for weighing and loading onto the packer's shipping trucks. The pens were so dilapidated that Milton tore them down and built new ones. Winter, he drove daily pickup loads of sorghum hay, a supplement for the withered winter grasses, to drop spots at the water holes. Oldenburg hired extra help for spring roundup, working the new winter calves. Summer, Milton roved on horseback, troubleshooting. The fence-line would need repair. Oldenburg taught him to recognize cancer eye, which could destroy a cow's market value. A low water tank meant Oldenburg must overhaul the windmill. Throughout the year Milton inspected the herd, groomed the horses, maintained the buildings, kept tools and equipment in working order.

Certain moments, standing high in the stirrups, surveying the herd and the land which stretched from horizon to horizon as if mirroring the sky, he could believe all belonged to him.

Every two weeks, when Oldenburg drove into Casa Grande for supplies, Milton deposited half his wages — his first savings account — and mailed the rest to C.C. These checks were like money thrown blindly over the shoulder. So thoroughly had he driven his family from his mind that he couldn't summon them back, even if he wished to. When, just before sleep, spent from the day's work, he glimpsed C.C. and Allen, the faces seemed unreal. They were like people he had met and loved profoundly one night at a party, then forgotten.

The night of the first November frost, soon after the wild horse roundup, Oldenburg had asked Milton if he played cards. Milton didn't.

"Too bad," Oldenburg said. "It gets dull evenings. Jenkins and I played gin rummy. We'd go to five thousand, take us a couple of weeks, and then start again."

"We could cook," Milton said.

On Sunday he and Oldenburg baked cakes. Milton missed the pressurized frosting cans with which he'd squirted flowers and desert scenes at the CETA bakery, but Oldenburg's cherry-chocolate layer cake was so good he ate a third of it. Oldenburg complimented him on his angel food.

Oldenburg bought a paperback *Joy of Cooking* in Casa Grande. Though he and Milton had been satisfied with their main dishes, they tried Carbonnade Flamande, Chicken Paprika, Quick Spaghetti Meat Pie. Milton liked New England Boiled Dinner. Mostly they made desserts. After experimenting with mousses and custard, they settled on cakes — banana, golden, seed, sponge, four-egg, Lady Baltimore, the Rombauer Special. Stacks of foil-wrapped cakes accumulated in the freezer. The men contributed cakes to charitable bake sales. Milton found that after his nightly slab of cake sleep came more easily and gently.

The men were serious in the kitchen. Standing side by side in white aprons tacked together from sheets, Milton whisking egg whites, Oldenburg drizzling chocolate over pound cake, they would say little. Milton might ask the whereabouts of a spice; Oldenburg's refusal to label the jars irritated him. Then they sat by the warm stove, feet propped on the crates, and steamed themselves in the moist smells.

As they relaxed on a Sunday afternoon, eating fresh, hot cake, Oldenburg startled Milton by wondering aloud if his own wife were still alive. She had left him in 1963, and they'd had no contact since their second son was killed in 1969, more than ten years before.

"She wanted a Nevada divorce," Oldenburg said, "but I served papers on her first, and I got custody of the boys. I prevented a great injustice." He had sold his business in Colorado and bought the ranch. "The boys hated it," he said. "They couldn't wait to join the Army."

In Hashan, Milton said, she and her lover would have been killed.

Oldenburg shook his head impatiently. "He's deserted her, certainly. He was a basketball coach, and much younger than she was."

A Pima phrase — he knew little Pima — occurred to Milton. *Ne ha: jun* — all my relations. "Here is the opposite," Milton said. "We should call this the No-Relations Ranch."

Oldenburg sputtered with laughter. "Yes! And we'd need a new brand. Little round faces with big X's over them."

"You'd better be careful. People would start calling it the Tic-tac-toe Ranch."

"Or a manual, you know, a sex manual, for fornication. The X's doing it to the O's."

Light-headed from the rich, heavily frosted cake, they sprayed crumbs from their mouths, laughing.

At the Pinal County Fair in May, Oldenburg entered a walnut pie and goaded Milton into baking his specialty, a jelly roll. It received honorable mention, while Oldenburg won second prize.

Milton wrote C.C., "I'm better than a restaurant."

C.C. didn't answer. When Valley Bank opened a Hashan branch in June, Milton transferred his account and began meeting his friends for the first time in a year.

They needled him, "Milton, you sleeping with that old man?" His second Friday in town, Milton was writing out a deposit slip when he heard Bosque say, "Milton Oldenburg."

"Yes, Daddy just gave him his allowance," said Helene Mashad, the teller.

Bosque punched him on the shoulder and put out his hand. Milton shook it, self-conscious about his missing finger.

Bosque was cashing his unemployment check. The factory where he'd manufactured plastic tote bags for the past six months had closed. "Doesn't matter," Bosque said. "I'm living good." Before leaving, he said to come on by.

"You know what Oldenburg's doing, don't you?" Helene said, smoothing the wrinkles from Milton's check. She still wore her long lavender Phoenix nails and a frothy perm. After years in Phoenix she'd relocated at the new branch, closer to her home in Black Butte. "Oldenburg wants to marry you. Then he'll get some kind of government money for his Indian wife. Or he'll adopt you. Same deal."

"It's not me who's the wife or child. I run that place." Nervous speaking to a woman again, Milton rambled, boasting of his authority over hired crews, what Oldenburg called his quick mind and fast hands cutting calves or constructing a corner brace, his skill with new tools. Even his baking. "He has to be the wife," Milton said. "He's a better cook." Milton leaned his hip against the counter. "Older woman. He's so old he turned white. And he lost his shape." Milton's hands made breasts. "Nothing left."

They both laughed. Elated by the success of his joke, Milton asked her to dinner. Helene said yes, pick her up at six.

Milton was uneasy in Hashan. The dusty buildings — adobes, sandwich houses of mud and board, slump-block tract homes — seemed part of the unreal life that included his family. To kill time, he rode to the trading post in Black Butte, a few miles in the direction of Oldenburg's ranch, and read magazines. When he arrived at the bank, Helene slapped her forehead: she hadn't known he was on horseback. Phew, she said, she didn't want to go out with a horse. Milton should follow her home and take a bath first.

They never left her house. She was eager for him, and Milton realized that as a man he'd been dead for a year. They made love until early morning. Milton lay propped against the headboard, his arm encircling her, her cheek resting on his chest. She briskly stroked his hand.

"Your poor finger," she said. "I hear Lopez has little circles in his shoulder like where worms have gone into a tomato."

"It was bad," Milton said, closing his hand.

"I can't stand the men in this town, the drunken pigs," Helene said. "I don't know why I came back."

Helene wasn't what Milton wanted, but he liked her well enough to visit once or twice a month. Because she lived outside Hashan, few people knew of the affair. They would eat dinner and see a movie in Casa Grande or Phoenix, and go to bed. Sometimes they simply watched TV in bed, or drove Helene's Toyota through the desert, for miles without seeing another light.

When Milton returned from his second weekend with Helene, Oldenburg was peevish. "You drink with that woman?" he said. "You going to send her picture to your wife?" Emergencies arose that kept Milton on the ranch weekends. After selling two wild colts to a stable, he took Helene to Phoenix overnight. Oldenburg berated him, "The cows don't calve on Saturday and Sunday? They don't get sick? A shed doesn't blow down on Sunday?" Still the men baked together. At the beginning of the school year they entered a fund-raising Bake-Off sponsored by the PTO. Oldenburg won first with a Boston cream pie, and Milton's apple ring took second.

Helene transferred to Casa Grande, and Milton brought his account with her, relieved to avoid Hashan. Conversations with his friends were strained and dead. He worked; they didn't. They drank; he didn't. They had families. Milton nodded when he saw them, but no longer stopped to talk.

Fridays after Helene punched out, they might browse in the Casa Grande shopping center. Milton was drawn to the camera displays, neat lumps of technology embedded in towers of colorful film boxes. The Lerner shop's manikins fascinated him — bony stick figures like the bleached branches of felled cottonwood, a beautiful still arrangement. "Imagine Pimas in those," Helene said, pointing to the squares and triangles of glittering cloth. She puffed out her cheeks and spread her arms. Milton squeezed her small buttocks. Helene's legs were the slimmest of any O'odham woman he'd known.

During the second week of October, when Milton and a hired crew had set up shipping pens and begun culling the calves, a rare fall downpour, tail end of a Gulf hurricane, struck. For six hours thunder exploded and snarls of lightning webbed the sky. The deluge turned the ground to slop, sprang leaks in the roof, and washed out the floodgates at the edge of the granite mountains. Cattle stampeded through the openings; one died, entangled in the barbed wire. When the skies cleared, Oldenburg estimated that a quarter of the cash animals, some three hundred dollars apiece, had escaped. The shipping trucks were due in two days.

The next morning a new hired man brought further news: over the weekend a fight had broken out at the Sundowner. The fat end of a pool cue had caught Audrey Lopez across the throat, crushing her windpipe. Her funeral was to be at two in the afternoon.

Milton stood helplessly before Oldenburg. In the aftermath of the storm the sky was piercingly blue and a bracing wind stung his cheeks. Oldenburg's collar fluttered.

"You have to go," Oldenburg said. "There's no question."

"You'll lose too much money," Milton said stubbornly. "The cattle are in the mountains, and I know every little canyon where they run."

"There's no question," Oldenburg repeated. "The right way is always plain, though we do our best to obscure it."

The service took place in a small white Spanish-style church. At the cemetery the mourners stood bareheaded, the sun glinting off their hair. The cemetery was on a knoll, and in the broad afternoon light the surrounding plains, spotted by occasional cloud shadows, seemed immensely distant, like valleys at the foot of a solitary butte. Milton imagined the people at the tip of a rock spire miles in the clouds. The overcast dimmed them, and shreds of cumulus drifted past their backs and bowed heads.

Afterwards the men adjourned to the Lopez house, where Vigiliano Lopez rushed about the living room, flinging chairs aside to clear a center space. A ring of some twenty men sat on chairs or against the wall. Bosque arrived carrying three cold cases and two quarts of Crown Russe. More bottles appeared. Lopez started one Crown Russe in each direction and stalked back and forth from the kitchen, delivering beer and slapping bags of potato chips at the men's feet.

At his turn, Milton passed the bottle along.

"Drink, you goddamn Milton Oldenburg," Lopez said.

Milton said, "I'll lose my job."

"So?" Lopez shrugged distractedly. "I haven't had a job in a year. I don't need a job." Lopez had been the only Pima miner at the nearby Loma Linda pit until Anaconda shut it down. He pushed his hair repeatedly off his forehead, as if trying to remember something, then turned up the radio.

Milton sat erect in the chair, hands planted on his knees. He gobbled the potato chips. No one avoided him, nor he anyone else, yet talk was impossible. Grief surged through the party like a wave. Milton felt it in the overloud conversation, silences, the restlessness — no one able to stay in one place for long. Laughter came in fits. Over the radio, the wailing tremolos of the Mexican ballads were oppressive and nerve-wracking. The power of feeling in the room moved Milton and frightened him, but he was outside it.

Joining the others would be as simple as claiming the vodka bottle on its next round, Milton knew. But he remembered standing tall in the stirrups, as if he could see over the edge of the yellow horizon, the end of Oldenburg's land, and he kept his hands spread on his knees. At the thought of vodka's sickly taste-lessness, bile rose in his throat. Pretending to drink, tipping the bottle and plug-ging it with his tongue, would be foolish and shameful. Out of friendship and respect for Lopez, he could not leave. Their wounding each other, Milton real-ized, had bound him more closely to Lopez.

As night fell the men became drunker and louder. Bosque went out for more liquor. When he returned, he danced with the oil-drum cookstove, blackening his hands and shirt.

"Hey, not with my wife," Lopez said, grabbing the drum and humping it against the wall. "Need somebody to do you right, baby," he said. The drum clanged to the floor. The men cheered. Lopez, knees bent and hands out-stretched as if waiting for something to fall into them, lurched to the middle of the room. A smile was glazed over his face. He saw Milton.

"Drink with me, you son of a bitch," he shouted.

Milton motioned for the Crown Russe, a third full. "Half for you, half for me," he said. Marking a spot on the label with his finger, Milton drank two long swal-lows and held out the bottle for Lopez. Lopez drank and flipped the empty over his shoulder. Side by side, arms around each other, Milton and Lopez danced the *cumbia*. Lopez's weight sagged until Milton practically carried him. The man's trailing feet hooked an extension cord, sending a lamp and the radio crash-ing to the floor. Lopez collapsed.

Milton ran outside and retched. Immediately he was refreshed and lucid. The stars burned like drillpoints of light. Patting the horse into an easy walk, he sat back in the saddle, reins loose in his lap, and gave himself to the brilliant stillness. As his eyes adjusted to the night, he could distinguish the black silhouettes of mountains against the lesser dark of the sky. Faint stars emerged over the ranges, bringing the peaks closer. The mountains were calm and friendly, even the jag-ged line of the Ka kai.

That night Milton dreamed that a chocolate-colored flood swept through Ha-shan. The O'odham bobbed on the foam; from the shore others dove backward into the torrent, arms raised symmetrically by their heads. Receding, the flood left bodies swollen in the mud — Milton's brother Lee, their mother, belly down, rising in a mound. Milton, long hair fixed in the mud, stared upward. His hands were so full of fingers they had become agaves, clusters of fleshy, spiny leaves. Peering down at him, C.C. and Allen were black against the sun, arms crooked as if for flight. Milton was glad they had escaped.

Milton woke serene and energetic, the dream forgotten. Over breakfast Oldenburg studied him intently — clear gray eyes, a slight frown — but said nothing. The penned calves were weighed and loaded onto the shipping trucks. Many remained free, and the year would be a loss.

Milton wrote C.C. of Audrey Lopez's death. "I had a big drink to keep Lopez company," he added, "but I threw it up. It was the first booze in more than a year. I don't like it anymore."

Lying beside Milton the following weekend, Helene said, "Poor finger. I'll give you another one." She laid her pinky against the stub so a new finger seemed to grow. Her lavender nail looked like the fancy gem of a ring. She lifted, lowered the finger. "And Lopez with the purple spots on his shoulder like the eyes of a potato," she said. She shifted and her small, hard nipple brushed Milton's side. "It's a wonder you two didn't fight."

"Shut up," Milton said. "His wife is dead."

"I know. It's terrible." She had worried for him, Helene said, knowing he would be at the funeral with Lopez. He should have brought her.

"I didn't want you there," Milton said. "You don't have the right feelings." He left before dawn and hadn't returned to Helene when C.C. replied.

"I was shocked to hear about Audrey," C.C. wrote. "I feel sad about it every day. Hashan is such a bad place. But it isn't any better here. At Allen's school there are gangs and not just Mexicans but black and white too."

She wrote again: "I miss you. I've been thinking about coming back. Allen says he won't, but he'll come with me in the end. The money has helped. Thank you."

Milton threw up his arms and danced on the corral dirt, still moist and reddened from fluke autumn rains. Shouting, he danced on one leg and the other, dipping from side to side as if soaring, his head whirling. Oldenburg's nagging — where will they live? — worried him little. Over dinner Oldenburg suggested, "They'll live in your old place, and you can visit them on weekends. We'll have to move our baking to the middle of the week."

Milton knew he must be with the O'odham. Announcing a ride into the mountains, he saddled up and galloped toward Hashan. Because he couldn't see the faces of his family, his joy felt weirdly rootless. The past year he had killed them inside. The sudden aches for Allen, the sensation of carrying C.C.'s weight in his arms, had been like the twinges of heat, cold, and pain from his missing finger. As if straining after their elusive faces, Milton rode faster. His straw hat, blown back and held by its cord, flapped at his ear. The horse's neck was soaked with sweat.

Bosque's fat wife said he wasn't home. Milton made a plan for the Sundowner: after one draft for sociability, he would play the shuffleboard game. Tying up at a light pole, he hesitated in the lounge doorway. The familiarity of the raw wood beams crisscrossing the bare Sheetrock walls frightened him. But Bosque, sliding his rear off a barstool, called, "Milton Oldenburg."

"C.C.'s hauling her little tail home," Milton announced. "And the boy."

"All riiight." Bosque pumped his hand up and down. Milton's embarrassment at his missing finger disappeared in the vastness of Bosque's grip. Friends he hadn't spoken to in months surrounded him. "When's she coming? She going to live on the ranch? Oldenburg will have a whole Indian family now." Warmed by their celebration of his good luck, Milton ordered pitchers. His glass of draft was deep gold and sweeter than he had remembered, though flat. Others treated him in return. Someone told a story of Bosque building a scrap wood raft to sail the shallow lake left by the rains. Halfway across, the raft had broken apart and sunk. "Bosque was all mud up to his eyes," the storyteller said. "He looked like a bull rolling in cow flop." Everyone laughed.

Fuzzy after a half dozen beers, Milton felt his heart pound, and his blood. He saw them then — C.C., wings of hair, white teeth, dimpled round cheeks. Allen's straight bangs and small, unsmiling mouth. Their eyes were black with ripples of light, reflections on a pool. Milton was drawn into that pool, lost. Terror washed over him like a cold liquid, and he ordered a vodka.

"I'm a drunk," he told the neighbor on his right.

"Could be. Let's check that out, Milton," the man said.

"I never worked."

"No way," the man said, shaking his head.

"I didn't make a living for them."

"Not even a little bitty bit," the man agreed.

"Not even this much," Milton said, holding his thumb and forefinger almost closed, momentarily diverted by the game. "I hurt them."

Holding up his hands, the man yelled, "Not me."

"I tortured them. They don't belong to me. I don't have a family," Milton mumbled. Quickly he drank three double vodkas. The jukebox streamed colors, and he floated on its garbled music.

Shoving against the men's room door, Milton splashed into the urinal, wavering against the stall. He groped for the Sundowner's rear exit. The cold bit through his jacket. He pitched against a stack of bricks.

Waking in the dark, Milton jumped to his feet. C.C. was coming, and his job was in danger. He was foreman of a white man's ranch. Allen and C.C. would be amazed at his spread. With a bigger bank account than three-quarters of Hashan, he could support them for a year on savings alone. The night before was an ugly blur. But his tongue was bitter, his head thudded, he had the shakes. Cursing, Milton mounted and kicked the horse into a canter. To deceive Oldenburg he must work like a crazy man and sweat out his hangover. The fits of nausea made him moan with frustration. He kicked the horse and struck his own head.

Milton arrived an hour after sunup. Shooing the horse into the corral with a smack to the rump, he stood foggily at the gate, unable to remember his chore from the previous day. A ladder leaning against the barn reminded him: patching. He lugged a roll of asphalt roofing up the ladder. Scrambling over the steep pitch didn't frighten him, even when he slipped and tore his hands. He smeared tar, pressed the material into place, drove the nails. Every stroke was true, two per nail. Milton had laid half a new roof when Oldenburg called him.

"Come down." Oldenburg was pointing to the corral. The gate was still ajar. Milton's horse, head drooping, dozed against the rail, but the other three were gone.

Milton stood before him, wobbly from exertion, blood draining from his head.

"You lied," Oldenburg said. "You abandoned your job. The week is *my* time. You've been drunk. I'm going to have to let you go, Milton."

Milton couldn't speak.

"You understand, don't you?" Oldenburg said more rapidly. His eyes flicked down, back to Milton. "Do you see what happens?" His arms extended toward the empty corral.

"So I lose a day running them down."

Smiling slightly, Oldenburg shook his head. "You miss the point. It would be wrong for me to break my word. You'd have no cause to believe me again, and our agreement would be meaningless."

"Once a year I get drunk," Milton burst out. "We'll put a name on it, November Something Milton's Holiday."

Oldenburg smiled again. "Once a month . . . once a week . . . I'm sorry. I'll give you two weeks' pay, but you can leave any time." He turned.

"I've worked hard for you!" Milton's throat felt as if it were closing up.

Oldenburg stopped, brow furrowed. "It's sad," he said. "You've managed the Box-J better than I could. I'm going to miss our baking." He paused. "But we have to go on, Milton, don't you see? My family leaves me, Jenkins leaves me, you leave me. But *I* go on." He walked away.

Two long steps, a knee in the back, arms around the neck, and he could break the man in half—Milton's arms dropped. He had lost the urge for violence. Long after Oldenburg had disappeared into the open green range where the horses were, he stood by the corral. Then, arms over his head as if escaping a cloudburst, he ran into the adobe, packed his belongings in a sheet, and that afternoon rode the exhausted horse back to his old home.

To C.C., Milton wrote, "I don't have my job anymore but there's plenty of money in the bank." Weeks later she replied, "Milton, I know what's going on. I can't come home to this." But she would continue to write him, she said. Milton saw no one. Pacing the house, he talked to the portraits over the TV—Allen's eighth-grade class picture, a computer-drawn black-dot composition of C.C. from the O'odham Tash carnival. He disturbed nothing, not even the year-and-a-half-old pile of dishes in the sink.

For several weeks he laid fence for a Highway Maintenance heavy equipment yard. Working with a new type of fence, chain link topped with barbed wire, cheered him. The foreman was lax, married to one of Milton's cousins, so when Milton requested the leftover spools of barbed wire, he said, "Sure. It's paid for."

Milton dug holes around his house and cut posts from the warped, gnarled mesquite growing in the vacant land. As he worked, the blue sky poured through chinks in the posts, reminding him pleasantly of the timeless first days repairing the line on Oldenburg's range. When he had finished stringing the wire, Milton's house was enclosed in a neat box—two thorned strands, glinting silver. Sunlight jumped off the metal in zigzag bolts. In Hashan, where fences were unknown and the beige ground was broken only by houses, cactus, and drab shrubs, the effect was as startling as if Milton had wrapped his home in Christmas lights.

Milton sat on the back doorstep, drinking beer. Discouraged by the fence, no one visited at first. But dogs still ran through the yard, as did children, who preferred scaling the fence to slithering under it. Their legs waggled precariously on the stiffly swaying wire; then they hopped down, dashed to the opposite side, and climbed out, awkward as spiders. Milton's fence became a community joke, which made him popular. Instead of walking through the gap behind the house, friends would crawl between the strands or try to vault them. Or they would lean on the posts, passing a beer back and forth while they chatted.

Keeping her promise, C.C. wrote that Allen had shot up tall. Even running track he wore his Walkman, she said. But he smoked, and she had to yell at him. Last term he'd made nearly all A's.

Milton grew extremely fat, seldom leaving the house except to shop or work the odd jobs his new skills brought him. Through spring and summer he drowsed on the doorstep. In November, almost a year after he'd left Oldenburg's, he fell asleep on the concrete slab and spent the night without jacket or blanket. The next day he was very sick, and Bosque and Lopez drove him to the hospital. The doctor said he had pneumonia.

Milton's first day in ICU, Bosque and Lopez shot craps with him during visiting hours. But as his lungs continued to fill with fluid, his heart, invaded by fatty tissue from his years of drinking, weakened. Four days after entering the hospital, he suffered a heart attack.

In the coronary ward, restricted to ten-minute visits, Milton dreamed, feeling as if the fluid had leaked into his skull and his brain was sodden. In one dream the agaves again sprouted from his wrists, their stalks reaching into the sky. He gave the name *ne ha: jun* — all my relations — to his agave hands.

The next morning C.C. and Allen appeared in the doorway. Huge, billowing, formless as smoke, they approached the bed in a peculiar rolling motion. Milton was afraid. From the dreams he realized that his deepest love was drawn from a lake far beneath him, and that lake was death. But understanding, he lost his fear. He held out his arms to them.

Rita Maria Magdaleno

The Summer Dances

For Lita

Inevitably, we lose all our innocence.
— JUDITH ORTIZ-COFER

Those nights were damp as small
chains of watermelon vines
ready to blossom. That summer,
we wanted to go to *Miami*,
to the *Plaza* to go dancing
on Sunday nights. We always washed
our hair with jojoba. Oh,
we had beautiful hair. And
those young men, our secret
admirers, had black hair,
glossy. My two *hermanitas*
and I would pretend like we
were moving in dreamy circles,
that we were dancing and being
held in those warm male arms.
But my dad would always say,
*"Oh, those boys . . . they all just want
one thing."* All that summer,
I remember the sweet smell
of jojoba and the way
our hair would flow, black
silk, secret wishes. My twin
brother never learned
how to dance, and we never
did go to the dance hall
in *Miami.* But I remember

the music of those *cumbias*
and the sweet rhythm
of those boys. Each night,
they floated up, dark angels
in my dreams. And each night,
my father would pause in
our doorway, stand in that space
between the light and the dark.
There, he would bless us, fragile
rain of holy water entering
our room and descending silently
upon us. I still remember that
wet smell, and the rain. Each night,
it hovered in the Pinales and the yellow
pines waited patiently. They waited
for that first summer rain.

Rita Maria Magdaleno

Zapatos

This is a poem to you who have found
my shoes — soft, olive green,
generous leather straps, air-
cushioned heels, Clarks
from America. They were new
and I left them on a frantic
counter, past 9 P.M. in the exhausted
bus terminal #1, Guadalajara moist
and dark, the small rain coming.

It's late May and I'm travelling
alone to San Miguel de Allende.
You'll never know me, the woman
who planned to wear those shoes,
to walk the cobblestoned ways
through Mexico. I try to imagine
the look on your brown face
when you discover my loss, open
the white plastic bag, see
my shoes nestled inside
like two airy birds, green.
You'll never know that this
was my first time travelling so far
into the land where my father's blood
began running through his infant
veins. But I'll tell you anyway:
This is my virgin journey
and I'm going with or without shoes.

Now, I'm almost in Celaya
and I see two brown colts

nibbling wild grass near
the roadside. Now, you are
probably slipping into my shoes;
and I imagine you in Guadalajara,
you, strolling the gardens,
bright red. You, amazed
that there could be so much
softness inside the sturdy leather
of my shoes.

Paul Morris

Salome

To ocher long ago,
The small towns of the desert surrendered.
Heat makes every movement futile.

Adobe houses refuse fences and have forgotten grass,
The ground too hardheaded and alkaline.
Skipping two seasons without a thought,
Plants here are deeply confused.

When the interstate passed around,
The chain grocery store closed along with the café.
Gas stations moved to chase the road
And sell bad shocks, leaving the one bar
To hunker down.

The young leave here with the regularity of buses.
The dull Sabre jet in the park
The town's only dream of flight.

At night the road to Yuma is so long it forgets to turn;
Car lights are set on bright and forgotten.
This radio croons in Spanish or shouts a fervent gospel.

With one hand you tune in the cool air north.

Paul Morris

Learning Spanish

For Mary Malherek

The parts of the body are easy.
Only so many parts can be removed.
Look on the sides of roads at night:
The places rarely change.
Methods are simple, just a few verbs.

The moist scent of coffee flowers.

Then a man across the table
Pulls up his shirt to show
Three bullets, here and here, here.
Or by a kitchen door a woman stirs
Black beans and weeps, her mother
Macheted by soldiers,
Or the man without thumbs who sits
Looking out the car window, saying little . . .
And I know I've learned nothing
Of the language they speak.

Paul Morris

A Resonance of Emerald:

Hummers in the Desert

It is spring here in the Sonoran Desert, and I am hanging a damp sheet across the clothesline on my patio. I hear the whirl of a fan blade, and suddenly six inches from my nose is a hummingbird, poised to drink from the red plastic feeder hanging from the eaves. Wings beating eighty times a second, it is an arrogant explosion of light. A male with a crimson cap and gorget bib, its rapid fire chick-chick feeding squeaks give it away: an Anna's hummingbird, the noisiest of the hummers. In sunlight, its feathers take on a dramatic iridescence until the bird retreats into the shade. Once out of the direct light, this hummer has no colors, its chest and neck only muted shades of gray.

The hummer pauses, inspects me only briefly, then moves to feed, first perching on the plastic seat. It leans forward, begins sipping the sugar water, and I am forgotten. My life is too slow, a pace too sluggish to be a threat. To these souped-up three ounces of feathers, I move like an avalanche of cold syrup. Last week I watched a television nature show on underwater life, and as I stared at the patient movements of starfish and sea slugs, I knew suddenly that this must be how hummingbirds observe humans: dull, stupid creatures glued in time. The brief moment we call a second must seem an hour to this bird with its frenetic drum-solo heartbeat — 1,260 beats a minute. How it might regard a human holding a damp sheet in the same way we might suddenly realize that a stone has somehow moved to a different spot.

As it drinks, the hummer pauses, lifts its head, and looks over its shoulder, constantly watching for the Black-Chinned hummingbird that is battling for this source of food. It drinks again. I stand transfixed, forgetting the wet sheet. It takes no notice of me.

But why should it? The hummer is living life at a pace I'll never see. We snicker at the drowsy inertia of the tortoise and marvel at the drifting lethargy of the basking shark. Don't we consider speed a virtue and sloth a sin? When I replay a freeze-frame memory of a traffic accident hurtling across an intersection, time floats slowly in a bubble of adrenaline. Some days the momentum of my life seems perilously fast as though I sense the axial rotation of the earth, spinning at a frightening 1,038 miles per hour. Fill me up with espresso till I vibrate or frighten me till time crawls to a stop, but I'll never understand the quickened world this hummer inhabits. Perhaps this bird, the basking shark, and I all orbit some distant center, only at different spiraling velocities.

The Anna's raises its head and lifts off to hover at another hole on the feeder and drink again. Both feeding spots must taste similar—it's the same sugared water after all. But this is a constant quest for motion. This is a bird that never walks, that even flies upside down. It is a life that would rather move than rest. The hummer enters the light and suddenly becomes a tantrum of rouge.

"Birds are flowers flying," says A. R. Ammons. If we plucked the feathers from this hummingbird like petals from a blossom, we'd find no brilliance in the down. Beneath the microscope, a feather reveals layers and layers of translucent prisms set atop sections of inky blackness. Light enters the feather and is either absorbed, revealing only a sooty darkness, or is bent in the prismlike platelets and reflected back to your eye. Depending upon the layers of feather and the angle of the light, you suddenly see the flash of the spectrum, a dramatic rainbow of feathers that pulses with each motion. And when seen in a tiny bird beating its wings 4,800 times a minute, fireworks can happen.

The matchless iridescence of hummingbirds attracted the interest of Europeans during the nineteenth century. Between 1849 and 1861, John Gould produced a remarkable five-volume book featuring exquisite color illustrations of all the hummingbird species known at the time. What Emily Dickinson calls "A Resonance of Emerald — / A Rush of Cochineal" immediately became the fashion craze as dressmakers, haberdashers, and clothing designers sought out the minute feathers to adorn their work. Reports tell of twelve thousand hummingbird skins traded at a London auction in 1888, with thousands more on the block a month later.

Just sixty-two years earlier in what is now San Francisco, a priest, Padre Tomás, introduced the naturalist Emile Botta to an unusual new hummingbird. Intrigued, Botta preserved a specimen, returned to Paris, and passed it to the noted ornithologist Reme Primevere Lesson, the era's leading expert on hummingbirds. As Adam did with the animals in the Garden, Lesson realized that our understanding of a new species begins with the most essential act of definition. Can we really begin to know anything without a name?

Like any practical scientist with an interest toward future grants and financial support, Lesson thought of the generous Duke of Rivoli, Prince Francois Victor

Massena, a man noted for sponsoring birding expeditions around the world and owner of one of the largest private collections of bird specimens in Europe. Lesson had already named a bird after the Duke: the Rivoli's hummingbird. What better flattery than to use the name of the Duke's delightful wife, Anne de Belle Massena, a woman whose charm and beauty John James Audubon mentions in his writings. And thus we know this bird as the Anna's hummingbird (*Calypte anna*).

The Duke of Rivoli went on to play a pivotal role in Audubon's career, purchasing his *Birds of America* portfolio and, more importantly, introducing him to French society and future patrons. In 1846, the American Academy of Natural Science in Philadelphia purchased the Duke's collection of twelve thousand bird skins (including the original bird Lesson used to describe the Anna's hummer). The Duke's story continues until 1983, when changes are made and his namesake, the Rivoli's hummingbird, is crossed out in everyone's field guides and renamed the Magnificent hummingbird. His wife's bird fares better and continues to carry her name.

A printer explained to me once that certain colors cannot be reproduced exactly on paper: the neon hues of tropical fish, the infinite variations of the morning glory, and even certain auto body paints, for instance; all are beyond the range of inks we now have. Fortunately, the human eye does not remember color well. We can compare and discern subtle differences in hues, but if we look at them singly, we cannot remember the variations. Bring a chip of paint to the store and we can match it nicely; forget the chip and who knows what color you'll take home. We are unfaithful lovers of the world around us. Give us a brief moment of flashing wing and we are lost in evanescence.

Ironically, the hummingbird never sees its own colors. Its great brilliance only occurs with distance. Get too close and beauty disappears. As with the great Rose Window at the cathedral in Chartres, the stained glass that Rilke describes as possessing a brilliance that "would seize a soul and tear it into God," one's vantage point is everything. Stand in the plaza outside the church and see only the stone framework and gray glass; enter and risk being transformed by luminous glory. Sometimes I think people exude light in a similar manner, a brief vibrating luminescence we cannot perceive in ourselves but depending upon how the sunlight strikes those around us, we might see momentary flashes.

Here's a snapshot taken at my sister's wedding last summer. We are frozen in midtoast, caught as the slender flutes of champagne flutter momentarily above the centerpiece. The brief flash has caught the red luminous pulse in our eyes, that crimson reflection of the deep blood behind our eyes. Everyone in that photo is brilliant with the momentary life within us, exhilarated with something that suddenly disappears like a hummingbird.

Jonathan Penner

This Is My Voice

Before I speak, can I say one thing? This has all been very upsetting. But I know you've got a job to do, and I know you're extremely intelligent people, and whatever punishment you decide I deserve is fine.

I guess it all began in August, when I first came here. Professor Delavette was still on Martha's Vineyard then. Her house sitter got pneumonia and had to be hospitalized. His name was funny, something Saint something.

A saver, this guy was. I found drawers of empty Yoplait containers. He'd wash out the 9-Lives cans after he fed Professor Delavette's cat.

George St. George.

So I was looking for a place to get some writing done before the fall semester began, and the secretary had the keys to Professor Delavette's. St. George had developed something with his liver. He went home to Baltimore, I believe it was.

The secretary phones Professor Delavette and tells her a very large, very young man is available. "Extremely," she says, looking up at me. I'm standing there in front of her desk, keeping my arms behind me, because all I did in high school was lift weights. And then I talked, and Professor Delavette said it was fine, so I stayed in her guesthouse and took care of things.

I have to tell you, and I know Dean Beechel has a meeting. This will be quick. I just have to tell you that Professor Delavette was the main reason I came here in the first place. I consider her one of our finest living writers. You know how informal she is, and the other students call her Gina and so forth, but for me it was thrilling just to cut her grass. Her power mower broke down, so I used a hand one. Once I turned over a wheelbarrow behind the toolshed, and underneath was a footprint in the hardened mud, and every day for the rest of August I came back and looked at it and wondered if it was hers.

I need to explain about me and writing. Too many ideas is what my trouble is. Even for the first word! And the crazy thing, what's so frustrating, is I feel like I already *know* the stories. Is that possible? I could swear they exist, I already know them, somewhere in here, or in here. Writing them down should be so easy, like unwrapping presents, and I'm so amazed when I never can.

Of course, I signed up for her workshop. And that's really where I should have begun — I shouldn't have told you about St. George, and the cat, and the secretary. That was a terrible beginning. I signed up for her workshop, and next thing everyone else in the class is handing in stories. She'd get them duplicated, and we'd all discuss them.

And what do I know, I'm the last person who should criticize. But I always felt terrible reading those stories. The characters in them were always learning something important about life — they never just wasted their time, not a minute.

It was enough to make any actual human being feel poor. Is that good writing?

But I couldn't write any stories at all. After three weeks, I showed her a paragraph. Professor Delavette read it fast. Then she gave me a funny look and sat down and read it slowly, with her finger moving down the margin and stopping sometimes to rub the paper in little circles. Then she hands it back and tells me, "I'm impressed. You have a voice."

Why did she have to say that? I sat and stared at that paragraph. It was something about the vacation I subbed at the post office. It was about carrying mail. It was idiotic, the things I remembered, like my shadow humping over the lawn, and songs I'd hear in my head all day, and places on the route where I could, you know, relieve myself. I tried reading it aloud, alone in my room, and I had to stop in the first sentence. I think it was right then that I started getting angry at Professor Delavette. When she told me I had a voice. Because it stank, and I'd written it the only way I could.

Whatever punishment you gentlemen decide is O.K. with me. I'm grateful to you and Professor Delavette for not calling the police. But what I want to emphasize is this. All this time, I was taking care of her place, and all through the semester I tried to do my best.

I swept her steps. I washed her windows inside and out. I kept her grass cut and raked out her hedges. Somehow she got her power mower going again, this old beast of a reel type. It'd run awhile and stop. I'd pull the cord until my muscles felt like balloons, and take off my shirt and keep yanking, sometimes jerking the whole machine off the ground, until my right hand was cramped into a ball. Then I'd go up to the house, and Professor Delavette would come out and remove the air filter, or clean the plug, or just whack the carburetor, and it would run awhile again. She told me she couldn't afford a new one. Maybe that was my fault, because she'd said I didn't have to pay any rent for the guesthouse, except the value of my labor.

I guess it actually began when this young kid arrived, the Maharish. His friends call him that, now. I don't want to get him mixed up in this. He's from my hometown. I used to baby-sit him and his sister. He quit high school and came to find me at the university, and I was amazed how he's changed. He brought a calendar with scenes of his guru doing yoga between vases of flowers. When I used to take him and his sister to play on the swings, he was a regular kid with a regular name.

Now he wants to be an artist, but he doesn't know how to paint. He doesn't have any paints. He said the first step was getting himself in tune. That's why he came to me, because he thought I was a writer and I'd inspire him. He's been sleeping on my floor in his dhoti. Like a loincloth?

I was afraid to tell Professor Delavette, but I made him phone his parents. He won't eat meat, and I've been trying to get some protein into him. But all he does is read all day, and meditate, and do his tantrum.

Tantrum. You sit a certain way and breathe a certain way.

Well, he saw I wasn't doing any writing, and he gave me some stuff to read. Stories from the Orient. The people in them learned wisdom from locusts and fish.

Next he brought out a magazine, *Ursa Major.* Fantasy. I love that stuff, but it was trash. I assume you gentlemen have all been shown one of those stories, the one where the couple become the slaves of their dog. At the time I just passed over it.

With the Maharish there, things got harder. He never left the room, and I didn't know what to do with him. By this time I'd dropped all my classes except Professor Delavette's, and I'd spend hours every day, sitting with cotton in my ears, staring at my typewriter, until it made me sweat just to roll in a piece of paper, with the Maharish doing his tantrum on the floor behind me. Even with the cotton, I thought I could hear the rhythm of his breathing.

No matter how I tried, I couldn't write a story, and sometimes I felt like I'd kill Professor Delavette, or else the Maharish. The only other thing in the world I could imagine doing was delivering mail again. So I went down to the post office and applied, but I'd gotten a bad report the time I worked for them as a sub.

The postmaster told me forget it. "Trouble with you," he said, "you got an attitude." He looked me up and down, and just from his body type, which was pitiful, I knew what was coming. "Like most jocks," he says, and starts shaking his head, "you think you can get through life on muscles."

No matter how you dress, if you lift for too many years they know. They know from your neck.

In October there were leaves to rake, and you've heard about the fire. Professor Delavette came out with the garden hose. Then in November a pipe burst in the guesthouse bathroom. The Maharish discovered it, because he slept on the floor. The next thing I knew he was standing in the middle of my bed, dripping on me.

I pulled on some pants and went outside to shut off the main. Then I looked for a mop, but all there was was a handle with an empty clamp. Professor Delavette came out and said her water had gone off, and for some reason I felt shy, even though I had my pants on. I leaned around the guesthouse door and told her the story.

"I've seen a naked man before," she says.

I'm sorry. I shouldn't have told you that.

I finished getting dressed, and she gave me her car keys, and I went to the hardware store for a mop. They had mops. They had mops of every kind and size and shape. It was just the same as writing a story. Then I saw a replacement head, and I was happy, and I bought it. But when I got it home, I couldn't get it into the clamp on Professor Delavette's old handle. It was too big.

We were on the porch of the guesthouse, and she stood there watching me. I went and got a hammer., I thought maybe I could just modify the clamp a little. Professor Delavette didn't say anything. She just looked at me so — seriously, or something — that I felt like I'd explode. I was kind of trying to hammer the clamp on my lap, and I could see she was afraid I'd hurt myself, but that she knew I'd be hurt more if she even opened her mouth. Then I did mash myself, a good one on the forefinger. "My God," she says and throws away the hammer. I'm squeezing the finger. "Let me see that," she says, pulling at my wrist.

Just then the Maharish comes out of the guesthouse. He stands there in the doorway in that loincloth of his, blinking at the daylight. "Something's happened," he tells me. "I'm in tune. I can feel it."

Well, Professor Delavette just looks at him, this practically naked little kid. He smiles at her. "Shanty, shanty, shanty," he says, kind of blessing her with his hand. She nods at him and says, "Shanty, shanty," herself. Then she says she'll go call the plumber.

I knew what she was thinking, and I followed her up to her door. "He's just this kid," I tell her.

"He's lovely," she says. "Whatever helps. All I want from you is a story."

"I'm having trouble."

"You've got a voice," she says. "Use it." It was a command, like from a queen.

I should have told you that first, because this is when the bad part really began. The Maharish painted all day, except he didn't use paints. He couldn't afford them. He used food. Peanut butter, ketchup, mayonnaise. He used toothpaste and mud. He finger-painted. All this time I was trying to write. Then he said that since I'd helped him, now he was going to help me.

And that's when he came up with the idea for me to hand in the *Ursa Major* story. The one where the couple become the slaves of their dog. Just to get me started, just to get me going. I stood up and I felt like strangling him.

I sat down and tried again to write, and my ideas were like bugs around a streetlight—all the people I could write about, everything I could make them say and do. And that's when I knew, I really understood for the first time, that there was no way in the world I could write a story.

"Let's see that magazine," I said.

And you know the rest. I stole it.

I was scared to death Professor Delavette would catch me, so you've seen the changes I made. It didn't need to be a couple that got enslaved, so I made it a guy. Instead of a dog, I made it a hobo woman that he befriends. She doesn't exactly enslave him—in fact, he makes her hit the road, at the end—but she does, in a way. I thought I better slide in some things, about the job he works at, cleaning up alcoholics—that's where he meets this hobo woman—and about this old Thunderbird his girlfriend is after him to buy. It's more confusing than in *Ursa Major*. At least there the story was clear. And in *Ursa Major* they had good writing, all soft and bouncy. Anyone would know I couldn't write that well—the sentences made me think of actual pillows—so I had the guy tell it the way I would, if it were me. If I were him. I titled it "His Master's Voice."

When I finished, my shirt was sticking to me. I didn't know if I could hand that story in. But it was that or give Professor Delavette nothing at all. I knew I couldn't put it in her hands, so I left it in her mailbox at school.

It was about two weeks after the pipe broke, and we were having Indian summer. The grass needed one more mowing. I started at the back and was working my way forward toward the house, when I saw Professor Delavette coming toward me across the lawn. Right away I was sure she had me. Something was in her hand, and I guessed what it was.

I shut off the lawnmower, and you know how quiet that makes it. She just stood there. There were *tears* in her eyes, and I didn't know exactly what or how, but I knew right then that something terrible was going to happen.

"This is beautiful," she said. "This is wonderful."

She held it out to me, and I took it. I just looked at the first page. She'd filled the margins with notes. "Rings true," and "Captures it," and "Good!" and "Yes!" all over the place.

I handed it back. "It's garbage," I said. "It isn't even mine." And I told her how I'd gotten the story from that trashy little magazine. But she just kept standing there, smiling and shaking her head.

"This is *yours*," she says. "*This is your voice.*"

Then she must have seen that I was starting to feel pretty bad, because she reached out and touched my arm, and said, "We'll talk about it later. Come up to the house when you're done." She gave the lawn mower a kick. Then she walked away with that awful story in her hand.

Well, I pulled the cord and it started right up. Exercise helps. You go to the weight room all in knots and come out after your shower all peaceful. I pushed that lawn mower back and forth faster than most people jog.

But it didn't help, not this time. I went roaring past the guesthouse, where the Maharish was out in front on a blanket, trying for a tan in his loincloth. It was probably the last afternoon of the year that would be warm enough. The guy had inner peace, you've got to give him that. He'd given up his tantrum and had just told me that morning he didn't need to paint anymore, either. He thought he was about ready to go home to his parents.

He waved his hand at me to slow down, but I couldn't. And the faster I went, the worse I felt. And I'm ashamed to admit it, but you know what bothered me? She had no idea who I was. If she really liked me or my writing at all, she should have known that wasn't my work. And you know what else? Not the fact I plagiarized the story, though I'm ashamed of that too. It was the fact that she let herself be fooled. The more I thought about that, the longer I mowed, the more I lost all my respect for Professor Delavette, like I was cutting it down one row at a time.

By the time I finished the lawn, it was all gone, and that's the only way I can explain what happened. I was right outside her living room. I shut off the lawn mower, and I knew I would never push that thing again. I felt like throwing it away. I lifted it by the handles, and I never felt so strong in my life.

I began to turn, stepping backward in a circle, leaning against the weight. It's all in the forearms. I got it a few inches off the ground, then higher. I leaned back and got it knee high, thigh high, until I could get my legs and shoulders into it, and the lawn mower and I were just whirling each other around, and then

I gave it everything I had. It barely cleared the sill of her big living room window and went crashing through.

You could hear the thump and clank as it hit the carpet, and the glass tinkling like wind chimes. Then an upstairs window opened, and Professor Delavette leaned her head out.

"What in the world," she says, "was that?"

I tell her, "That was my voice. *That* was my voice."

Well, I know Dean Beechel has to go. I guess all you gentlemen do. I guess I'll be getting a letter after you've decided.

I just wanted you to understand what happened. Naturally, I feel different now. In the last week I've read Professor Delavette's books again, and I can't be angry at her — only grateful. She truly is one of the finest writers alive.

And I realize that's the problem right there. For her, writing is just so easy, it doesn't take any effort at all. She can sit down and write a story anytime she wants to. So how can she understand the fact that I can't?

I know you gentlemen will be writing an official report. I hope you'll say I tried my best. Please put that in my permanent file. But say it was like trying to burn an ice cube.

Say it was like trying to teach a gorilla to dance.

Or no: a sewer to sing.

Then if anybody, some future employer — if anyone ever wants to know about me — they'll simply look it up. I waive my right to privacy, and they'll know. Or the government. They can just read your report, and they'll know the truth. Teachers, in case I ever come back to school — they can look too. I waive my right to privacy — do I have a right to privacy? I don't care who sees it, even Professor Delavette herself, in case someday she needs to put me in a story, and she's trying to get my voice, but all she remembers is a broken window and the smell of grass coming up her stairs.

Jean Rukkila

Risking the Reach

A friend asked hummingbirds
to stand on her hands.
Her fingers cupped the feeder,
thumb touched thumb,
to create a tiny mountain range.
Birds paused on her knuckles,
a merry-go-round of collapsed flight,
still wings tucked tight
to throbbing hearts.
Sugar moved through them,
a whispered shower against her skin.

Those tiny toes, that fine sensation,
teased out delicate memory.
A river place with willows,
where wind trailed feathers of leaves
against the glass of water.
Still liquid changed to pulsing rings.
The distinctive caress
of a leaf that had only felt wind before.

Leaves on the water
like a ring of hummingbirds.
A sensual bouquet, an empowering joy,
to hold spoonfuls of breathing feathers.
It was not an embrace,
though willing hands quivered.

Dean Stover

Bill of Sale

Oatmeal sticking to my ribs,
long johns hugging my body,
I walk into a deep freezer day in February
to help place shovels, rakes and tools
around the combine, tractors and hayracks
so farmers from several counties away
who've seen the bill of sale in the local paper
could inspect it all
before the auctioneer
rattled Money-Money-Money,
Money-and-a-Quarter, Money-and-a-Half,
Going Once, Twice, Sold
for Money-and-a-Half, his voice
dancing like a blizzard.

I act like an adult
while watching all the men and a few women
dressed in overalls and gray thermal jackets
with hoods pulled up over their heads
and John Deere or Pioneer Seed Corn hats
against the rolling hills where snow caps
the hard, clotted earth.

I aim for the garage where women
serve from big urns of coffee and sheets of cake,
and huddle around a heater the size of a kettle drum,
its electric fire pouring through
half of me hot before I turn
to warm the other half, freezing,
my body bitterly changing temperatures
like a planet rotating through the seasons.

I am out of control, no choice
in the matter, my connection to the land cut
as I wander away
from the planting, weeding, harvesting
where God's face is the weather.
My life pulled from sweet hay and the stiff ammonia of manure,
the feeding of livestock and the day they're sent to slaughter,
the machines droning in fields and the oil spots on the ground.
I wander back to hear what the tractors bring,
and feel the earth, hard
as any truth that can be told,
being sold from under me.

John Sullivan

Jack Duluoz Hangs This Note on Maggie Cassidy's Fridge and Heads Out for Mexico

Maggie: Last night we hit Absolute Zero, and the long
slide stopped. It was good, it felt natural to freeze
like that, so finally, but I need my old motions back.
Staying here, I can't buy urgency or angels.
I've got to scrape this saggin' skin away and clean
myself for real, so I'm heading out for San Luis.
There's light there, Maggie, so much pure light
locked up in the sand. And I've got to burn
my own pale ass back to dust because it sounds
like some kind of new plan.

But you persist, Maggie, you're the resident diver.
These stone canyons, these bleached-out faces and
their noise are your sea. At your window, slouched
against an old iron light pole, reeling, jagged from the
slow crawl of morning up your spine, you get to run
the scam again, you get to run the old scam again, until
the scam's too flat to jag our old bones,
and our skin won't dance no more.

Don't you see, Maggie? It's all come unwound.
The goddess holds a dead young god in her arms.
Every afternoon or so, it's Chrysalis time, again
for the children. They make their happy rictus.
They launch themselves through cold glass toward the sky, like
in the birdman bit, their bodies arc across the sky,
spitting red, making red mist turn molecular like grace,
like pain vectors cranked down hard, or contrails of frost
over gristle, they make it bleed, all the time, bleed.

It scares me, Maggie, watching this.
Have these babies dropped their love wires?
Have their talkin' brains sucked up too much
Doppler from the subway?
Fine Lady, would you have these silly birds lie down
in grass and asphodel, and endless public evil?

Well, I say bare your arms, Sweet Lady, prepare to grunt
and sweat for it. I say wine, Lady, I say velocity
and hard at it too. Keep your bruises cookin', cookin', keep
'em polished till the lie glows true for starters.
Walking South: I wave the thighbone of a large meat
animal, I wave its torn meat in all their baby faces.
Look at this, I say to them.
I bring back some real evidence.

Lynne Weinberg-Hill

Walkers and Other Tribes

Epi and Chachita are pioneers in an old neighborhood recently resettled by young families. They are out for their evening walk. For at least twelve years, they had a routine. They walked to the park and back. But since Thanksgiving, Epi hasn't gone to the park. She and Chachita have wandered the alleys and streets, reluctant explorers of unfamiliar blocks. Epi wears her green dog-walking sweater. Chachita, a faded gray mongrel, sniffs a large orange garbage can.

"Hello." Epi acknowledges a young couple pushing a baby buggy. Chachita stops and sniffs another garbage can.

This morning Epi heard an expert, a garbologist, speak on a local talk-radio show. The garbage expert examines everyday folks' refuse just like archaeologists examine Indian ruins. Turns out differences exist in what people say and what their garbage reveals. The example she recalls is beer. People report drinking six beers, yet twelve empties appear in their garbage. Epi reflects on her garbage. The usual waste plus newsletters from Saint Peter and Paul's Church and Gilberto's pension stubs but not a trace of her baby-sitting job. She gets paid cash and tucks that money away, so she can spoil the grandkids. It's not the money anyway. Epi likes an excuse to get out of the house, and children are like fresh *sopapillas* to her, light and airy and delicious to smell.

That's why she surprised herself Thanksgiving, yelling at the grandchildren and making them turn down the television. Her run-in with the law pushed heavy on her chest, and when Fina asked if something was wrong, she blamed her irritability on a touch of the flu.

By not telling the family what happened, Epi travels unknown ground. She decided not to confide in Gilberto. He would tell her not to make a fuss, and expect her to listen to him. After forty-four years together, Gilberto still bristles when Epi's opinion differs from his own.

She cannot share this with Tomás or Fina either. They are busy with work and children. If she were to tell them about the incident at the park, they might think Mama had "lost it" (as the grandkids say). Or, worse yet, they might decide Mama is a silly old lady with too much time on her hands.

Epi looks north toward the Catalina Mountains, the highest range hovering over the basin. Today they are dulled by pollution. She used to be able to see the Tucson Mountains if she looked west down Drachman or Elm Streets, but years ago University Medical School blocked her view on Drachman. And in the last year, a university parking garage on Elm eliminated that skyline. When they moved to this neighborhood almost forty years ago, the town only went another mile or so east, and then there was lush vegetation. Now they are in the very middle of the city, and developers have chased the desert miles away.

When she and Chachita get home, Epi checks the beans cooking for dinner. The young doctor at the clinic told them to cut down on fats and cholesterol, but if she goes more than a few days without making *chile rellenos* or *chorizo*, Gilberto gets crabby. What's better? For him to live a long grumpy life or to die with a full belly?

She's making beans the way he likes them, with salt pork, bacon, onions, and lots of *chiltepines*, and earlier she made fresh tortillas like when the kids were small. The smells will put Gilberto in a good mood. If he's content, he'll leave Epi to herself after dinner, so she can figure out what to do about court the next day.

"Hi Chachita, how was the park tonight?" Gilberto speaks to the dog in Spanish, but really he's talking to Epi. Over the years they have communicated first through the children and now through the dog. "Dinner smells good."

"Beans the way you like them, and homemade tortillas." Gilberto smiles his approval. He has been out in the garage, repairing a broken chair. He is always working around the house or visiting with Manny, the school crossing guard at the corner. Since he took his pension from the city, Gilberto looks for ways to keep busy. For forty-five years, he worked for Parks and Recreation and felt proud of his civil service job. Like a *patrón* surveying his land, Gilberto would drive Epi around the city, showing off charming parks tucked inside old neighborhoods.

"Is Chachita ready for the big sale this Saturday?" Gilberto and Manny have planned this yard sale for weeks. They have repaired old furniture, picked up discarded fencing and latticework from the alleys, cleaned out closets, even searched through the junk in the side yard. They remind Epi of her mother and aunts fussing over spring cleaning. At least Gilberto has been too busy to notice Epi's agitation. She's been waking up during the night with a start, occasionally recalling a vivid dream.

Epi picks light words. "Chachita only has a few things to sell. You know how she can't let go of stuff."

Gilberto smiles, "Oh, you had a call, a Christine Green?" questioning with his eyebrows.

Epi has her reply ready. "A young woman from the park. She has a recipe for me."

Curiosity satisfied, Gilberto begins talking about the yard sale. He is painting six big signs and lists the information. Then he reads aloud the newspaper ad, anticipating Epi's approval. "A big sale not to miss. Household items, yard and porch furniture, forty years of souvenirs priced cheap!"

The idea came to Epi over a week ago while she was listening to the radio. A man described today's society as tribal, similar to earlier civilizations, divided into groups with common interests. Callers from all over the country telephoned in their agreement and mentioned their tribes—a national science fiction club, bird-watchers, families, religious groups; someone even suggested talk-radio listeners. Each caller spoke proudly of such associations. That's when Epi thought about her tribes. Family and church, of course, but she identifies with another tribe—one nobody mentioned, one without a name.

She has seen these foot soldiers, day after day, year after year, and she feels a kinship. The retired European tailor and his wife who walk together. A young woman who runs, backwards. A middle-aged gentleman who walks his beagle the same four blocks several times a day. Bicyclists. Joggers. Many different travelers populate the neighborhood streets. Some, like the short woman with the three large black dogs, Epi has greeted for at least ten years.

These are people, like her, who can't be confined indoors. They need to feel their soles touch the ground, even if the earth is topped with concrete. If they stay away from fresh air more than a day, they get irritable. They have to get outside to smell the creosote bushes after the rain, feel the choke of hot air on a summer night, listen to the doves chirp in the morning. With these people, Epi shares a word and a wave, the way children signal a secret code.

Christine Green belongs to this club. Epi has seen her for four or five years now with her two well-behaved golden retrievers. Whenever Christine sees Epi, she makes a point of coming over and asking after Chachita, who likes to nuzzle and smell the retrievers. Christine has worked her way through law school and will become a lawyer as soon as she passes an important exam. Epi remembers her last name because one day they were noting the greenness of spring, and Christine said green was her favorite color and also her last name. Epi looked up her number and phoned. When the machine answered, she gathered her courage around her like a shawl and identified herself as Mrs. Gamez, the woman who walks Chachita. She has been waiting almost a week for Christine to call back.

After dinner while Gilberto is watching *Matlock*, Epi sneaks off to the bedroom telephone. Initially she worried about imposing on Christine, but the young woman invites friendliness. "I'm sorry I didn't get back to you sooner. I was out of town. I hope you didn't give up on me."

"Oh, of course not." Epi pauses a long moment. "I feel sort of silly, but I need some advice — about the law."

"Sure," Christine replies. "How can I help?"

"Well, it's a long story," Epi hesitates.

"Go ahead, Mrs. Gamez. I have time."

"It was Thanksgiving." Epi begins slowly. "You remember how rainy and cold it was?"

"Yes."

"Well, Chachita and I took our walk anyways, before we went to my daughter's. The park was about empty. That nice young couple with the two Dobermans came, and Chachita was so glad to see them she forgot about her arthritis." Epi is not clear whether Christine needs all these details, but she has kept the story so tight inside, the words begin spilling out like air escaping from a balloon.

"Then they left, and I sat down at the picnic bench. Chachita was a little bit away from me, smelling the leaves. That's when the animal control officer came up from behind and startled me. He raised his voice and told me I was violating the leash law. I called Chachita to me. When I hooked on her leash, the young man accused me of having a leash over six feet long."

Epi takes a breath. "Am I taking up too much of your time?" she asks, embarrassed.

"Oh no, go on, Mrs. Gamez. I'm curious to hear what happened."

"Well, then he looks at Chachita's dog license and says it expired in October. I told him we had the new one at home, but I forgot to have Gilberto put it on the collar with his pliers. That was another ticket. Then he asked for a driver's license and was about to start writing again when I said I don't drive."

"How many tickets did he give you?" Christine asks.

"Three," Epi replies.

"That guy hated working the holiday," Christine jokes.

Feeling supported, Epi tells Christine about the leash law she found at the library and copied down. It says a dog has to be under control, and Chachita was under control, so Epi didn't send in any money for the fines. Now the court date on her tickets is tomorrow. It's not just the $75 in fines that upsets her. She has walked her dogs in Tucson all her life and never had to keep them on a leash before. Epi finishes by asking Christine, "Can you be my lawyer for the court appearance tomorrow?"

"Gee, I'm just back from vacation and have to be at work." Christine sounds truly sorry. Then she explains it's Justice Court, like *People's Court* on television. Epi needs to bring proof Chachita is licensed and whatever else she thinks will help her case. "There is the letter of the law and the spirit of the law. Judges have discretion, and it's two weeks before Christmas. Maybe the judge will be in a better holiday mood than the animal control officer."

When Epi hangs up, she feels better. Christine has been so sympathetic and understands dog needs. Her unleashed golden retrievers chase after their tennis balls. They behave within the spirit of the law, and so does Chachita.

Epi contemplates telling Gilberto what happened and asking him to come to court with her. She has never been to court in her life, and Gilberto has experience. Once he pleaded not guilty to running a red light, and even though he lost, he had his say.

She goes back to the living room where Gilberto is watching Matlock talk with an old couple whose dog is accused of biting. Epi is alarmed, imagining even Matlock knows her secret. Gilberto is chuckling.

"Come watch TV with me." Gilberto pats his hand on the couch, signalling Chachita to jump up next to him.

Epi considers sitting down but decides to bake brownies and goes into the kitchen. She takes the butter and eggs out of the refrigerator and is setting up the Mixmaster when she remembers chocolate is high in cholesterol. Wondering what to do, she turns on the radio and hears Larry King interviewing some celebrity who's written a book about dependence. Or is it child abuse? So many problems. Drugs, cigarettes, coffee, love, gambling. They blur together like commercials. Maybe she has a radio addiction. Whenever she's nervous, she switches on the radio, just the same as a drunk reaches for the tequila. Epi turns the radio off, puts on some hot water for tea, and stares out the kitchen window into the Christmas lights flashing on the house across the street.

When their neighbor was on the ladder hanging those lights, Gilberto saw her and went over to help. "Let me give you a hand there," he shouted up to her.

"Oh, Mr. Gamez, how kind of you, but I'm all done," she responded.

As Gilberto headed back across the street, Epi saw a sadness wash over his deeply lined bronze face, a brief instant where his age and vulnerability stood out against his features. Then he waved good-bye to the neighbor, and when he turned back toward Epi, he looked composed again.

Now Epi notices how the lights snake around the arborvitae trees, dancing in the dark night. They are out of sync. One moment the lights blink the same. The next moment, everything looks different.

"The water's boiling." Gilberto's voice in Epi's ear startles her. "I'm getting up early tomorrow to count parking spaces at Himmel Park."

Gilberto's a member of the Himmel Park Neighborhood Committee. The city wants to put a horseshoe-shaped parking lot through the middle of the grass, so people won't have to walk so far to reach their cars. The park committee doesn't want this city oasis redesigned around a parking facility.

"I'll be gone when you get home. I'm baby-sitting until lunchtime," Epi says quickly.

"Chachita doesn't like you working too hard," Gilberto tells her. "You're ready for the yard sale Saturday, aren't you?"

"No problem!" She imitates their youngest grandson, and both of them laugh. Gilberto goes to bed.

Epi can't think about the yard sale. She can't think past the next day. She's determined not to pay the fine, but she's never before taken such a stand. What if she can't go through with it?

She turns on the radio, thinks of addictions and turns it off again, takes out the garbage and watches Chachita sniff around, choosing just the right spot to squat. Then Epi and Chachita come in to watch the news. Epi has almost forgotten about the homeless. Next time she goes to church, she'll take some canned tuna for the Community Food Bank.

After watching the weather, she goes to bed. Her mind is filled with leash laws and doesn't turn off like the radio. She lies still for a long time, thinking about going to court. Then she recollects the radio doctor explaining how to relax, and begins unburdening her mind as she would unpack groceries from a sack. That's the last thing she recalls.

When she awakens, a snatch of her dream floods back. She is a young girl, living in Barrio Libre. She and her older sister Concha are in front of their small adobe house, the house they lived in as children. Epi steps into the house and is at the park with Chachita. Young families drive their minivans through the grass.

Epi hears the back door shut and Gilberto's truck start. She gets up and goes into the kitchen. Gilberto has squeezed fresh orange juice and made their coffee. She turns on the radio to listen for the weather.

A rumbling goes through the kitchen, loud, like a UPS truck driving past. Epi looks out the window and sees the young woman next door hauling out her garbage can. This neighbor owns her house all by herself. Epi cannot imagine what it's like to live alone. She has lived first with her family in the Barrio and then a few miles away with Gilberto. Young women today move across the country by themselves. They would think nothing of going to court alone.

The thought of court makes her stomach jump. She decides to attend early morning Mass. Maybe praying will give her the courage she lacks. She turns the radio up and listens for the weather as she looks in the bathroom mirror, brushes her short, thick gray hair, and puts on some lipstick. When she's ready, she takes her purse, the dog license, and Chachita's leash. Chachita doesn't even move. Her back leg is stiff, and she doesn't hear the jingle of the leash.

Epi buttons her sweater as she walks the six blocks to church. The morning is chilly, but the sun is already at work. She never did hear the weather, and she forgot her cans of tuna.

After lighting a candle and praying to Our Lady of Guadalupe, she walks briskly to Speedway Boulevard to catch the bus. Early morning, the street is crammed with traffic. Before all the newcomers moved here, Tucson had no rush hour. Now the bus is crowded with college students, men in business suits, middle-aged women, a young mother and her baby. Epi steps down the aisle and takes a seat next to a fashionably dressed lady. A retarded girl boards the bus. While the girl is waiting her turn to pay, she picks up her skirt and scratches her crotch, totally unaware of judgment in the air.

The ride downtown carries Epi back to Barrio Libre where she grew up a few blocks from the Pima County Courthouse. She seldom goes downtown anymore. The old stores have closed, and the adobe house of her childhood was demolished during the urban renewal of the 1960s. Barrio Libre is now the Tucson Community Center, the shops of La Placita Village, and a huge parking lot. She recalls her dream and feels a heaviness in her heart, again grieving the death of a loved one.

When Epi gets off the bus, she looks across the street at the courthouse, tucked between glass and concrete skyscrapers, a low pink adobe building topped with a yellow and blue Mexican-tile dome. Inside, it smells like elementary school, the odor of bodies mixed with dust and sweat.

In the courtroom, she takes a seat on a long pew. The room is huge under a thirty-foot-high ceiling, outlined by wooden beams. The judge faces into the room, behind a massive bench, an American flag to his right and the Arizona flag on his left. Two large tables separate him from the wooden pews. The first table has a sign reading Plaintiff. The second table says Defendant.

The courtroom is full of people — lawyers, public safety officers, policemen. A woman and man take turns presenting cases for the state, but they don't do every case. Some cases are settled quietly before the judge. All the activity stirs Epi's uncertainties. She considers pleading guilty and paying the fine.

The light bounces off the judge's bald head as he smiles at a young woman's story. He cautions her to use better judgment in the future and dismisses the case. Other cases follow. A landlord who requests an eviction notice against a tenant. A man who swerved to avoid a javelina and hit two mesquite trees. Then they call Epifania Gamez.

Epi is sworn to tell the truth and told to sit at the table marked Defendant. The animal control officer is in the witness stand.

"I encountered the defendant at the picnic table in the park." The young man is somber. "Her dog was about twenty feet away."

"Do you wish to interrogate the officer?" The judge is speaking to Epi.

She asks the first questions that come to mind. "What was the dog doing? Was she hurting anything?"

"She was sniffing the leaves." The young man's tone condemns the act.

Epi remembers that the law stresses control. "Didn't the dog come when I called her?"

"You had to call the name two or three times and then clap your hands." The officer speaks with accusation in his tone.

"The dog is going deaf," Epi says to the judge.

The officer squints into the light. He looks about the same age as Epi's oldest grandson. The judge smiles at Epi and looks down at his paperwork to read the other charges.

"Is your dog licensed, Mrs. Gamez?"

"Yes, Your Honor. I have the proof here." She rises from the table and walks to the bench. The judge takes the paperwork and looks it over.

"And this is the leash I had, Your Honor." Epi lifts the leash up toward the judge.

"Well, Mrs. Gamez. I didn't even know a ten-foot-long leash was against the law."

Epi stands before the judge, who takes a few minutes to read over the paperwork. Finally he looks again at her. "You seem a responsible dog owner to me. I'm going to dismiss all charges."

Epi doesn't move until the judge tells her she can go. When she turns to leave, her legs feel spongy, and her hands are shaking. She walks slowly out of the courtroom, down the hall, and outdoors into the warm winter air. Stopping at the top of the stairs to steady herself, she feels like a young woman leaving her first dance. She takes a deep breath, straightens her back, and descends with a firm step.

She walks two blocks to the bus stop by La Placita Village. These streets used to be filled with children and families. Epi recalls a picture of two little girls, Concha and her, standing under a huge paloverde tree, not too far from where she stands now, waiting for the bus.

The number five arrives, and Epi climbs aboard, leaving the barrio behind. The bus turns north on Sixth Avenue. Out the window, Epi sees old houses mingled with newer buildings. She is surprised how the newer buildings already look old and blend in with the houses that have been there for as long as she can remember.

At home, Gilberto and Manny are in the carport, setting up tables and painting signs. Gilberto is excited. He asks how the baby-sitting went but doesn't wait for an answer.

"There are one hundred ten parking places at Himmel Park," he tells her. "If they put that horseshoe parking lot through the middle, that's only five extra spaces. You don't think they'd ruin the park for five more parking spaces, do you?"

"Yes," Epi almost shouts. "I believe they would." She turns and enters the house, as surprised as Gilberto at the anger in her voice.

When she steps into the kitchen to heat up the beans and tortillas for lunch, Epi hears that conservative fellow on the radio, damning the homeless like an evangelist leading a revival meeting. She turns him off and picks up the ten-foot-long leash. Chachita moves more quickly than usual toward the door. They head out in the direction of the park. At the corner Epi hesitates. She sees an orange garbage can Chachita has never before sniffed. Tomorrow they can return to the park. Today they will explore new blocks.

Colorado

Like most writers, or, for that matter, artists of any stripe, I am obliged to serve a great many other roles in my daily life. In most of these roles, the artist is unknown, or irrelevant, or at least a secondary function. The pleasure of travelling to a small town in the mountains to be the visiting artist is that for once all those other roles and obligations fade to background. In Craig, Colorado, I was, for two days, primarily a poet.

One middle-school girl who attended a workshop I taught in the morning came to my reading in the evening and enthusiastically — before parents and friends — took my hand. "There!" she announced. "I've shaken hands with a published poet!" And her business with me was done: she paid me no further attention.

A rare high-school boy (How many high-school boys are National Merit Scholars and have written over a hundred poems?) followed me about all evening, hovered at my car, loathe to let me go. "There's no one here I can talk to about poetry," he apologized, and asked, if it was O.K. just one more question?

Preparing for the workshops, I select poems children will relate to, poems that may serve as models or introductions for a particular writing exercise. Selecting poems for the reading, I lean toward the humorous and accessible. Some of what I consider my most ambitious work I almost never read in public. That's as it should be, I think. Some poems are meant mainly for the printed page.

PATRICIA DUBRAVA

Chip Bissell

In the Clearing

In memory of Clyde and Carol Bissell
July 1, 1992

This day, two years ago now,
a last time I saw you both alive
as it turned out.

I talk with you, my forever young brother and sister,
in the backyard
at the house you built together.

"How do you like your steaks?"
last question you might ask me,
and mine about whippoorwills.

I wish I could hear them now,
always toward June's twilight
mixed with honeysuckle breath of childhood memories.

"Both gone, you say?"
"An accident . . . Clyde and Carol are dead,"
this day, three months passing.

"Rare, I like mine rare, not really,
but rarely do I get them."
Old joke, real laugh, real life.

I want it back now (without preoccupations).
I want to slow it down — frame by frame —
it's not supposed to happen this way.

You, younger and too young and . . .
"My God, the children . . . what will become . . . ?
How did it . . . ice on the road . . . a fox crossing . . . ?"

Too soon your light gone
and so close to our hearts. . . .
Did you know that?

"Remember the times . . . on the river,
lightning close and thunder . . . you poking
your head out from under the blanketed kayak,

asking in a seven-year-old innocence,
"Are we dead yet?"
No . . . and I thinking older would teach you

of rivers, rapids, and finding the current:
now you teaching me the hardest lesson of all,
letting go.

Memories are not enough. . . . I want to hear your irreverent laughter. . . . God,
you loved to laugh at life's little jokes. . . . I just don't get it. . . . You both loved
life so much and so proud . . . your children growing. . . . You lived to make
things grow. . . .

    Can we be real for a moment?

    So much to say now without the words:
    you taught me about limits and how it is
    to have something to say too late.

    I will listen and ache for the whippoorwill sound,
    soulful in the echo of your woods,

    will listen for laughter as shadows deepen
    and light falls below our horizon.

    You carved in our hearts a clearing,
    where memories green turn forever golden.

Ramon Del Castillo

Violence in *Los Barrios*

It's a place
where young hoods
with pockets full
of spray-paint cans
sucked until
they are bone-dry
so *vatos*, both old and young,
can get high
congregate
to spread the good word
of false *carnalismo*
leaving gang graffiti
imprinted against the barren walls
of empty buildings
in *los barrios*
with the blood
of their own *carnales.*
It's a place
where young *vatas*
are forced to spread
a sense of false morality
through initiation rites
that debase
nuestra cultura
where young men
become exploiters
of their own mothers
by killing
the leaves
of young trees
leaving them to weep

while watching
lonely tears silently
fall only to greet
an angry mother earth.
It's a place
that is slowly losing
the smell of *aristas*
replacing it
with the melancholy
smell of death
where long lines of *la gente*
solemnly march
to another funeral
where rosaries are recited
in vain
causing a lot of pain.

Lorna Dee Cervantes

Ode *a Las Gatas*

(a Bird, Tiny, Mousie, Grumpy, Cat-Eyes, Flaca, Sleepy, Princess, y Betty la Boop)

We were nine lives, cat claws plunged in
the caterwauling of *la llorona* and the crying saints.

We believed in witches, wild cards, jokers,
and the tricksters who lived without it.

Disciples of the pride, we preyed on fury's wing.
We lied. We stole the heart's desire. We never

got a cent, but, feral, flew to another side
of glory. We came — this close to dying,

we gunned the engines of our grief — and gained.
Taught to live from hand to mouth, the moratorium

of our lives began at blood's first quickening.
Given to the beck and call so fast, we primed.

our lives that instant when we slipped into the gap
between child and man — and slave. We chose

to stay, tough in the fist of our fathers'
mercy. No face cards in our deck, we dealt

the devil back his hand, we scorched the virgin
from our breasts, as the sweat of heat upon us

did not free us but did not bind us either.
We had the power then, between three worlds,

to fuse our *bruja* pack, our pact to faith — not
in our futures but in a present we could fix within

the diamond decks minted in our carboned eyes.
We were crystalline, runaway *rucas* on the prowl,

edge of night in our glassy throats, cut of class
in flyaway manes, the blood of oils in our slapped

cheeks and with bit lips we smiled to
circling owls. No angles, no novenas, no past

spirits that we recognized, nobody's business
what we did, we know we earned our freedom,

and we did.

Jack Collom

Kit

This is a little story
About Christopher Carson; you won't be sorry.
Now Kit was a Mountain Man and Great Plains Hero
In a geographic vise that'd buck you down to zero
Any minute. A quiet little kit mouse, locally born and raised,
Then Continen-tally praised.
Kit went to Santa Fe across the wide western ache
When he was still knee-high to a piece of johnnycake.
He liked his corn best boiled down to brown whiskey,
Which translation made its transport both possible and frisky.
He studied the natives and became so cool and wild
He went over them like a man and under them like a child.
Kit had a taste for the chopped bit of action,
And piled luck with the patience of a cold desert fraction.
He done large deeds — he could afford to be humble
Because, even in that age of seriously retarded media rumble,
Books'd crop up and stumble eastward, the rapid penny dreadfuls,
And young dudes in Boston, 1845, 'd receive headfuls
Of such inspiration as might be lodged in a drawing of Kit
About nine foot tall, poised Bunyanesque in some Arcadian glade, a fit
Of heroism whirling in his stalwart brown (actually blue, like most killers')
    eyes,
Curling under one giant arm a buxom white lady jelled twixt terror and trust,
    carelessly — by the thighs
Whilst fighting off a slavering grizzly bear with the other
And sensing the approach behind him of the "Murderous Red Brother."

Well, one such Boston boy, Quentin Peabody, grew up with that light
Of possible manhood, and though he was not "meant to fight"
Did at last go West in a Conestoga caravan to Bent's Fort
On the lower Arkansas, where life was just getting over being the sort

Of passage the average coyote knew, kind of a quotidian arson,
As himself might've put it (literary dude) — and there he met Kit Carson.
Kit was middle-aged, gray-haired, bespectacled, still five foot six,
Untouched by all his ferryings across the dry-gulch River Styx,
And they became acquainted.
Well now, the boyhood mental picture painted
In young Peabody's head went through macro/micro shifts,
But dust has its way of pinpointing the drifts,
And one day the Journalist felt bold enough
To trot out his dog-eared volume and *enquire* about all that stuff.

He showed Kit the lurid sketch described above,
And the little guy mildly put on his glasses and studied it a couple minutes —
    like a dove
Examining some legendary golden eagle rage —
Then folded up the page
(more to just put it away than to hold it, much less resurrect it).
He said,
        "Waal — I hain't
Sayin' hit never happened, but I sure cain't
Recollect it."

Outside the dirt-floor room, some half-coyote pup
Was still yip-yap-yodeling at nothing, but the silver and the sugar beets were
    coming up.

(yodel)

Jack Collom

From "Truck Trip with Reed"

switch in Brush (last stint 119 —
total for me 908 miles), salad, numbers.
Brush off, Reed's last Stint
roll on
12:13 P . M . roll on roll on
abt. 75 miles as the raven flies
from the mountains, lost in blue-sky haze
"Royal Gorge — open all yr. round"
rolling on
Irish music, sunflowers
South Platte rolling on just north of us
white silos of sugar
in the form of beet pulp, wch. smells
like shit tastes roll on
big black semitrailer
"West Coast Theatrical"
pulls in to get itself weighed
sore butt, rolling on
little white clouds
clumps of sagebrush
fading away
roll on roll on
black & white cows &
cream-colored interstate w/ sandy sides
speed limit 55
Brighton 48
roll on
"mountains!" says Reed
as we crest a sandy roll
"snow on 'em"
dim in the distance

rolling along
all but the snow dissolves in air

painter road, roll
Stuckey's Texaco
vegetable fairy rings in open sand
yucca swords —
silver semi — Coors beer
Longs Peak dark Meeker mass
barely discernible
Reed looks around
w/ tiny smile, rolling on, rolling on
machine spits alfalfa hay
into red truckbed, rolling slowly
pigeons on the farm —
alarm!
roll on, the river's gone, roll on
roll on, roll on
blue car
red car
off 76, Boulder 37
whites of its eyes
prairie dogs left, winter wheat right
roll on by sheep
roll on by 3 Mexican girls
roll on by miles of air
rolling along
Reed sings
indistinguishably
big black grasshopper sucks planet
w/ ominous head bobs
alkali
distinguish Indian Peaks
Audubon, Arapahoe
Ft. Lupton U-Pump-It
coming home
great blue heron!

flies by, never looks down
roll on
"super foods"
we roll along the rumble strips of life
half-aware who's waiting for us
rolling on
one more time
roll on roll on
sip hot orange juice
down into Boulder Valley
Sugarloaf visible
pass purple-brown pond
ringed with Russian olive &
1 buffalo
Boulder 12
the hills emerge & tilt & shift
as we roll a little
dream of detail
down the road
now snow peaks sink
behind the blue-green foothills
Down to a daily brown —
diagonal into town
roll out the barrel
sweet roll
(silver plane)
Mt. Sanitas like a piece of cake
rolling in my
sweet baby's arms
drumroll
stoplight, hot day
"feel like I should go trim a tree
or something,"
says Reed,
mutters something abt.
the Pacific Ocean

Abelardo Delgado

El Barrio

I'm that piece of land
always getting out of hand,
that which *la ciudad*
                              tries to hide.
I house *la gente*
to whom
              the American dream
has lied.
In my corners stand
moreno youth with no future.
Monday's wash on the
t e n d e d e r o s
tells a torn fable.
A *chisme* is also drying up
on some *comadre's* mouth.
My *calles* clutter with litter,
with the weight of many needs.
My mood is
              a constant SOS
that no one heeds.
I am the alma mater
for lost souls
              and bodies.
Yo soy the unkempt
              l a b o r a t o r y
where the new social worker studies.
My alleys are hammocks
for would-be *prostitutas*,
ambition's burial place.
Yo soy el barrio,
              the slum,

the ghetto,
progress's sore thumb.
Collectively I am a spirit
that is defeated . . . explosive.
Yo fabrico trouble
of the plausive kind.
Conservatively, comfortably,
soy la casa
             for all who suffer,
thirst, and hunger for justice.
I am a well-guarded prison
with no rhyme or reason.

Abelardo Delgado

La Llorona

In each religion,
in each region,
in each culture,
in each country and city,
there is a legend of *la llorona*.
Nature intended
for grandparents to die first
and then the parents.
When the process is reversed,
nature itself pierces the
                 h e a v e n s
with cries of anguish
in her own language.
La llorona, the wailing one,
keeps crying for her lost son.
When Cortés conquered the Aztecs
in Tenochtitlán,
                 he took
a beautiful woman,
La Malinche,
                 and they had a son,
one of the first Mestizos,
one of the first Chicanos.
When the child grew up,
Cortés wanted to send him to Europe
to be educated as a white man.
La Malinche rather than giving her son
to such a fate
                 sacrificed him to the sun.
La llorona, the wailing one,
keeps crying for her lost son.

T e n o c h t i t l á n
is now Mexico City,
and many are those who swear
that in the dead of night,
when the wind blows cold,
La Malinche, symbol of all mothers
who have lost a son,
gives out her deafening wails.
Ay, ay, ay, her crying is a warning
to the descendants of the Aztecs
to stay away from technological monsters,
from the dangers that materialism fosters.

Margie Domingo

La Mujer Azteca

I am Azteca,
The root of your ancestors.
From the earth I rose,
Pure and innocent.
Know your earth,
Smell the sacred soil,
That is mixed with clay,
And blessed by the rain.
Hear the southwest wind whisper,
The chant of the Gods,
Believe the faith,
Of your ancestors.
Listen to my talk,
Feel the breath
Of your father and mother,
Who followed me.
I linger in your blood.
Your blood is from the heavens,
The heavens that nourish,
The golden brown skin,
Of your people.
It has been blessed,
By the four directions,
Look to me in the South,
I am your Mother Earth,
I am Tierra who gave birth,
To the children of the fields,
The sacred maize,
In this land where you walk.
I am your blood,
Your spirit is in you,

The southwest wind is in your soul,
Mother Earth protects your walk,
The voice of your people,
Is in your talk.
We lost our land to the Europeans,
Who brought us death,
With their disease,
We lost our Gods and Aztec spirit,
But rose again,
With the God of seed.
Have faith my children of the corn,
Look to the South where I was born,
The Gods are with you,
Your spirit won't die,
At least one child of each family,
Will hear my heart and speak of me.
It is not a curse, my only hope,
You'll keep the faith,
Learn the talk,
And love the land,
You are destined to walk.

I am the seed of hope.
The sacred maize that was chosen,
Above the mud and the wood.
The children of mud had no minds,
They could not think.
The children of wood,
Had no blood or heart,
And could not love.
The children of corn,
Sprinkle the four directions,
Speak the truth,
And love the land,
From where they are born.
Honor the heavens,
That bring the sacred rains.

Tlaloc the God of Rain,
Will bless this land,
Beneficial waters,
Cleanse your soul,
Feed the corn,
The grass, the trees,
So they may grow.
Beware Tlaloc with the power,
The Four Rains of destruction:
The fiery rain of heat,
Burns the seeds of hope,
The fungus rain of disease,
Rots the food of strength,
The wind rain,
Blows a planted seed,
To halt its growth,
And flint blade, frozen water,
Tears and cuts,
The leaves and earth,
To eternal damnation.
Beware of exploitation,
Coming in disguise,
Of a soft gentle rain,
Listen to the raindrops,
Wash the path,
You are destined to walk.

I am the salt of the earth,
La Mujer de Aztlan
I face the four directions,
Throw my fist to the wind,
Bless our children across the land,
Save our culture, speak our talk,
Stand with pride,
Where we're destined to walk.
¡Que viva Aztlan!

Patricia Dubrava

After the Earthquake

He was either in Mexico City
or Puerto Vallarta —
what would it be like without Carlitos
to insult me about my age,
keep me posted on Chicano *chisme*?

Texas-born, Tulane-educated,
acid-tongued, on learning my friend
es del valle San Luis, he asked:
"Oh, and does she wear shoes?"

Artist, philosopher and snob,
he declared (humbly):
"I'm just another Mexican,
crying in the wilderness."

Perhaps Mexico shook herself
like a *panzona* who's eaten
too many frijoles and suddenly does aerobics,
and in that shuddering Carlos "Panzon" Martinez
died, reclaimed by the land
which let him move a generation away
from thatch-roofed towns
before bringing him home
to a Mexican death of multitudes.

The phone rings.
Carlos, from P. V.
"Damn you, Martinez, I was composing
your elegy."
"Hey, finish it," he says,
like a good Mexican fatalist.
"You never know."

Anthony J. Garcia

The Day Ricardo Falcon Died

Today I opened the mail to find an invitation to join a new Hispanic brain trust. I could be part of the "Mandate Hispanico" and develop the new agenda for the 1990s. The mandate was sponsored by the local reactionary beer-brewing family. It proclaimed itself the "training ground for future Hispanic managers, business leaders, and politicians." Noticeably absent from a shopping list of agenda items were questions of land rights, workers' rights. There was not even an allusion to cultural and language freedoms.

The "Mandate" talked about "marketing" ourselves. It's funny, in the old days we talked about "liberating" ourselves. I guess today the goal is better living through modern capitalism.

My invitation had been signed by none other than Vern Gallegos. It is no wonder the whole thing smelled funny. As his name left my lips, the bad taste remained. I had always hoped he could have died young, but I guess that honor is reserved for the good.

Vernon (God Bless America) Gallegos, pronounced *Gal-egg-us*, was an unrepentant, dyed-in-the-wool, rightwing, kiss-ass creep, a fact long acknowledged and well documented, so much so that I'm sure he included it in his résumé.

My thoughts raced backward as I sat on the couch and torched up a smoke. Could it have been sixteen years ago since that day? That year. That lifetime. I was seventeen years old, just out of high school, wandering the campus in awe. I hung out in the office of UMAS, that is, the United Mexican American Students. Today I suppose they are the Hispanic High Achievers or some shit like that.

Being the youngest guy in UMAS, I learned early to shut my mouth and observe. As I walked into the office that day, everyone was in the process of packing for a trip. Carlos Santana and Chepito Areas could be heard soul sacrificing on the office radio. It seemed that a caravan was leaving today for El Paso, Texas, the site of the first and to my knowledge last National La Raza Unida party convention.

Two nights before, Ricardo Falcon had spoken to the UMAS general membership. He was inspiring. Falcon was already a campus legend. Having grown up in a small rural Colorado town, he recruited Chicanos from farmworking families into college. He was from campesino stock. Although a member of the university administration, he was one of us. He fought for us daily, and when the university tried to fire him, we fought to get his job back.

He spoke with compassion. He was fearless, and after forcing the university to back down, we thought him invulnerable. His words had moved us and fanned the "revolutionary flames" burning within us. El Paso would be the site of the Chicano version of the Constitutional Convention. The Chicano movement would give us many a different "plan," but La Raza Unida would give us organization. It would be a national body that was both institutional and revolutionary. So everyone packed and loaded the vans, to answer the call.

Everyone, it seemed, had heard the call but me. I entered the office and moved toward the hub of activity. Armando Quiñones was the organization's chairman. He was on the phone trying to nail down housing for two hundred students in El Paso. Oso Madrid was in charge of security for the trip. "The Bear" was six foot three inches and two hundred and fifty pounds of dedication to *La Causa*. He was the organization's benevolent protector. He and a few of the "heavies" spoke of taking precautions, carrying pieces, and what to do "when the shit comes down."

Raul Lucero was Armando's rival for organizational leadership. It was somewhat of a friendly rivalry. Raul was the previous year's chair. While Armando was cool, calculating, and cerebral; Raul was brash and aggressive. He was also a hound dog, a womanizer of the worst sort. Armando had neither the looks, the charisma, nor the interest to follow such diversions, except when it came to Evelina Mondragon.

Eva was my first encounter with the complete woman. Her father was a district court judge in New Mexico, and her mother was a schoolteacher. She was an honor-roll graduate who was given a full scholarship to the University of New Mexico but chose to strike out on her own in Colorado.

It took me years to overcome the dreams of this beautiful, brown-skinned, dark-haired, India-looking Chicana peering across the room at me. The crowds of people surrounding us would melt away into the walls, the walls evaporating into some watercolor surrealist image, as Evelina would stare and hold me frozen in her eyes, her brown breasts growing larger with each inhaled breath. Or was that my breath or maybe even my breasts? I'm not sure, because I could not avert my eyes from her. Her full pink lips would part, and she would say, *"Gracias,"* then she would pause and with tremendous affection, she would punctuate her statement, *"carnal."*

To say that I idealized Evelina would be an understatement. It would be an eternity that I would hold onto my infatuation with the "Goddess Evelina." She would remain a tender vestige of my youth. I guess I wasn't the only one. Raul was overtly manipulating the van passenger sign-up sheet to include Evelina in his van; while Armando covertly did the same for his van. Conversely, Evelina announced that she would be the driver of a third van. It would be the Chicana van, which would develop questions and positions central to "La Mujer." Raul's van would become the party van; while Armando would take the intellectuals.

It was at this point that Vern Gallegos enters the picture. Vern would often come to the UMAS office to use the phone, the typewriter, or just to pontificate on his experiences as a Marine who had volunteered to kill "Gooks in Nam." Vern agreed with none of the principles of UMAS, but as someone who was "Spanish-surnamed," he was entitled to all the resources of the organization.

As the sleeping bags were taken out, rolled, and rerolled, amid the chaos of the pressing business at hand, Vern's banter continued. He ranted on about little boys playing a man's game. He badgered Evelina about women staying home barefoot and pregnant.

His run-ins with Raul, Armando, and Evelina were notorious. He bore the traces of a broken beer pitcher from Raul, a pen stabbing from Evelina, and numerous crushing ego assaults from Armando. But still he persisted.

As much as I hate to admit this, Vern considered me somewhat of an ally. I believe it was because one frozen night at a party, in a drunken moment, I accepted a ride home from him. He seemed to recall this incident with much more interest than I could or cared to. Vern was not one to let you forget the slightest favor proffered, perhaps, because doing something for others was rare for Vern, and something he often saw as a weakness.

So on this day, since I also was not going on the trip, he insisted on drawing me into his sarcastic baiting. And try as I did, I was having difficulty distancing myself from his idiocy. He continued to feign conversation with me as a means of reaching the others. Ignoring Vern would not dissuade him, and confronting him would only fuel his antagonism.

It was into this confusion that a telephone rang, providing the chilling interruption. I could hear Armando's voice tensing as he asked questions. "When? How? Where?" And "What will happen next?" When he replaced the receiver, we all quieted to hear Armando's words. His voice quivering and his eyes blinking rapidly, unable to focus, he spoke: "Today in Alamogordo, New Mexico, Ricardo Falcon was shot." Armando continued, "He stopped to fill his radiator with water.

His car was overheating. The gas station owner claimed that he was trying to rob him, and shot him in the chest." Armando stumbled on his words. "The police have arrested Florencio Granados, who was travelling with Ricardo, for being an accessory to armed robbery. They refused to allow Priscilla Falcon to ride in the ambulance with her husband." Clearing his voice Armando finished, "Ricardo Falcon died on his way to the hospital. All this took place a couple of hours ago."

His words fell like lead on the twenty-five boisterous dreamers crowded into the tiny office area. The room was now struck sullen. The air became thick, making it tough to breathe. A couple of the women could be heard sobbing. Evelina crossed the office to the window and opened it to allow the crisp spring air into the room.

I did not know Falcon as the others had, so he had not been a flesh-and-blood person to me. At that age, I had no idea of the historic impact this event would have. However, the sense of loss was so strong, it was as though a brother had departed the family.

Into this somber moment Vern (the Mouth) chose to venture. He rose from his seat near the corner typewriter and walked to the corner of the room. Vern the crew-cut hawk, Vern the sexist, Vern the Linda Chavez predecessor who wrote articles about how Mexicans were stupid and lazy, belched forth, "Good riddance to bad news."

Before anyone else could do it, Evelina lunged into Vern's face, slashing it with her nails, quickly drawing blood. Vern, ever the gracious gentleman, doubled up his fist and crushed it squarely into the center of the beautiful Evelina's face. Seemingly out of nowhere, through a crowd paralyzed by grief and shock, the large frame of Oso (the Protector) cast its shadow across the room, as he picked up Vern by his feet.

The force of Evelina's lunge, Vern's retaliation, and Oso's intercession had brought the two struggling men to the wall, near the open sixth-story window. It was too convenient, too righteous. As Vern flailed helplessly, Oso held him head-first out the window. No one dared move closer to the two, lest they be drawn into the struggle and conclude their lives on the sidewalk six flights below. Out of the silence I began to hear Vern whimper. He was now crying as gently and helplessly as a baby. He begged The Bear to hold onto him. He pleaded for his life, promising, denying mother and country, apologizing, offering anything in the world just to be allowed to retain another moment of precious life.

I then realized what a sacrifice men and women like Ricardo Falcon make for us. To be willing to forgo the only proven level of existence in order to preserve principle and dignity. They place their lives at risk for an idea. Vern had no principles to die for; he also had none for which to live. Oso released him. Vern's eyes grew to saucer size, as he knew that in the next instant he would be plummeting to the ground below.

You know, there are instants in a person's life that pass, split seconds that we will question over and over again and for which we never arrive at a satisfactory answer. What would have happened if I had done such a thing or another? In this case, as I sit here on my living-room couch, looking at Vern's obnoxious invitation, torn into pieces lying on the floor, I keep asking myself, "What the hell was I thinking?" In that microsecond during which Vern (the Sleaseball) Gallegos was hanging out the window, suspended between life and death, I dove forward. Grabbing his military boots, I worked my way down his body, until he was able to steady himself and climb back in through the window. No one was more astonished than I was.

Someone had seen Vern dangling out the window and had called the cops. Just as Vern was back on his feet and was readjusting his ripped clothing, they arrived. "What's going on?" the big ugly one demanded. Everyone stood silent. I stepped forward moving to the nearest unrolled sleeping bag and said, "Nothing, just packing for a trip, Officer." My face felt flushed, and I found it difficult to breathe. From across the crowded room Evelina smiled, her cheeks red and her eye swollen, "*Gracias*," she said, "*carnal*." Vern kind of slithered out behind the police, and we all went back to packing.

I didn't make the trip to El Paso, but I did go to Falcon's funeral. I wore a black arm band, and I think I cried. Within a couple of years Florencio Granados and five other *compañeros* would be dead, victims of violent explosions. After that the campus became like a police state — if you were connected with UMAS you were watched. The idealism and the innocence of those early days were lost.

The irony would haunt me, how a man would rise from such a humble background to shake the foundations of the university and the state, only to die on the same day that his moral opposite would be given a reprieve. Vern would continue to live, and Ricardo Falcon would no longer know that pleasure.

Today we no longer identify ourselves as Chicanos. We attribute our lineage to the rapist and oppressor Spaniards. We call ourselves Hispanics. Our children are encouraged to speed the acculturation process, as we attempt to emulate the new colonizer's culture. And our departed leaders have been replaced by blow-dried Hispanic politicians committed only to increasing campaign contributions and perpetual reelection. Their idea of being progressive is not to be Republican.

I often sit on Sunday afternoons with my children, on the weekends that I have them. I sip beer, and we watch the sun go down in the west. From my back porch, we can feel its warmth until the very last moment on the horizon. I tell stories, just as my mother and father told me stories about Emiliano Zapata and Pancho Villa. I tell them stories of Ricardo Falcon, Ruben Salazar, Cesar Chavez, and Reies Tijerina. I never mention Vern, or that I saved his life. I don't think of it that way. Oso was a good man. All I did was help him maintain his principles. And maybe Falcon would have done the same thing.

But the ex's car will pull up the alley, and the horn will blow. The kids will grab their stuff, kiss me good-bye, and run off to their mom's car. They tell me that they love me and that they are proud to be Chicano. I'll go into the house, grab another beer, click on the stereo. I still own records, vinyl as the kids call them. Tonight Santana is playing "Samba Pa Ti" over and over. I sit down at the typewriter and let myself drift back years to Evelina's smile. Someone told me that over the years she put on weight. "No," said someone else. "She always was kind of heavy."

Funny, she always seemed so perfect, but then we all were, except Vern.

Rachel E. Harding

splendour

there are some gods / you can't talk to
long-toothed and
big-handed they
      have been in cane fields
      bent like a black rainbow
      slicing sugar
            in the full length of day

digging canals in the muck
till death grabs a shoveling arm
a snake-bitten heel
and holds like some kind of desperate
lover

you can't tell them
anything   no singing rod will steer them
no drum knows their name

they come
inside their own time
touch you on one shoulder
if you look
your tongue will swallow
      give you no words
      to tell
      take your language out to wide water
      and push it from shore

Judith Jerome

The Secret Life of School

It was not such a big deal, the thing that happened to me that day in 1957 when my life changed forever, but it was the smell I noticed first, the second I stepped in the door. School, for the seven years I'd known it, had always smelled the same. But here it was different, sweeter — sort of perfumy — and acrid at the same time. Like the zoo, a little. Or like when they castrated pigs at my uncle's. Plus, I stood in this enormous, cavernous sort of lobby, with halls going off in two directions and an enormous gymnasium to the right, and all of it filled with the most unbelievable noise. Clutching new sharp-cornered Pee-Chees and my first three-ring binder, I felt, unaccountably, like throwing up.

I'd walked right past my old school to get here. And I was excited, like always on the first day of school, anticipating: a few new kids, a new teacher, the smell and feel of new texts, writing my name in the front, folding the book covers on, greedy for the contents. Really. But anticipating especially the secret life of school — you know, who sits by whom, and row monitors and boyfriends and lunch, the whirl and intricacy and tension of the social order. I came alive here, woke up. It used me up entirely. I had the biggest feet in my class. I'd been the tallest girl until last year. I'd gotten straight A's since kindergarten. I sang solos in the talent shows (knew every song from *Oklahoma*, boy's and girl's parts); wrote plays, directed and starred in them; gossiped; made alliances and misalliances. I threw spear grass and chinaberries, heedless of putting out eyes; plotted; pumped the long-chained swings to horizontal and the spine-jarring snap. I fought girls full out, especially Patty Duncan, rolling in the dirt. I had three or four boyfriends at all times, and I chased boys, kicking. I kicked boys. I kicked boys. I kicked boys. Joy.

I'd walked on the opposite side of the street from my old school, and from that distance I could not see detail in the gray chiselled bas-relief at the wide front doors. But I knew that two lines of granite, straight-limbed boys and girls, with books in their arms, stood, at about a child's waist level, flanking the doors. And I knew that pencilled drops of urine sprang from the front sides of these children; while chunks of feces, clearly, though they were the same size, dropped from behind. They'd been there as long as I'd been there, the lead worked permanently, barring sandblasting, into the grain of the stone.

Still, graffiti aside, it was an entrance of dignity, an entrance of dignity in an otherwise modest flat-roofed little building. The main part was built in 1948 in a low L and connected at one end with the two-story white brick box that was the original school. At the time I was there, sixth and seventh graders used the second floor of the old building, and P.E. took up the lower floor. The floors were wooden, and they creaked satisfyingly.

The new junior high, on the other hand, was red. It had opened only the previous year, and it was huge, mazelike, with its many wings. And a terrifying casualness, really, with frankly exposed red metal beams, and a lower roof still, as though there was a sort of disintegration of form, of a sense of edifice as the decade moved to a close.

People streamed toward it. At my old school the playgrounds and lawns were already empty and silent, the tops of heads visible through the casement windows, in the art room, in Miss Fisher's first, in Mrs. Gilbert's second, in Dahlia's (my secret name for Mrs. Becker) third. Inside things went on, presumably, rich, profound, mysterious. I'd always been certain of adults' envy and deep curiosity, especially during fire drills when the school turned itself inside out onto the lawn, displaying briefly, tantalizingly, its secret life. I would always try not to look but would look once or twice, glance sidelong and smug as the people in their cars rolled past. It went without saying that their lives were unimaginably dull by comparison. Only now I, with my notebook over my chest was, like them, without access.

And standing now in that vast and raw entryway, here was the whirl and intricacy and tension, but at an unfamiliar pitch, a shrillness as strange as the smell and kin to it. And there was not a person I knew. No one paid the slightest bit of attention to me.

Even last year, at the beginning of the year, the P.E. teacher had announced that seventh-grade girls could no longer run out to the kickball field, *or* to recess. No one knew why, though there was whispered speculation. And it wasn't fair. You never got a swing anymore at recess. And you could still run the bases in kickball, which didn't make sense, but you couldn't run in Field Day at the end of the year. Not that I cared about that anyway. In sixth grade, for the first time in that many years, I lost the hundred-yard dash. Bob Ackerman beat me. And in the two-hundred-yard dash Bob Ackerman and Ernest Portula, the crossing monitor who never took off his diagonal white plastic sash, both beat me.

"Will!" He looked for the source of the voice. We'd gone to school together since third grade, had been copresidents of the I Hate Patty Duncan Club. I

started toward him. No running. He saw me, with almost a look of recognition —
and then his eyes shifted and lit up. I turned.

The girl was pretty. She had brown hair curled in a soft pageboy and brown
eyes and pink lipstick, for which last year she would have been sent home. She
was smiling, presumably at Will.

Will started toward the girl. "Hey Filene," he said as he went past.

That was it. I mean, it wasn't like Will was anybody special. He didn't get good
grades. He'd never been my boyfriend. But in that moment I knew for sure what I
had been about to know for a long time. And that was that everything, everything,
everything had changed. And all the logic of the new rules was just out of reach.
The next year I would stop singing solos and fail physics. And I could curl my
hair in a pageboy and wear pink lipstick — and I would, I vowed — but I was never
going to do it like that girl, whom I loved now just as much as Will did.

In fourth and fifth grades I'd had to sit by Charles Hawkins in P.E. because of
the alphabetic proximity of our names. He was skinny and smelled of urine, and
he tortured me by scraping fingernails full of dirt off his arms and wiping them
on me. I was not mean to him like most everybody else was, but . . . now I felt —
and this was brand-new, like the smell and the sound — a lot like Charles
Hawkins now.

And it's been the same, more or less, ever since.

Ricardo La Foré

The Upwardly Mobile Professionals

On the day when our people become extinct
Having fallen victim to the good intentions
Of the "Upwardly Mobile Professionals."
It shall be remembered that they,
These "professionals" stood by
And rather than align themselves
With what they considered the dregs
Of our society, stood by and watched
All the traces of our people disappear.

These "Upwardly Mobile Professionals."
Who cleaned up after mayors, governors
And presidents of our country.
Shall be reminded on that day
That the real hearts who bled
Did so from neglect and indifference
Inflicted on them by those
Who deal in rhetoric from public forums
There to represent their people
Because they had several degrees
But not one degree of love or compassion
For those who breast-fed them while they
Got their degrees.

These "Upwardly Mobile Professionals."
Rationalized and gave credibility
To dreams born in the deep dark corners
Of boardrooms and patent-leather briefcases
But the only dream they realized
Was that which espoused total assimilation

At the expense of the few who still believed
And would risk their lives and flesh
To remain that which we truly are.

These "Upwardly Mobile Professionals."
Never even questioned this subtle form
Of benign genocide.
They guided the lambs to the slaughter
And unknowingly participated in the obscene act
By their upwardly mobile but
Ill-intentioned aspirations.

Just before the final hour
The proud history of those who they betrayed
Shall pass in review
For all to see the scars and the shame
Just before the final hour
The shallow ramblings of the mediators
And entrepreneurs shall ring empty
And unheard, by the obliterated offspring
Of the hopeless, but pure of heart
And so in the final hour
Sick from grief and worry
Assimilation and upward mobility
Finally accomplished what
War, police, drugs and racism could not.

And so we were laid to rest
With the usual fanfare and hoopla
That we are all so good at.
The governor made an obligatory speech
The mayor did the same, and the president
At the behest of yet another upwardly mobile
professional sensing a photo opportunity
Sent a telegram.
We finally got our hero's burial

And these "Upwardly Mobile Professionals"
Content that they had done all they could
Set out to plan another conference
To network with other people in danger of
Becoming extinct!

Jeannie Madrid

N-Words

A negative name from a black slavery
With no language no knowledge of African glory
From a Riqueno Chicano trying to be white
When you're not that type not that light
You've the mouth of a whale and the brain of a bird
Or you'd save your nasty nutcake N-words
Mom's African obvious Native American and White
Fraternally I'm Scotch-Irish That's right
My ties to Africa America and Europe are secure
About your background it's hard to be sure
Fugitive slaves in the closet hoping only white shows through
I reject your rejection but I don't reject you
Because I know who I am I know what is true
That my beginnings are not as American slave
But way back in Africa among intellectually great
So I work for the time when all people are free
I travel the road to permanent Peace
Always all ways on to permanent peace
You may briefly distract but you can't detain me
I'm nobody to rape have nothing to pillage
Besides I know your face 'cause we live in the same village
Wake up little brother and I'll drive you to school
You're not one of the good citizens who rules
You don't have the connections You don't have the money
And besides . . . you ain't no plantation owner honey

Jacinta Taitano Martens

From "dear mama"

dear mama,

sometimes i get so angry with this family, i can't stand to be
around them. and sometimes i like all of you at the same time.
do you ever have those feelings?

when i was sitting on the hamper in the bathroom saying how
much i hated everyone in the whole world, i didn't mean you.

this is a terrible day!

j

dear mama,

it's been a long time since we've had any babies in our house.
are we done?

your curious daughter,

j

ps. i think we have very nice babies.

dear mama,

i know what i did. i used your lipstick without permission.
i am very sorry. you have so many beautiful things on
your dresser, and your lips are always so beautiful that i wanted

to see if mine would look as good. and the other thing is that
you said you didn't use makeup until you were twenty-one,
and you know how worried i get about things like that.
i hate to keep reminding you, but in america you start things
a little earlier. americans are good people even though
they wear makeup when they are young.

uncle pepe said that anybody could die crossing the street, so
you have to make sure every day you live is rich and full.
now that i have tried lipstick, i feel my life is rich and full.

your fulfilled daughter who will not use lipstick ever again
without permission,

j

dear mama,

the reason my confession took so long was because the
monsignor was telling me that confession is not a good place to
be creative.
i didn't know that.

first, he asked me to repeat my entire confession because i said i
had impure thoughts five hundred times. then he asked me to
say everything over again. finally he asked me what an impure
though was, and i told him it was on page ninety-two in the
Baltimore Catechism. he was coughing hard and told me
to go to the altar and tell god i would never confess this sin ever
again.

he also said not to confess any sins now that i might commit
in the future or my act of contrition wouldn't work.

i am very happy to have learned so much about confession.

with the grace of god,

j

dear mama,

when i watched the clothes hanging in a line — all of our white underwear all in neat rows — i started laughing. i don't know why.

i was watching the clothes while i was lying on the grass looking up at all that white underwear and beautiful blue sky.

i just laughed and laughed.

what do you think about this?

your happy daughter,

j

dear mama,

i know you believe that eating lima beans is for my own good, but i'm not sure. that's all i wanted to say. i wish uncle joe had never planted lima beans.

your child who doesn't like green vegetables, cooked or uncooked,

j

Wardell Montgomery, Jr.

Do I Have To Live Like This?

Today, times are hard, good jobs are few
Even computers are looking for work to do
When liquor and drugs for many are a way of life
It's no small wonder we're losing folk via gun and knife
Pushers at parties and on the street
Liquor stores on too many corners
If I depend on them to exist
I ask my wretched self:
Do I have to live like this?

Do they supply junk because I demand
Or do I demand junk because they supply
Are these scapegoats for our pleasure
Or only to bring us heartaches and pain
Remaining sober, I could see through this silly game
Am I caught in a thunderstorm
thinking it's only a light rain of mist
I ask my wretched self:
Do I have to live like this?

In rugged bygone years my people — poor and proud —
Have done so much with so little
By comparison, I have had so much,
Yet have done so little
I tried to keep up with the Joneses
And ended up with a jones I could not keep up with
If Harriet Tubman, Sojourner Truth, Crispus Attucks,
Denmark Vesey, Nat Turner, Frederick Douglass
And others too numerous to list
Could rise above slavery and oppression, teaching
their people of the evils they had to resist — then

I ask my wretched self:
Do I have to have to live like this?

Did I let Hollywood and Madison Avenue turn my American Dream
To a nightmare while I lay stretched out on the sidewalk
With children dancing around me singing
Is he sick? Is he asleep? Is he drunk? Is he drugged?
Is he dead? What a shame! Let's call the police
To take him away so we can play another game?
When I think of the many strong Afro-Americans
Who were their own analysts
I ask my wretched self:
Do I have to live like this?

Jacqueline St. Joan

Red on Her Fingers

[I]t came from everywhere. Which is to say it was
always there, and that it came from nowhere.
      — WILLIAM MATTHEWS, "Mood Indigo"

Every morning it was waiting on the other side of her
eyelids; lingering near the coffeepot until fed;
it didn't eat much, though it ate often; at first

it was only a sound in her body, racehorses crossing
her chest; her breath and her heartbeat panting at the gates;
her bowels rumbling with the winner; it became

other people's opinions, something gray that soiled
the town, selecting victims by the size of their hearts; it
was a challenge in black and white; knight to queen's fifth,

two pieces given a few moves, even fewer places to move;
She: Come sit here beside me; He: Let me pour you a drink;
each empties a glass vial when the other's back turns; she

knew the envy of a baritone for the soprano who sings the bass
line; but she caught the rare whiff of hatred in the piano
bench, a small mirror hanging in a tin frame; she found it

red on her fingers from forcing open the hard nut of
compassion; and it was worn like calluses for a gui-
tarist, green bruises inside the gymnast's tired thighs;

but truly it was also confession, an old shame trickling
down her leg; she felt bellows pumping, the open wings
of a heron flapping; and thick freckled arms stoking

the fire in the living room of its childhood, where at Christmas
the black engine and four cars circled and circled back into
grievances, admissions, and closed fists pounding;

rosaries began to murmur about it, and quickly
everyone would take sides.   Once
in the back of a drawer she found an old

photograph of it: 1949; she stands
barefoot, alone on a sidewalk, little shoulders
strapped in a sundress; her hair long

and light; one hand on her hip;
that hip cocked; the other hand shades
her eyes; she's squinting at it, daring it to shoot.

Idaho

I talked a great deal about nonfiction during my visits as a TumbleWords writer. Although I've written both poetry and fiction, I am currently at work on a memoir, and I've been intrigued by the lines that we draw between story and memory. The writers I met with were often caught up in the same dilemma I faced each time I tried to force my "just the facts, ma'am" approach onto the "truth" of my and my family's history: where exactly is the truth in memory?

What I've found is that we often find truth not in memory itself but in the story we make of memory. As I toured through Idaho, I heard again and again this sad refrain: "I don't have a story." Many of the people who spoke this were young as writers go, thirty-five, maybe forty. They believed that because they had not lived the lives of their elders, they had no legitimate claim to tell the stories of their people in any way that did not adhere to fact (whatever that may be). Is it any wonder they felt lost and disconnected?

All I could give as encouragement is what authors of nonfiction such as Mary Clearman Blew, Bill Kittredge, and Terry Tempest Williams have given me: the conviction that the story of the individual is the story of the family, the community, the tribe. One woman in a small Idaho town confided (near tears) that she did not feel she had any right to tell the stories of her family. What if she remembered wrong? What if her memory was that of a child — unreliable, fantastic, distorting — and her siblings and uncles and parents rose up against her? I took her arm. "The blood that is here," I said, touching the pulse of her wrist, "is your story. Your memory, your history, your family's history, belongs to you, is as much a part of you as the blood in your veins."

I believe this absolutely, and seeing the empathetic faces of my audience — writers and readers, mothers and daughters, grandfathers and sons, from Twin Falls, Tetonia, Montpelier, Bonners Ferry — as they listened to me read from my memoir made me understand that they were giving to me as much as I was giving to them. They believed not in the factual details of my presentation, but in the spirit of memory and our need to make sense of our lives through narrative. "Thank you," said one man after a workshop and a reading, "for giving me permission to tell my story." I was stunned by this sincerity and the realization that this is what so many of us as writers desire: permission to say, to write and record, what we believe to be true.

KIM BARNES

Rick Ardinger

Planting Day

For Rosemary

She walks barefoot,
bent in the garden, poking
seeds and molding mounds
of soft wet earth
for cucumbers. Snow
still caps the mountains
as she stakes tomatoes
and peppers perfect
with yellow ribbon,
ties sticks in a makeshift
fence against dogs
and rabbits and to make
it pretty, marks rows
with seed packets,
measures time in inches.
She knows how soon
weeds thicken, rounded
mounds erode, vines
strangle crooked fences,
and Ball jars boil
September in the kitchen.
She'd like to pickle
the moon in its own
rhythms, shelve the sun
like honey, or just
hold planting day
inside a locket's memory
raging forever
with crickets.

Rick Ardinger

A Mountain Disappears in a Cloud
While I Eat Beans for Lunch

After the chill this morning,
the birds will consider going south.
All summer with the birds.
The meadowlarks in May,
the robin squatting in her nest
in the tree beside the porch,
cliff swallows in the barn
and under the eaves already gone.

I knocked down their elaborate
empty nests, stacked firewood
closer to the door all morning.
The old boney cat basks
in noon sun while she can.
I watch her close
to see that she still breathes.

Tonight coyotes in the canyon's
hollow echo will mimic winter wind,
and the dog will lie awake
and growl till dawn when
he can sleep again.

There's wood to split,
the car to fix,
some windows still need putty.
Meanwhile, I stand arms akimbo
on the porch, staring down a mountain
as if I had the time. Summer
flies in the distant bird.
My plate of beans turns cold.

Kim Barnes

From *In the Wilderness*

The first man to prophesy my future was a grandfatherly missionary with hair the color of new dimes, who sold us beautiful wooden boxes carved by the natives of Haiti. In our second week of revival, two people had been healed: one of an ulcer, the other of a slow-knitting rib, cracked when his saw kicked off a limb and knocked him flat.

Meetings lasted for hours, every night, beginning with the opening prayer, a few answering amens, then singing. As our voices rose, people began to clap then sway, palms raised to the ceiling. When the missionary took the podium, we were primed for his outpouring of God-given wisdom and spiritual insight. By the time the sermon ended, the pitch of our praise had built to the point of drowning out his closing words, and he called on us to confess and be reborn in loud outbursts that sounded more like commands than entreaties. Finally, the entire congregation shouted and stamped, those gifted in tongues adding their heavenly language to the booming chorus.

Each preacher was different. One might holler and wave his arms; another pounded the pulpit with his Bible until the spine broke and pages flew. The missionary from Haiti danced in the aisles, twirling with his arms outstretched, head thrown back, heels clicking the wooden floor in the measured beat of flamenco. It was he who called me out one night after the sermon, after Sister Barrack had prophesied in tongues and Sister Hanson had interpreted God's message, a message of warning lest Satan rally his army, jealous of our praise. Several women had fallen under the Spirit and lay on the floor trembling and weeping; others less stunned draped the women's legs with lap clothes to ensure modesty.

He found me, head bowed, a little sleepy, muttering my prayers and unprepared for his attention. The voices quieted as he called me to the altar. I stepped away from my seat and made my way toward the front, weaving through the prostrated bodies. His eyes were serious and piercing, as though there were something I was hiding, as though he could read in my face what had roused in him the need to clasp my head between his sweaty palms and drive me to my knees.

I felt no fear. I felt the roughness of his hands and the eyes of the church upon me, but I believed in this man of the Lord. I had seen him heal the Payton boy, seen the short leg lengthen in the preacher's cupped hand. What wound or fault he might find in me I could not discern, but I waited calmly to be free of it, newly whole.

"What is your name, child?"

"Kim," I whispered.

"Sister Kim, God has brought us here together tonight for a very special reason. Do you know what that is?" He let his gaze sweep the room. "Sister Kim walks among you with a gift. Sister Kim, do you know what that gift is?"

I heard the voices behind me: "Yes Lord!" "Thank you, Jesus!" I thought I heard my mother crying. I shook my head, filled with a growing curiosity as though a stranger were about to read my palm, uncover a family secret. I steadied myself against the weight of his hands.

"You, my daughter, have the gift of healing. You are a healer," Behind me the praise grew louder. The room felt suddenly hot, and I wished for an open door, a window letting in the cool night air. His hands were heavier than my legs could stand, and I fell, sweat trickling down my sides.

Sister Hall pounded out chords on the upright. I don't remember the hymn or what other hands came to bless me. I only remember my knees on the cold wood floor and wondering what my father thought then, what would be expected of me in the days to come. I wondered if Lynn witnessed my anointing, what desire for me it raised, what part of him I might touch.

The next Sunday I sat at the table of Brother and Sister Barrack. They ran cattle outside of Weippe, an even smaller town than Pierce, twenty miles southwest. There were others there my age, children still wobbly in their manners at the table's far end, eating silently while the adults pondered the day's sermon and praised the wife's fried chicken. If there was a lull in the conversation, if the discussion had turned to the past week's revival, I don't recall. I only know I felt a sudden pain, as though a nail were being driven into my ear. I whimpered and my fork clattered to my plate.

I had never had an ear infection, had never felt the kind of pain I now felt, both throbbing and sharp. I remembered the missionary's words, and with absolute certainty stood up and announced, "Someone here has an earache."

Looking from one unperceiving face to another, I pressed my hand to the right side of my head.

"Someone's ear hurts."

I stood with my neck bent to ease the pressure. At the other end of the table a woman let out a single sob.

It was Sister Barrack. I moved from my child's place and walked to her chair. She bowed her head, softly crying, and I placed my hand on her right ear. I could feel the heat there, the drumming pain. Others joined me, clasping my shoulders, touching my back.

"Dear Lord, our sister has a need. She needs you, Jesus." My words were met with a chorus of amens and hallelujahs. I drew a breath. My eleven-year-old awkwardness was gone. The words flowed.

"We ask that you take this pain from her. Heal her, Lord! In God's name we pray."

The chorus became a chant, loud and encompassing, until the body I touched and the hands touching me melded. I floated in a swell of sound, a humming of breath and blood.

"You will be healed!" I demanded it, surprised by the sound of my own voice. The woman shuddered and groaned. The heat from her ear spread from my fingers into my arm and shoulder — my neck and face flushed with it. I opened my eyes and found myself in that room, the chicken half-eaten, gravy scumming the plates. The woman shivered in my hands.

Later I played with the other children in the barn. The woman's one daughter and I hid from the boys in the stubble of corn, giggling with pleasure at their blindness. We rooted tadpoles from the shallows and stabbed them onto rusty hooks. The creek held catfish, and we bobbed for them in the manure-silted water. Each one we pulled from the muddy stream seemed a miracle, so different from the blazing trout I caught in the clear runoff of Reed's Creek. I held their sleek black bodies in my hands, smoothing the spiny backs, careful of their poison.

That night, after evening service, the wife slipped into bed beside her already sleeping husband. When she woke the next morning her pillow was sticky with pus. The fever was gone. Whether it would have been so had I not touched her, I don't know. I can explain the progress of illness and infection but not that moment when her pain took hold of me as though it were my own affliction. She testified at church that a miracle had been wrought, and I felt the weight of expectation fall on me, heavy as the missionary's hands. My parents allowed me to walk in front of them. The other children began to resent the way the adults nodded whenever I spoke. I wasn't sure I could do it again. If I failed to discern an illness, or if I prayed for someone to be healed and nothing happened, would it mean I had sinned, that I was unworthy to bear such a gift?

I thought of Lynn's hands, how they touched me accidentally or on purpose but always in a way I remembered for days. We spent many Sunday afternoons in the parsonage. While the women made stew or fried venison dusted with flour, Danny, Lynn, and I hunched together on the narrow stairway leading upstairs, sharing the dirty jokes we had heard at school, guessing what went on in the bed of their sister.

It was always dark there, and we spoke in whispers. The closeness of our bodies took my breath away. When Lynn's leg rested against mine I could no longer hear what was being said. Once he put his hand on my knee. The sweet shock traveled to the bone and began a fire that spread its warmth to my crotch, a feeling so pleasurable I shuddered with the sure sin of it.

When we returned to the company of our parents, I could still feel the heat of his hand. I burned with shame to have given that much of myself so easily. I prayed for forgiveness, for strength, for whatever temptation this was to leave me. But even in sleep I remembered his palm pressed against bare skin beneath the hem of my skirt. Something had begun its slow possession. How could I be both healer and sinner? How could I close my eyes in prayer when all I could see was the face of the preacher's son? I was lost, no language to describe how I savored this sin, no one to prophesy my salvation or damnation. I huddled beneath the covers of my bed, hearing the wind rise, the pinecones tacking the ground. Surely God would cause a tree to fall, send it crashing through the roof. I imagined Lynn's kiss, then the slide of his hand between my legs. The night held still. I could dream of no more.

It had been three years since my mother stood at the kitchen window, pointing up and out into the haze of August sky.

"How many, Kim? How many birds on the wire?"

I looked from her to the square of light and back. The clues lay in the words — bird, wire — just as they did in my father's riddles: If a plane crashes on the border between the United States and Canada, where do they bury the survivors? If a rooster lays an egg on the peak of a roof, which way will the egg roll? Kits, cats, sacks, and wives, how many were going to St. Ives?

I could no more find the true meaning in my mother's question than I could see the birds and the wire. The distance from the window to the table where I sat, nose rubbing the pages of my history book, was no more than ten feet, but even that distance would have been enough to fade her features to an air-brushed silhouette.

Some weeks afterward, I sat in the optometrist's office, surrounded by cases of heavy frames, trying on pair after pair. I could not see myself in the mirror the assistant held out for me: the dark plastic lines faded into the peachy canvas of my face, which I obediently studied for a weighty minute before reaching for the next pair. Days later, when the doctor slid them over my ears, the glasses settled onto my nose with surprising heaviness. Even more startling was my mother's face peering into my own, so close I could see gray flecks in her pale green eyes. Behind her, the doctor and assistant leaned toward me as though I had just been given the power of speech and were about to utter my first word.

What had I seen before? The birds on the wire I had imagined as leaves on a branch; now when I saw them from the window I could count their feathers, watch the small beaks preen for dust, see them tense for flight before rising into the air and disappearing. I described for my mother the colors of grass, the movement of shadows, the ever changing shade of my aunt's hair.

The language of vision had always been with me — pale, clear, bright, deep — but my sense of the words had been tactile, palpable, something I felt rather than saw. I remember the smell of smoke, the auroral glow of my father's cigarette as we drove the dark road to town or back to camp. The trees and river flew by, miles I knew by heart but could not describe any differently in daylight than at night, although I never doubted their existence any more than I doubted the presence of angels, whose wings I imagined the cloudiest white, softly downed without quills or striation, large enough to carry me aloft in huge breathy beats.

In the stairway I came to believe the absence of light a blessing. I prayed for the counterfeit night and the sound of Lynn's voice husky with desire. I prayed we not be found out, knowing God's grace covered a multitude of transgressions, knowing my wickedness lay in the very prayer I offered — the prayer of a sinner jealous of her sin.

It was Lynn I thought of one Sunday night as I waited for my parents to finish their prayers. Brother Hall's sermon had been a long one, and everyone seemed ready to file from the pews and head home. No one had a special need or pressing confession to present to the congregation — not even Sister Payton, a large, dark woman given to fits of lumbago, who normally went forward to have her swollen knees anointed with the thick green oil kept pushed to the back of the lectern. People had already begun pulling on their coats and shaking hands with their neighbors when Brother Hall stepped from the stage and clapped his hands together for attention.

"Our work here tonight is not done," he announced loudly. Everyone stopped still, eyes widening with sudden interest. "There is one among us who has a weakness, a need." He released one of his hands and held it out, fingers together, pointed at me like a hatchet. "Sister Kim, will you come forward?"

My parents looked from Brother Hall to me then shuffled back to let me pass, their hands lifted in prayer, palms up, as if to catch rain. Those who had left their seats, thinking the evening's worship closed, settled back into their rows.

What was it I needed? My throat wasn't sore. The pain in my shins had stopped, healed by the woman revivalist in Orofino who told me I lacked calcium, pressed her thumbs into my temples until my head pounded, then released me with her encouragement to drink more milk. As I walked down the aisle, mentally checking my stomach for pain, the balance of my shoulders and hips, I passed Lynn. He sat in the front, leaned casually into the pew's hard corner. Even the backs of his ears were beautiful.

Brother Hall grasped my shoulders then gently pivoted me to the congregation. I looked out over the room, into the upturned faces and moving mouths of God's people. Lynn, only a few feet away, met my eyes with such intensity I felt suddenly paralyzed. He was seeing something in me no one else could see, something that threaded through the soles of my feet and into my leg bones like the ancient canes of berries, piercing my bowels and lungs, twining its tendrils around my throat so that I labored to breathe. The intimacy of his vision was not holy. The way his mouth, lips slightly parted, drew me in with all the air in the room made me reel. The hands gripped my shoulders tighter. I felt each finger and thumb into my flesh; I counted them under my breath, eyes closed.

"Sister Kim," the voice spoke to the back of my head, "how long have you been burdened with poor sight?"

I opened my eyes slowly, blinking for a moment to force the room into focus. My mother stood with her hands clasped in front of her breasts. Her lips seemed to tremble.

I thought back to that August afternoon, to the birds on the wire. How old had I been? That girl was another life ago. Was I eight?

"At least three years," I whispered.

"These glasses are a heavy burden. The Lord can heal these eyes, and will," Brother Hall turned me back to face him, "if she will only have faith."

I looked into his own eyes, so dark the pupil and iris bled together. Like the eyes of an animal, I thought.

Until that moment, I seldom considered my vision. The glasses were a part of me, an extension of my body. Because of them I could see my way from one room to another without holding to the walls and shuffling my feet. Now their presence seemed less a gift than a flaw, a mark of weakness.

I felt a sudden growing shame, the same shame I felt at the new roundness of my breasts, the hair in hidden places. I lowered my head. I remember my hand cupping Sister Barrack's fevered ear. The image reviled me. How foolish to believe that I held in my power the gift to discern the infirmity of another: I could not even see the reflection of my own face in the mirror without the grotesque magnification of glass.

"Sister Kim. Do you have faith?"

I nodded slowly.

"Do you believe God can heal your eyes?"

I nodded again. I had never before been afraid of prayer. Many times I had felt the laying on of hands. I had healed and been healed. Now the preacher's fingers seemed locked, digging into the soft pockets of flesh between my neck and shoulders.

I did not want to be there, my ears filled with moans and high singing building into the staccato rhythm of tongues. I did not want others to see my disgrace: my pride had blinded me to the blemishes of my own body. In believing that I, a silly, stammering girl, could work miracles, I had drawn attention to myself. My spiritual vision had clouded to match my eyesight. I thought of Lynn, the cloistered stairway. Had I really believed God could not see through such blackness?

I waited, eyes closed, for the touch of pungent oil, Brother Hall's finger sliding twice across my forehead in the shape of a cross. Instead I felt my glasses lifted from my face. I opened my eyes to see the blur of his hand tucking the dark frames into the pocket of his white shirt.

I lost my balance and grabbed for his arm. He steadied me then pressed his thumbs against my eyelids. The prayers rose higher, a loud thrum of joined voices, like the amplified murmurings of bees.

"Hear us now, Jesus. We come to Thee to ask that these eyes be *healed. Heal these eyes*, Dear Lord, so that our sister might see clearly all you have created."

He made short, sharp jerks with his hands. I strained with the effort to keep rigid.

"She knows, Lord, that if she has enough faith, if she will only believe, *she will be healed!*"

Others were shouting now. Their feet stomped the wooden floor as they called on the Spirit, *"Jesus. Sweet Jesus."*

Then the hands pulled away, the voices quieted, and I opened my eyes.

"Sister Kim, how many fingers am I holding up?"

I blinked, my vision still dark with the print of his thumbs. His hand floated so close I could see the half-circle of his wedding band.

"Three," I answered. Somewhere behind me, Sister Hanson called out, "Praise the Lord!"

"Can you see your parents?" The hand was at my arm, turning me once again to the room. I looked to where I left my family. Browns and blues washed together as though I were looking through water. I peered harder. Sister Hanson twirled in the aisle — I recognized her high-pitched voice, the characteristic trilling of her glossolalia. But I could not see my mother and father, only the arms raised to heaven, undulating like meadow grass. I shook my head. No one seemed to notice. The room vibrated with the loud praise of men and women given over to the Spirit. Sister Hall pounded out a hymn on the upright, and I knew the meeting would last long into the night.

"You must believe and you will be healed. Go home tonight and pray for faith to accept this truth." Brother Hall released me, and I felt my way up the aisle until my father caught my wrist.

Three days passed before I regained my sight. Three days of not seeing the blackboard, of being unable to find the swings at recess. I told my teacher and friends my glasses were broken and let them lead me like a pet dog. I clutched my mother's sleeve when we walked to and from the car, and even though I had never needed it before, I began to leave a light on at bedtime: If I woke, I could not see beyond the lamp's dim silhouette. I was no longer a child secure in my parents' bed, their closeness giving boundaries to my nighttime world.

Did my mother feel her own faith waiver, watching from the window as I stumbled up the driveway to catch the bus, holding to my brother's coattail, clutching the books I could not read? Did she long to take from that preacher the glasses he had pocketed and lay them beside my bed as I slept? I'd wake and find them there, my prayers answered, the prayers of a child wandering scared, lost in the waters, waiting for a hand to reach from the bank and pull her to safety.

I imagine my mother kissing my eyes when she believed I was deep into dreams, as I now kiss the fluttering and delicate lids of my own children. I heard her whispering, *"Believe."* I open my eyes and see her disappear into a rectangle of light.

At the next Wednesday night prayer meeting, Brother Hall slipped the glasses into my hand, as though he himself were embarrassed by my failure. I waited until the singing began before I put them on and reached for the hymnal, thrilled to see the black letters distinct against white pages. It seemed miracle enough. With the book held straight out before me, I began to sing.

Later, in the stairway, air damp with close breathing, Lynn reached to slide the glasses from my face. I caught his hand.

"You're so much prettier," he whispered.

I folded the hard frames in my palm and clasped them tightly. I closed my eyes and waited in darkness for his kiss.

William Johnson

Ice Fishing on Lost Valley Reservoir

The lantern's so bright
they're attracted like
flies are to rot
though it's only bacon fat
jammed on steel hooks
like tufts of gin-soaked
cotton a drunk smells
even in sleep. Me,
I've come for the moon
spilling its change in snow,
that high light show
the aurora puts on
at no charge, plush tourmaline
rainbows that mimic the
one I've laid out quivering
in a pantomime of breath.
In the bucket charcoal
simpers like bone dust.
Even in down-lined gloves
my hands grasp the emptiness,
no tingle answering
the Morse of stars.
Adrift in slush the bobber
throbs its commandment—
stand, jerk hand, if there's
a tug, twist line on the
spool, if not, squat, breathe
deeply, wait. How the sky
Deepens toward hinterspace,
like lights of the city
lovers glimpse from Highdrive

above instead of below.
All those lives up there
pretending that nothing has
ended, and the dreamer absently
watching them, half in,
half out of the body,
hooked and soon to be landed.

Leslie Leek

Searching for Star

For two days I had searched for Star. I could only go after school, and Daddy said I had to be back before dark. I couldn't go at all on Friday because Mother said I had to have my tap lesson. She wanted me to take ballet, but there wasn't anybody to teach it. So every Friday it's step-ball-change, step-ball-change on the hardwood floor beneath the front room carpet that is rolled up at Francis's house. Francis is a high-school girl. She's okay. I can tap things like "Three Blind Mice." I try to get it right for Mother, who wants to see what I learn every week. She props herself up on pillows on the roll-out sofa bed in the living room.

"You can do it, Jessica. You can do it, my love," she says. She tries to make her voice sound like always. But it seems far away. She tries hard to watch me. Her eyes, she calls them hazel, a color that can change from brown to green, burn their darkest color toward me from her pale face.

On Saturday Daddy said he'd help me find Star. Star is my friend, my beauty of a black mare with the white diamond mark on her forehead.

We get up early. Daddy takes me to Annie's Café next door for sunny-side up eggs and country fried potatoes. Asa Green is there saucering his coffee. It makes me sick to watch him. His beard has egg on it. He's worn that same wool shirt since I can remember, and there is snot on one ragged cuff.

"Lost your mare in The Rocks?" Asa says. "You'll never find her." He slurps more coffee. "Place is haunted. Like that Ber-muda Triangle, energy so strong it pulls cars and trucks right off the highway; semis even. I seen it. They say they built that highway right over a Shoshone burial ground. Big Chief's gettin' even." He starts to laugh. Little explosions of air come out of his mouth, puff, puff, puff. "You'll never find her."

Annie tells him to shut up. "Don't mind him," she says to me. "Nathan, you want more coffee?" she asks my dad. She sounds awful nice, like women do when they talk to him. She pours his coffee, clears our plates. "How's Helen today?" she asks.

"About the same," Dad answers.

"Strange things go on out there," Old Asa says, like he's just caught up to us. "Stock disappears all the time."

"Asa, you old fart," Annie gives him a stop-it look, "that's enough."

Asa slurps his coffee but doesn't seem to have his feelings hurt.

"Let's go, Jess," Dad says.

"Good luck." Annie smiles at us as we go out the door and back to the apartment above the newspaper office to get our warm clothes so the cold won't catch us. We are careful to be quiet. Mother is asleep.

We crawl under the barbed-wire fence about a mile from town. We have our halter, ropes, and bucket of oats. Daddy puts his foot on the lower wire and holds the one next to it up so I can slip through. I do the same for him from the other side, except I can't get the wire high enough. He snags the back of his jacket but makes it through.

"Thanks," he says.

On the other side of the fence he puts his arm around me. "Okay, Jess, we'll find her. We'll find her and bring her home, and she'll have that colt. It will be a dandy. She has just found some warm place in the rocks where the grass is still tender and delicious. She's lazy and greedy and doesn't want to leave. Don't bother about Old Asa."

I wish Mother was here to take a picture of us like the one we had taken in Virginia City, Montana, with the old-time clothes on. Daddy in a fake mustache sits on a straight-backed chair. I stand with my arm on his shoulder, looking serious. I wish we didn't have to go anther step, that we could just stay here, his arm around me like this.

We decide to walk together as far as the rock canyon where the stock path splits and goes in two directions, one on top of the lavas, the other through the bottom.

If you drive past The Rocks — that's what everyone calls the place, The Rocks — if you drive by, say you're on the highway going to Pocatello, or maybe coming back from there, and you look out, you think it's just country, sagebrush — ordinary. Mostly I don't think people even look at it because the mountains on the other side holler loudest at the eye. Most people don't know there are secret places here: rock canyons, meadows, Hidden Lake surrounded by cattails and strange birds. Last fall I saw a big fight between the sandhill cranes and the geese, everybody honking and squawking and circling, and setting down tough. The cranes won, I think because they sound the scariest, like pterodactyls. Then they just walked around, full of themselves. They made me laugh.

I don't care what Asa says, I know for myself about some of the secrets of this place. I spend a lot of time down here. I don't tell my friends. I don't know why.

I do tell my dad about the path of pictures. He's the only one I tell.

"What?" he says at first.

I tell him about the pictures on the rocks. He calls them petroglyphs. I tell him how there is a picture of one hand at the first to give a warning, then three hands that let you in. You must touch "Three Hands" in the middle, and they will let you see the rest but only with the sun to help in certain places. There is "Day Bending" and "Earth Turns Round to Look at the Animals," "Crazy Dance for Summer," "Stories Like Sticks That Tell the Future," "Old People Dreaming," "Magic Man," "Magic Flying Woman," "The Children with Words for Night," and "All the Signs Play Tricks on Wind."

"Wait a minute," Dad says. "What are you saying?"

"The names of the pictures."

"On the rocks?"

"Yes."

He looks at me funny. He smiles. I feel like he's hugged me again, but we're still walking over the lavas and the cheatgrass.

Adults are strange. They seem surprised when you know the simplest things, but they expect you to know the hard stuff, like about people. Like when I'm in the newspaper office. We have a weekly newspaper. Dad says we're a vanishing breed. We haven't gone to "offset" yet like most. He calls me a printer's devil. On Wednesday and Thursday I have to be in the office because that's the time when we mail the papers. We all work, the whole family. Well, not Mother the last few weeks, but usually. I fold the papers. Dad says I'm the fastest folder in the West. Anyway, what I want to say is that sometimes when I'm in the office some important person will come in to see Dad. Daddy always introduces me.

"Senator, this is my daughter, Jessie."

"Commissioner, this is my daughter, Jessie."

They'll say something dumb like, "She's sharp as a little tack," after we talk for a while. I'm not "sharp." I'm just polite like Mother insists. I don't understand why these men act like my old uncles, and I don't understand what often happens next as my mother leaves the linotype where she's been working and moves to the front of the office to join the conversation. She moves like a dark-haired movie star down the narrow aisle between the makeup stones — big tables where Dad puts the paper together — and the casting box and the type cases, in a matching straight skirt and sweater. Her high-heeled shoes clip-clip over the old wood floor that is sprinkled with metal shavings from the linotype and the casting box.

She shakes hands with the visitors. The men, the old uncles, stare at her and lose
the flow of their smooth words. I look at Daddy. He smiles.

"You're just the sweetest little lady," the visitors will say to me when they leave.
I'd like to punch them.

"I'm proud of you, honey," Dad says to me.

Out here in The Rocks, I know a lot. It's easy to know things here. I listen. I
do what the rocks say, or the wind.

It's easy to forget how scared I feel about finding Star while I'm with Daddy,
walking along, thinking, the halter and the oat bucket thudding with our steps.
The cold air nibbles my cheeks. I chew the gum that Dad taught me to make
from oats. You have to chew and chew a handful and finally it makes gum, but
it won't blow into bubbles. Dad looks at the pictures on the rocks as we go by,
but we don't put fingers to the middle of "Three Hands," so most of the pictures
stay hidden. Besides, the best ones are farther up the trail, and we don't have
time for them today.

I always try to walk just like Dad when we are out like this, when we go duck
hunting or walk along with the horses for a rest. When I was little, four or five,
he gave me a beautiful Jesse James toy pistol and holster set. Mother got mad.

"Nathan, you encourage her," she said. "She's never going to be a young lady.
She'll stay a little Barbarian." That word was new to me, like *petroglyph* and
cancer. Mother stomped in her high heels out of the office and slammed the
door so hard dust came from between the boards. The web where the old cat
spider Dad named Mark Twain lived shook so hard in the corner of the window
that old Mark curled up in a tight ball to protect himself. I reached in and pulled
out both pistols at once from their black leather holsters and twirled them better
than Jesse James.

Last fall Daddy's friend Gordon Crowley took Dad and me deer hunting. We
drove in his pickup with the horses in back to the head of Harkness Canyon. It
was dark and cold. Dad and I were excited, Dad the most. It was awful early in
the morning. Dad and Gordon drank whiskey in their coffee.

"Gotta open your eyes," Gordon said.

I got coffee too, from the thermos and a chocolate bar before the sun came
up. We rode our horses to the top of the mountain. I was on Star. It was a hard
ride because it was barely getting light, but Star picked her way perfectly over
the shale. At the top, Dad and I sat under a tree. Gordon said he'd see what he
could scare up.

"This is the life, Jess, girl. This is all a guy could ask for." He put his arm around me. We were very happy. We could see the world from up there. After a while I got confused about what was his face and what was the day opening up around us.

We hunted all day. The horses carried us up and down the mountains. Maybe I got a little tired, but I wouldn't tell anybody. I don't think you could feel any better than we did. Dad didn't shoot at anything. He never does. On the way home I fell asleep hard and, as big as I was, Daddy carried me into the house. Mother thought I was dead or something. She gave a little scream that woke me up. When she saw I was fine, she got mad.

"Look at you. You're a mess. Into the tub right now!"

"Jess," Dad says, "we're at the fork in the path." I'm surprised to hear him because I've been thinking about the hunting story. I look up at him. I would rather die than have him know how scared I feel about him leaving me. I've been out here a hundred times by myself or with Star. I know the county. I know more. But today is heavy with dark clouds and a few snowflakes that disappear the instant they hit anything. I'm cold. I feel something grow big and hard in my throat. I can barely swallow. I spit the oat gum out and imagine the cool handles of those silver pistols though I am much too old for them now.

"Okay," I say.

"Remember, we'll meet at the end of this canyon. I'll be there on the upper trail. You'll be able to see me from time to time. I'll whistle for you. You whistle back. If we don't find her, we'll come back and search another section tomorrow." He puts a gloved hand on my shoulder, which is buried beneath my old wool coat. Then he moves away from me.

I pretend to walk hard up the trail in my own direction, but as soon as he is out of sight, I stop. I wonder if Mother is awake yet, if she is sitting up in bed drinking coffee, or if the pain is too much and she hides her head under the covers so no one will see her cry.

"Don't worry Jess," Dad says, "she's getting better."

I look up in time to see a flash of my dad's red and black checked coat above the rocks. I start to move on, not keeping just to the trail but zig-zagging so I won't miss a place Star might be sleeping or grazing. She'd have to be sleeping though, not to know I was looking for her. I wonder what she could be dreaming about: the oat bucket, the corral with the lean-to and straw we got ready for her back in town, her baby, that colt she will have later than most colts should be born, how she will lick it clean and nudge it to stand up and nurse it.

I hear the whistle, the wave of sound that is our family signal. It's how we call the horses, how Dad calls me when it's time to come to dinner or come in from playing at night. The whistle if you drew it would start slow at the bottom and jump to a sharp peak and come back down the other side into a series of little hill sounds that go faster. I whistle back. One whistle, we said to check on each other, two if we find Star.

After the whistles, it is quiet. I start to think about something I heard in the office once.

"Milton, I'd like you to meet my daughter, Jessie. Jessie, this is Mr. Drummond. He's writing a history of the county."

Daddy is always interested in people writing things. He says when he retires he'll write stories, maybe a book. He doesn't say this to Mr. Drummond. I go back to what I'm doing, but I hear Mr. Drummond tell about the Shoshone, how they used to leave their old and sick people in The Rocks down by the creek, to die.

After I remember this I feel nervous about looking behind the rocks in the bare spaces. I'm afraid I'll find a skeleton or some old person dying, or my mother. This thinking makes me hear Old Asa's voice at Annie's.

"You'll never find her."

Should I worry about that energy that pulls cars and semis right off the highway? I walk faster. I don't know this until my ears pick up the quickening clink, clink of the halter and the oat bucket and my mouth seems to be gulping down the sharp air till it hurts. I make myself slow down.

Suddenly I see something dark, way off to the right, by a clump of juniper bushes. My heart beats so loud I think anyone could hear it. I try to run toward the hope of the dark horse shape, but it's hard because of the rocks, the sagebrush. I fall, get up, fall again. The halter slips off my shoulder. I save the oat bucket. When I'm almost there, I see how the dark shape that I thought I could see toss its head and enjoy the sight of me, falling all over the place, is only the dead trunk of another old juniper.

"Hell," I say. I know that no one can hear me. Mother can't scold me, and Dad can't give me that look with his eyes that is ten times worse than anything. I call that look the double whammy.

I begin to make my way back to the trail. I don't have far to go until the end where I will meet Dad. I feel tired and hungry, and I want to go home and find out I'm dreaming this like Star might be dreaming she's licking the smooth coat of her new baby.

I drag my eyes along the ground from habit. I follow a split in the rocks. The rocks grow into a wall. The wall is speckled with green and yellow and red stuff that grows all over it. I call this place Box Canyon. I read the name in the *Red Stallion* book.

I stumble, catch myself, look ahead. My breath stops. There it is. Not my old friend. Not the mare, lazy and greedy, eating hidden delicate grass. Not my Star. There it is, the colt, a shaggy, dark little thing curled up. I try to whistle, nothing comes out. I try harder and harder. My throat burns. My eyes burn. I throw the halter and oat bucket down.

"Dad," I cry. "Dad! Dad!"

I can't move to it. It raises its head when it hears me. It looks wild and scared. I hear my mother's voice.

"She wants me to die. She wants me to die. Oh, Nathan," she cried. All I said was maybe the operation would make her feel better, she wouldn't have to be so grumpy, and she started to scream and cry. Daddy tried to hold her. "She wants me to die." She kept saying it. "She wants me to die."

I hate that little horse below me. I hate that shaggy body. "You'll never be a beauty," I scream at it. "You'll never be a beauty."

I hear rocks fall from the other side of the canyon. I see a blur of red and black.

"Jess," Dad calls. "Jess." He can't reach me, so he sends my name wrapped up warm like that. He sees the little horse. He climbs and slips through the rock and brush to reach it. He goes right toward it. It tries to jump up but is too weak and wobbles and falls back down. Dad throws off his gloves and the rope he carries over his shoulder. He kneels down to it.

"It's all right, little filly, poor little filly," he says.

I move closer with his words.

"Little waif, little orphan." His voice is gentle. He strokes her little black neck and back. "Come on, Jess. Isn't she a beauty? We'll have to get her back to town."

I kneel down beside them. The filly makes scared grunting noises. I take off my gloves too, so I can feel her shaggy dark coat, her soft, soft nose with a little white star shape on it.

"A few days old," he says. "It's a miracle she's alive."

I ache to put my arms around her mother's safe neck.

"Jessie, I don't think we'll find Star. She'd never leave her foal like this unless something happened."

I make myself go tough and hard. I do it for the filly.

"Tough little girl" I whisper to her. "Tough little filly, little wild girl."

Ron McFarland

At the Correctional Facility

That November afternoon I ate in Cottonwood,
coconut cream pie like Mother never made
and coffee way too good for the circumstances.
I was waiting for the minute hand to come in line
with three to send me to the prison outside town,
minimal security, boot-camp poetry for first
offenders, those with just enough badness,
to use the old word for it, to lock behind
chain link topped with concertina wire.
"Don't kid yourself," the warden said,
"these boys know where they are."

A few miles past the gate on a gravel road
you can ski the Butte when the snow is right,
carve traces of your own design, fall down,
tumble over and over, and then get up as if
nothing has happened. And on that afternoon
the snow was right, say fifty inches at the base,
sun out, fresh powder, maybe girls from somewhere
out of town, where guys in trouble just get lost.

Go straight, and then bear left. You can't
miss it. And there I was, and they were
dress-right-dress and ready-front, and left-face,
forward-marching, crunching in the snow-ice-mud
with a military chant, almost a tune: "Mama,
Mama can't you see . . ." something, all words
scattered in the wind that sang among the pines.
The counsellor says they'll get the message here,
they'll get good time for this, they'll be co-
operative, and if they're not, it all goes

on their record. Right away they call me sir.

Of course, I'm flattered but not buffaloed.
I've been said "sir" to by the best and worst.
Even my own students have so demeaned themselves,
so lowered to me, so kowtowed on rare occasion
to my austerity. But something in these prisoners'
bitter metaphors rings true from time to time.
I move from one blue jacket to the green that
marks the veteran, back to blue, from one close-
barbered head on to the next. Too much silence.
Too much respect, perhaps, for words, or maybe
fear, too much concern for stepping out of line.

"Help me with this," a guy named Robert says,
and then they all need help. An inmate needs
to write, let's say, a villanelle, a poem that will
teach him to appreciate restriction, call it form,
locked firmly up between two lines of words,
mean lines and unforgiving, lines that will not budge.

That night I ate in Grangeville with some friends,
fresh salmon, salad, wild rice, a Cabernet,
and I stayed up too late that night and wrote,
words flowing free along the icy slope
of my imagination, hurdling vicious moguls,
down the two-black-diamond Devil's Chute,
and in the morning threw it all away.

Ron McFarland

Out Here

Even a stone can astonish us,
thrown or underfoot, rippling the surface
of some dark pond
or stumbling along in the dust
if we give it a chance.

In New York, L.A., Chicago, even Seattle
passions run riot in ways we cannot
feel with our stingy sensibilities.
People keep on living there as if
they were going to die
in the next minute,
so of course they do.
A friend who works for the *Wall Street Journal*
says it's the only honest way to live.

Out here we live as if
we're going to live forever.
We spend carefully.
The Forest Service and the BLM
send college students into the field
each summer to count sagebrush.
They are contemplating a program
to tabulate tumbleweed,
full employment year-round.
It's an education.

The friend from Manhattan
visits one of our short summers,
waiting daily for something to happen.
It never does. The whole summer

is like skipping stones
late in the afternoon on a placid pond.
We try to talk, but she's too deep,
like a stone seeking the bottom.
Out here we like those conversations
where no one has the last word.

Steven E. Puglisi

What Were They Like?

1) These people of Idaho,
     had they a common song to sing
     against the coming winter storm?
2) Did they draw near across great differences?
3) Had they special names
     for mountains, streams, and trees?
4) Did they practice a strict preaching,
     an eye for an eye, a tooth for a tooth?
5) Were their children taught the ceremonies
     of tenderness and concern?
6) Did they gather together in small groups
     to honor freedom, dignity, life?

1) Sir, their songs have turned to smoke.
     It is not remembered if they wept that winter
     before they sang
     or after.
2) Perhaps they met once
     amid some natural disaster,
     when their differences were young,
     when action was still possible.
3) Unfortunately, it is not reported.
4) Know that most were simple people; their life
     was 9 to 5. Peace was Friday night and hope
     was Sunday morning. For some, it was easy to annihilate.
     It was, oh, so much harder to defend, to protect
     without destroying, everyone, everything.
5) Strength is not the only position from which to choose.
     Fear and weakness are reasons, too. As for the children,
     we can only guess at what they learned.

6) Sir, they spoke in hushed whispers
   and hoarse cries
   of an angry god who screamed a flood,
   who promised to rain a fire
   next time, and did.

Bob Schild

The Long Ride

I was horseback on The Blackfoot
When a flutter turned my eye
To the curious contortions
Of a form up in the sky.
Then a twirling apparition
Angled upward on the fly.
I was rendered cold and breathless,
And my mouth turned powder dry.

First the sunlight bobbed and flickered,
Like its bulb was burning out.
Then it cast an eerie shadow,
Though there were no clouds about.
In that swirling, whirling madness
I could bare restrain a shout.
Though the day looked warm and cheery
I could feel the goose bumps sprout.

My old horse's nostrils quivered,
Then he whistled blasts of air;
While a frenzy of emotion
Seemed to leap from everywhere;
In an atmosphere so heavy
I could almost chew the air.
Though it ain't this cowboy's custom —
I knelt in silent prayer.

Then that cyclone of confusion
Seemed to melt into the sun;
While the day turned sudden pleasant —
As before this all was done.

When my pulse returned to normal
I had lost the urge to run;
But my mind still raced on blindly
As a bullet from a gun!

When I heard the story later
Why I bowed my head and cried;
While weird tangles of emotion
Pricked like brambles 'neath my hide.
It was not a dusty hillside,
Where you made your final ride;
But upwards to the heavens,
For I saw you pass inside.

William Studebaker

The Fall from Grace

I figure everyone's got a reason for being the way he is, and I've got my reason. Also I'm probably the reason my dad never got to give sermons in church. I mean, after I saw Annie and Grace naked, I couldn't think of anything else. . . .

Sunday school wasn't the same. I was lost. I couldn't remember nothing as complicated as the prophets or the Ten Commandments. All I could remember was Eve: first I'd see her with Grace's body, then I'd see her with Annie's. I guess I was just too stupid to keep things straight, and you can't have no stupid kid's dad give sermons.

It wouldn't have been so bad if I hadn't got caught. I can keep a secret, and I could've made a deal with the Lord to punish me, not Dad. Dad could've gone right on and given sermons that way. But that's not how it turned out. According to the new bishop's wife, De Jean, my folks are raising a "Peeping Tom." And what I did hurt her daughter, Grace, more than it hurt me.

I guess it didn't hurt my sister, Annie, none. At least, Mom hasn't said so, and Annie just twitters when she thinks about it. A twitter's not a sign of being hurt much. Anyway . . .

I can't remember everything. I guess the fall must have knocked some of the reasons out of my head, and if the fall didn't, opening my eyes and seeing De Jean looking down at me did. There I was, flat on my back, hugging a sewer pipe, peering up into two yellow cat's-eye marbles.

"What are you doing, *young* man?"

"Aaa."

"You had better have a good explanation."

I looked around for Dewight, but when the pipe hangers gave way, he made a run for it. I supposed he wouldn't come back either, unless I told on him.

"I, I," I said.

"See! He's a Peeping Tom," said De Jean.

"What makes you say that?" asked Mom.

"The girls were taking a bubble bath. . . ."

"They were?" said Mom.

"Yes, and he was peeping."

I knew I was had. I looked like a peeper, lying flat on the ground beneath the bathroom window, sewer pipe pressed to my chest.

"Dewight," I said.

"Oh, no you don't," said De Jean, "Dewight wouldn't let you peep at his own sister. Don't you try that, young man. Why, if Dewight had climbed that pipe, it would have come loose from the siding. He's too big to do such a thing."

"What did you see, Sterling?" asked Mom.

"What did he see? He saw everything. Those girls are developed. Why, Grace is shaving her legs now. Didn't I tell you?"

"No," said Mom.

"Oh, yes. She started a couple months ago. Last summer. She had just too much hair to look civilized. I thought Annie had started too."

"I'm not sure," said Mom.

"I'd keep track of those things if I were you," said De Jean. "Anyway, there was plenty to see, and he saw it all."

"Did you?" asked Mom.

"I did," I said.

"You did what?"

"I . . . I."

"If you tell the truth, it'll be better," said De Jean.

"I saw everything. I saw them naked. I saw *hair*."

"See! See!" said De Jean. "Poor girls."

"Go in the house and wait for your dad," said Mom.

"Poor girls, poor girls," said De Jean. "He saw . . ."

I pushed the sewer pipe off my chest, felt the knot on the back of my head. It bled a little, but I didn't say nothing to Mom. My chest hurt the most. As I walked toward the front door, I couldn't breathe. Air wheezing into my lungs made the sound of a vacuum cleaner trying to suck up a piece of plastic wrap. My whole body ached. I felt like I'd been body slammed by a giant, maybe by Goliath or somebody.

The only relief I got from the pain was when I thought of Grace all naked and soapy. She kept getting in and out of the tub like she was looking for something. It was enough to stop the pain, but then I'd remember I wasn't supposed to remember. I was peeping without even looking through the window. That's the way with real sin; it affects the imagination.

I sat for a long time waiting for Dad. When I wasn't thinking or trying not to think about Grace and Annie, I was thinking about my fall. Dewight and I took turns shinnying up the pipe. Well, not really. Dwight went up a couple times more than me because he said that on some of his turns they were just sitting in the tub. I noticed that the last time he went up, the pipe was loose, but Dwight said it was worth the risk. So I wrapped myself around the pipe and crawled up to the window.

If I hadn't fallen, it would've been worth it alright. Grace was sitting on the toilet with her feet propped up against the tub. She was cleaning between her toes. It was enough to make a twelve-year-old like me go stiff in the legs. I guess that's what pushed the pipe away from the house and started my fall. Hanging on to the pipe wasn't a good idea, but I was short of time, and I'm not a real fast thinker. Before I could figure just what to do, I hit the ground. I hit as hard as if I'd been Moroni tumbling off the Temple. That's how I got the lump on my head, and that's where I was when De Jean found me with her cat's-eyes.

I sat waiting for Dad for so long I thought eternity was going to pass. I had plenty of time to think about what I'd done. Some things were getting clearer, like Grace shaving the insides of her thighs, but some things were pretty hazy, like whether she'd shampooed her hair. That was more than I could remember. So I stayed with the easy stuff.

When Dad came, he didn't ask me anything. He'd already been filled in by De Jean. He just came into my room, looked around, and said, "I hear you had a little trouble today. I don't want you and Dwight hanging around together. You hear me?" I nodded. Before he left, he looked around my room some more, sort of like he gazes down the church aisles as he picks out a pew and sits down. It made me feel bad, like he was taking stock of the mess I'd made of my life.

I stooped over and picked up the clothes closest to me, but when he left, I threw them back down on the floor. Cleaning my room seemed pointless. But I had to do something to show that I understood the wrong I done, so I pinched the lump on the back of my head until my eyes watered. I thought Mom might come in, and I wanted her to know I was trying. But she never came in.

After another hour or so, I went outside, down to the Mill ditch where Dwight hid his Copenhagen. I decided to take a chew. I wanted to get real sick and throw up like Dwight said I would. I wanted to feel bad. I took a big pinch, but I didn't throw up or nothing.

Robert Wrigley

Majestic

The only word for it, his white Lincoln's arc
from the crown of the downriver road
and the splash it bellied in the water.
Two other passersby and I waded out and pulled him
from the half-sunk wreck, the high collar
of his vestments torn away for breathing,
a rosary knotted in his left hand.
It's an endless wait for an ambulance
there, that serpentine road between distant towns,
night coming on, August, the rocks we laid him on
still fired by the sun. And so we came
to know one another, three living men
touching tenderly the dead one's body,
tending mouth and chest, making
a pillow for the head. He did not look,
we understood, like any man of God.
It was Roy, the mill-hand from Orofino,
who saw the tattoo first — no cross at all
but Christ Himself hung out, crucified
to the pale, hairless flesh by needles of India ink.
Jim, the prison guard, had seen it all in his time
and looked up sweaty from the breath-kissed face
only long enough to say, "Keep pumping."
I cupped my hands behind the doughy neck
to hold the airway straight and knew
as the others knew there was no point at all
for him in what we did. After a while
we just stopped, and Jim began to talk about time
and distance, the site of the nearest phone,
the speed of the first car he'd sent there.
Roy lit a cigarette, traced the flights of nighthawks,

and I waded back out to the Lincoln,
in the open driver's door
a little eddied lake of papers and butts,
where the river lapped the deep blue dash,
a sodden Bible and a vial of pills.
There was something we should say
for him, we must all have been sure,
for later on, when the lights came in sight
around the last downriver corner,
we gathered again at the body
and took one another's hands,
bowed, our eyes closed,
and said each in his turn
what we thought might be a prayer.
Something huge sliced through the air then,
but no one looked up,
believing owl, saying *owl*,
and at last opening our eyes
just as the day's final light ripened purple
and the black basalt we knelt on disappeared.
In that one moment, that second
of uncertainty, nothing shone
but the cold flesh of the priest,
and on the breast, almost throbbing
with the outrushing dark —
the looming, hand-sized tattoo of Jesus
we could just as suddenly not see.
Bless the owl then, for passing over
once more and returning to us
the breathable air, the new, unspectacular night,
and the world itself, trailing beneath its talons,
still hanging on and making its bleats
and whimpers, before the noise
and the night above the river
swallowed it all.

Montana

Just before being introduced to a high-school library full of people who had braved a raging blizzard to hear me, the coordinator told me he thought everyone was more interested in hearing about life as a writer, rather than actually having me read anything. So I stumbled through an hour-long impromptu talk before someone in the audience finally held up a copy of Indian Creek *and said, "I came clear from North Dakota to hear you read from this book. Are you ever going to get to it?" So they got a reading at no extra charge.*

PETE FROMM

The room had been beautifully arranged, with lit candles to one side of the podium, a table at the back laid out with lovely things to eat and drink, a sense of occasion hanging in the room. Some of the local writers were nervous about reading, but in reading, their nervousness receded until they were fully inside their own words. You could feel the attentiveness in the audience, the empathy, the awe at what was most honest, most open. And I felt I'd been given the extraordinary gift of their words, their willingness to share with me who they were and what they did. In the break after their reading, there was time for coffee and cookies and wine and crudités — and time for me to talk a little with those who had read. By the time it was my turn to read, I was no longer a stranger, but in the presence of a caring and sympathetic audience, people I knew.

It seemed to me that this is what the TumbleWords project is about — that bringing literature to "underserved" communities means not only bringing in literature from outside the community, but setting up an atmosphere in which the words generated inside the community bear equal weight. I think there is such hope — so much possibility — in people's willingness to fully enter language.

RUTH RUDNER

B. J. Buckley

Night Fishing

There is a floating borderland
between light going down to darkness
and the humming rise of insects
into the drift currents
of cool wind over water,
over this lake, which holds the world
for a moment mirrored perfectly —
dry hills, sage, drowned
cottonwoods,
the buoyant angler
whipping the wild horses of the air
with a supple rod,
with the merest flick of the wrist
fly poised
on the surface before sinking
in a soft spiral bottomward,
where hunger follows,
where the eye cannot.

The strike, when it comes, is
quick
      hard
           down
an elephantine pull,
an ache —
      a sudden nothing.

Whatever it was
that leapt out of the dark water
wearing fish flesh and haloed in the moon,
that swallowed the mayfly's dance

then hung
by threads of starlight weightless
in the still air,
then fell
a streak of silver comet-sure
back into rippling heaven,
whatever it was cannot be betrayed
by naming, though it named me —
Castaway,
Night Fisher,
Ghost in the Shallows.
I am trying to learn to walk
like water.

David Cates

Either a Miracle or a Fluke

The night is busy, one call after another. Jack Dempsey Cliff's cab smells of ciga-rette smoke, and his pockets are tight with money. A roll of bills in one, a pound of change in the other. He orders fish and french fries at the Beachcomber but gets dispatched to 1818 Mission again while waiting for the food. He picks up Evey and Marie and begins to drive them across town to Alder for a house call. Both wear stylish dresses, a lot of jewelry, and high thick-heeled shoes. They look very nice, Evey and Marie. A little tired, but kind of sophisticated, like chesty models. Their conversation covers a wide range of topics, such as

How Marie cut her bottom on the spring sticking out of the seat padding in the last cab she rode in.

How she should be able to sue the cab company for a lot of money, but the legal system is fucked, so she probably wouldn't get a penny.

How Evey's getting too skinny.

How Marie's a smoker, so even though she's in good shape, she doesn't jog well.

How Evey has given up gin because of her stomach, but when someone offers to buy, well, what's she supposed to say?

How Marie is glad she doesn't have that problem.

How they all ought to jog together, get matching sweatsuits that say Eighteen Eighteen Camp for Girls and jog early in the morning along the bay.

How they could make up hilarious songs to sing while they ran.

How Marie wishes she could get a nice tan.

How Evey doesn't think Marie needs a tan, being Mexican, or whatever.

How the pizza they had for dinner wasn't sitting well with Evey.

How pepperoni will do that sometimes, but Evey should maybe go to a doctor for her stomach if it stays bad.

Then Marie says to Jack, "Haven't I seen you someplace before?"

"I ate a cheeseburger next to you at Solly's yesterday." It's true, but it's also true that Jack threw himself on the floor to look up her dress at the Pier Pub his first night in town. He doesn't mention that.

"A what?" Marie asks Evey. "What did he say?"

"He said a cheeseburger."

"At Solly's," Jack says. Just thinking about it makes his mouth water again. "I was sitting behind you guys yesterday. That's the last thing I've eaten."

"What are you, fasting?" Marie asks.

"No," Jack says. "Just working and sleeping, I guess. You were eating clams."

"Oh," Marie says.

"Were they good?"

"What?" Marie asks Evey. "What's he saying?"

"He wants to know if the clams were good."

"Yeah," Marie says. "They were fine. You know, something's wrong with your car. Noisy!"

"Bad injectors," Jack says.

"Bad what?"

"Bad injectors."

"Injectors?" She giggles. "That's awful!"

There's a short pause. Jack's got food on the brain. "The clams sound great, but I always get the cheeseburger. Best deal in town."

"You mean when you're not sleeping or going around with a bad injector!" Marie laughs. "You really ought to eat something besides cheeseburgers, you know."

"I do."

"What?"

"He eats something besides cheeseburgers," Evey says to Marie.

"Yeah, I heard him," Marie says. "That's very nice to know, but—"

"I like spaghetti too," Jack says.

"Clams are best," Marie says. "I really think you should try the clams."

"Clams are expensive."

"Damn right they are," Marie says. Then "Oh, *now* I know where I've seen you!"

After he threw himself on the floor between her legs that first night at the Pier Pub, Jack traced with his finger the inside of her calf and thigh up toward her black underwear. She could have stepped on his face, but she didn't. Instead she said, *That's an expensive touch,* and he said, *No problem, I'll do it for free,* and she stepped away, over him, smiled nicely but said, *You're broke, right? Well, I work for a living.*

Then Jack stood up and walked back to the bar, stared again at the wall above the mirror, the photograph of the Kodiak Island Boxing Champion, July 4, 1953, his father. A close-up of Kid Cliff's face, everything but his immediate features was slightly out of focus. The light gray of his cheeks melded with the lighter gray behind until in some places Jack couldn't tell where the man began and the background ended. His head tilted forward, and his dark gray eyes looked up almost seductively from under bushy eyebrows. His shiny hair was combed neatly back and plastered close to his head. A suppressed smile curled the corner of his pale lips.

Jack stood at the bar and looked at the picture and imagined his father hearing laughter. The irony galled him. There he was, Kid Cliff, just three weeks after he'd left his wife and infant son in Wisconsin. A soldier, a farmer, a fisherman, dirty tattoos plastered the length of his body, and hands—the bartender told Jack—he had hands like chunks of raw meat. Sure he did.

Yet in his photograph for posterity they have him looking like John Barrymore.

In the cab Jack can see Marie's dark eyes staring at him in the rearview mirror. Last time he was lucky to get away unhurt. This time he's got money to lose.

"Boy," he says, "I'm hungry."

She smiles. "That's your problem, mister."

"You know," Evey says, "if I drink just one glass of OJ when I get up, then I don't have to eat again until evening, sometimes never."

"Listen to her," Marie says to Jack. "She's worse than you with your cheese-burgers. She's going to starve herself."

Jack says he heard on the radio that a person can be overweight and still starve to death without the right vitamins and stuff.

Evey says that hunger can be gotten over with your brain—there's a point where you don't care anymore—and besides, her stomach hurts even more when she eats.

Marie says she's heard about that brain stuff but doesn't see much point in it or think anybody should push it.

Evey's sister had cancer and meditated her way out of it.

Marie can't even imagine that shit.

Evey says that a person never knows what he or she can do until faced with one of those big things.

Marie says that's true but still.

Evey doesn't have time to see a doctor anyway, at least not a stomach doctor.

Marie says she's feeling good tonight, feeling invincible.

That reminds Evey of the time someone laid a line of coke along the entire length of the Pier Pub bar.

Jack says he heard that too.

Evey says, "I could use a good bump right now, that's for sure."

At Alder, Jack drops them off and watches as they hustle up to the house. Under the porch light by the front door, Evey sags, puts a hand on her bony hip. Jack wonders if she's dying—and then he can see in the dark hollow under her eyes that she probably is. Marie lights a cigarette. She lets it dangle from her mouth while she giggles and straightens Evey's pale lavender dress.

Gil, the dispatcher, has radioed Jack that the Beachcomber called and his fish and fries are ready to be picked up. Jack's stomach hurts. He drives toward town, fast because he thinks he might start drooling. He thinks about the guy he met with the Chinese warlord tattoo on his back and wonders if anybody ever gets a hamburger-and-french-fry tattoo. He wonders if Evey's stomach feels like this all the time. He takes a left on Mill Bay and is starting up the hill when he sees three people on the side of the road raise their hands to flag him down. Jesus. He wants to drive by, but it's raining and he can't.

They're Filipinos. Filipinos never tip, and some of the cabbies won't pick them up, but Jack likes them, generally. These three smell funny. The old man wiggles his nose like a rabbit and can't even get into the cab. He keeps stepping up onto the seat, so the women, maybe his daughters, show him where to step so he can sit down. Foot on the floor, now lowering his hips, twisting slightly—that's it— ducking the rest of his body through the door, yes, and sitting. Poor guy must be sick or something. Only three fingers and a thumb on one hand, two and a thumb on the other. Maybe he's never been in a car, but that's ridiculous. What is it they smell like? Some kind of greasy vegetable or spaghetti-fed dog meat. Eating dogs is the one thing he doesn't like about Filipinos. But it's possible the old guy was at the Death March and saved Kid Cliff's life and was crippled by a Jap bayonet. Tortured. It could be Jack owes his life to this old man. It could be, and yet there's no way of knowing. Only doubting, of course. Millions of things could have happened to keep Jack from being born, to keep him from living as long as he's lived (thirty years in some cultures is old age), yet here he is anyway! When he thinks about the odds against any specific person being born . . . against himself . . . well, he's either a miracle or a fluke. But if certainly Jack is (and he is) when the odds were so stacked against his even being born, then this old man who probably didn't save Kid Cliff's life certainly must have saved Kid Cliff's life. And therefore he saved Jack.

For if this old Filipino's great-great-grandmother had died of some disease along with the rest of her family when she was ten, then she would never have become the mother of X, who became the mother of Y, who became the mother of Z, who became the mother of this old guy, who saved Kid Cliff's life by giving him water during the Death March, sure, an act that cost him three fingers, which allowed Kid Cliff to make the sperm that he would eventually deposit in Lorraine one autumn evening when nothing else in the world mattered except the sweaty union of two mortals in an upstairs bedroom of a Wisconsin farmhouse. And now here is Jack, sitting in his cab *not* not-being. A possible fluke, but he just can't chuck the possibility of a miracle either. Like the ideas of falling in love and being happy, the idea of a miracle is tenacious as hell.

Mary could still be in Wisconsin. Mary could be waiting for him. . . . Maybe Jack came to Alaska to realize only this: there's no such thing as an answer, only hope.

But there's more, he thinks. Of course. Kodiak is his father. He came here to put his face against his father's strong chest, feel his father's arms wrap around his back and shoulders. And more, too, which perhaps is the problem. His father is dead. Jack came to Kodiak to dig a grave and bury him.

But how? he thinks. And where? And how will he even know when he has?

All three passengers are dressed in their go-to-cannery clothes — rubber boots, colorful scarves, sweatshirts, cloth gloves on their laps. Maybe the old man is farting, and that's what the smell is. He's wiggling his nose like a rabbit, so perhaps he smells it too. His daughter has to pronounce the name of the cannery three times before Jack can understand. Jack's very polite — *What's that, ma'am? What's that, ma'am? Oh yes, ma'am* — imagining the sound of a bayonet slicing off a finger, another finger, another finger. The sound a man makes. Is enduring pain in itself an act of bravery? Is dying? Or is bravery *risking* pain, *risking* death for what you love or believe in? And where does Kid Cliff stand in all this? Did he sacrifice Lorraine and Jack, long before he came home from the prison camps, in order to survive? Or did he sacrifice himself one sunny day in June 1953 so that *they* could survive? Was it painful for him? Or easy? Was he lonely? Or simply forgetful?

The questions. They go on and on. After the Death March, Kid Cliff had three and a half more years of starvation and capricious torture to endure. Would the fingers of this heroic old Filipino man have been wasted if Kid Cliff had died on the Hell Ship to Japan, throat slit by a thirsty comrade? Those things happened. There are lots of people who weren't born because their fathers died on those ships in 1944, regardless of any heroism or providence that might have kept them alive until then. Does Jack's existence validate the old man's sacrifice? *Don't think of it!* They can ride for free, sure, and Jack himself is going to help the old man out of the cab.

In a book Jack read about the Death March, a veteran told about a thirty-year reunion of survivors back in the Philippines. Hanging on the side of their bus was a banner that said Defenders of Bataan. When the Filipinos read that, even the children, they held up their fingers in a **V**. "What do those kids know about us?" one of the veterans asked the bus driver, who answered, "Joe, they may not know English, or how to read and write, but they know about Bataan."

No matter how strange this old guy is, Jack thinks, if it weren't for him Jack wouldn't be alive. Sentimentality can be as seductive as pornography, so thinking this is irresistible, and by now Jack's almost convinced of its truth. Oh boy. It pleases him no end to feel goose bumps rising on the back of his neck. Sitting in the backseat between a couple of Asian princesses is a veritable king, a mortal god, a nose-twitching rabbit of a seven-fingered man in whose common-suffering corpse reek lies the naked seeds of miracles. Yessir.

When they arrive at the cannery, Jack hops out and runs around to open the door. He lends a hand to one of the princesses, but she's already standing, so he bends to help the king. Standing next to him now, on the gravel, Jack leans over and whispers "Bataan" into the royal ear. The king cocks his head, straining to hear. One of the princesses points to her own ear, then to the king's.

Jack whispers it again, "Bataan," louder; then thumb to his chest, Jack points at himself.

Wrinkling his nose, sniffing, shuffling uncomfortably, finally the king breaks into a grin. Jack feels flushed. The king extends his three-fingered hand, and Jack shakes it, thinking of miracles and torn flesh, falling in love with dog meat.

"José," the old man says. "Vedy, vedy fine, thank you."

Phil Condon

Walt and Dixie

It was after midnight. I stood on Interstate 80 in northern Indiana, heading toward New York City, hitchhiking. I had my summer savings from construction jobs, twelve twenty-dollar bills, under the innersole of my left shoe, just like in the movies. I was nineteen.

I'd had four rides since leaving Grand Island at dawn. The last, a Michigan salesman sipping from a tequila bottle, had let me off when he'd turned north toward home. I stood next to a light pole at the end of an entrance ramp, with my green canvas duffel bag at my feet and a sharp cone of light spread around me as if I'd stepped onstage somewhere. It was September and cool, but with no breeze I felt fine in a short-sleeved shirt. The stars were out. Michigan lay within the horizon to the north. I imagined it stretching away from me like the mitten I'd seen on the map.

It was only my second hitchhiking trip, and I felt as alone and free as I'd ever felt in my life. Yet the two separate feelings seemed to occupy the same space inside me, or maybe it was just two words pointing to the same exact thing, like those people from the South with double names, Jim Bob or Joe Ray. In the air was the raw scent of cut hay mixed with the lingering oily smell of the pavement in front of me, still warm from the day. I sat down with my thumb out, my neck craned back, counting stars.

A shiny white Cadillac with giant fins and bullet taillights, a '59 or '60, I thought, but restored to perfect condition, rolled by slowly and then stopped and honked. I grabbed my duffel and walked toward it. I didn't see another vehicle in either direction. The Caddy backed up slowly, its brake lights blinking like double red winks. I opened the front door.

"Hilo there, my friend. Need a lift?"

"I'm headed to New York City."

"El perfecto. That's where me and Dixie-Queen are bound." He stuck his hand out toward me, his palm up. "I'm Walt."

He wore an old man's ribbed sleeveless undershirt, and the white hairs on his chest matched the white stubble on his cheeks and chin. He looked older than my father. A black suit coat lay folded across the seatback next to him. His arms were as thin as I'd ever seen, twisted off-white ropes with large callused hands at the end. His collarbones disappeared like struts under his shirt. I shook with him, our hands horizontal. He didn't let go for several long seconds, just kept smiling, looking into my eyes in the dim light from the dome.

"Rob," I said. "Thanks for stopping."

"You can stow your bag in the back with her. Welcome aboard the Lost Angels–Madhatter Express." He laughed then stopped and spread his hand out as if he were inviting me into his living room. "Coast-to-coast comfort."

His eyes were gray, and when I looked at them I had trouble looking away until after he did. I didn't see anybody in the backseat.

"We're your last chance for tonight, I reckon," he said. "I know how it goes. I've spent many a night on the side of the road." He pushed a button on the panel in his door, and the lock on the back door popped up. "Many a night." He slapped the seatback. "Dixie-Queen, wake up, we got company. This here's Bob."

It was a frequent mistake. There wasn't really that much difference. Once I'd worked for two weeks on a summer roofing job, and the foreman called me Bob the whole time.

I opened the back door and looked in. A little girl straightened up in the seat. Her short legs rested on an open cardboard box on the floor. But she had nylons and high-heeled shoes on. She wore eyeshadow and lipstick.

"Just call me Dixie," she said, wiping at her eyes. "Isn't nobody but Walter calls me that other."

Her voice was a woman's, and as I looked closer I saw she was. Her face was like a miniature, painted on a doll. Twenty-five, maybe thirty years old. I wasn't sure I should take the ride, but I'd already shaken hands with Walt. I'd already hoisted my bag up off the ground. I put it on the seat.

"Will that bother you?" I asked. "I could keep it up front."

"It's fine," she said. "There's more room than enough. That's why Walter got this car. Isn't she just beautiful?"

I slammed the back door and sat down in the front seat. Walter stuck out his hand again. I felt just a little uneasy, as if maybe I should've waited for another ride. But I shook his hand again.

"Bob's got his own pair of eyes, DQ." He laughed. "He can see same as me that you're the beauty here. They don't make an automobile compares to my Dixie-Queen." He let go my hand. I was tired. I closed my door. Walt pushed the lock buttons for all four doors, and the sound of their snapping sounded final. I put my elbow out the window.

Walt steered back onto the highway. I watched the speedometer needle creep up to forty-five and hover there. You could hardly hear the engine.

Walt looked out at the farmland brushing by in the dark. "My friend, it's a gorgeous night in creation. Just look at it, slipping away in every direction like thick black satin."

I looked out the window. My head tipped to the side, and the breeze of us blowing through the night felt like somebody was washing my face.

"How tall are you, Bob?" Dixie asked from behind me.

I turned half around. I couldn't see her well.

"You look like over six foot," she said.

"Five eleven," I said.

"You look taller," she said. "I'm four foot one because I had a condition when I grew up. Walter's six foot even."

"Sock-footed," Walt said. They both laughed like kids who just thought a certain word sounded funny. When they stopped, the silence felt like a hole I had to fill up. "So you've come all the way from Los Angeles?" I asked.

"Every mile," Walt said. He scrunched toward the instrument panel and squinted at it over the steering wheel. "Twenty-one hundred sixty-two and four-tenths." He slapped the wheel. "Started out day before yesterday. Haven't stopped but to fill the Caddy's tank. Or drain ours."

"Walter," Dixie said. "Your language."

"When do you sleep?" I asked.

He winked at me. "I got some truckers' aspirin with me." He patted the jacket next to him. "I take two every state line we cross."

"Show him our pictures," Dixie said.

Walt reached over and opened the glove compartment. He pulled out a stack of Polaroids and clicked on the dome light. I thumbed through the pictures of the two of them standing by state-line signs: Arizona, New Mexico, Texas, Oklahoma, Missouri, Illinois, Indiana. The top of her head came to just above his belt. In each of them his big hand rested on her shoulder, and she had her arm folded up across her chest and her hand on top of his. They grinned like two retirees on the trip of a lifetime.

I put the photos back. "Those are great," I said.

"I got sleep tablets, too," he said. "If you need them."

"Don't take those, Bob," Dixie said. "I took one the first night, and I couldn't get my eyes open for the next picture stop. Which was that, Walter?"

"Texas," Walt said. "I just thought Bob might have trouble sleeping. It happens on the road. A man gets all vibrated up or something."

"Do you want a milk ball?" Dixie asked. She shoved an open box of malted milk balls over my shoulder.

"No thanks," I said. "Boy, you two got a little of everything."

"I buy 'em by the case," Walt said, smiling at me. "It's her weakness."

"You like screen magazines?" Dixie asked. She held out a *Photoplay* with Elizabeth Taylor on the front, offering it to me. "I like the old ones best," she said. "The pictures look better when they yellow out."

"She's got two more cartons in the trunk," Walt said. "I scour them up for her at the beauty parlors."

For the first time, I must have let the thoughts I'd been having finally show through. I gave him an odd look.

"Something kinda funny about reading old movie magazines, eh Bob?" He kept smiling just the same, moving his head around, looking at me, Dixie, the countryside. About every fourth look was at the road ahead. The speedometer still read forty-five.

"No. No. My mother subscribed to *Silver Screen* once. She bought it from one of the kids selling magazines to go through college."

"Something's on your mind, though. I saw it. I'll tell you the truth. I'm forty-six years old, and I can't read much more than road maps, street signs, and café menus. I can't write much more than my own name. But I can read people. Oh Lordy, how I can read people."

"Walter has a sixth sense," Dixie said.

I looked back out the window. Clusters of farmhouses and outbuildings were scattered across every knoll. A dog barked from a long way off.

"Well, the truth is, you two just aren't much like other people I've met, I guess. That's all." I tried to put it as mildly as I could.

"Good for you. Listen friend, the world's full of folks all the same as one another, like racks of summer clothes on the sidewalk. Nosir, not for me. Be an In-da-Wid-U-ul. Right, Dixie-Queen?"

"An In-da-Wid-U-ul," Dixie said. She laughed, tipping her head back and opening her mouth real wide. Walt laughed, too. Their laughter was so good-natured and unforced that this time it caught me up in it. When I got my breath back, I said "sock-footed." We laughed in little waves then, one of us stopping and then hearing the others and starting up again.

"Whew-eee," Walt said, wiping his eyes on his jacket sleeve. "Not too many things in this life bone-free," he said. "But laughing's one. DQ and me like the free ones."

I felt the little lump of bills inside my shoe, or thought I did. "The best things in life, they say," I said.

"Yeah, but they don't believe it," Walt said. "Do they now? You have some money, don't you?"

I didn't say anything.

"I have eight dollars," Dixie said. "You can have it if you need it."

"You don't have to answer," Walt said. "It's fine you do. Now me — I got this car and my helper pills and a trunkful of secondhand stuff. Dixie's got her magazines and milk balls and her eight dollars. I thought you spent a dollar at that rock shop, Dixie."

"Seven dollars," she said.

"How're you making it all this way?" I asked.

"You have me, Walter," Dixie said.

"And I thank the Lord for that," he said, craning around and smiling at her. "Of a night and of a day." He turned back to me. "Let me tell you about us making it." He pointed out the window with the flat of his hand. It came to me then how his voice didn't fit him. It was deep and strong, like dark wood with fine grain, but he looked unhealthy, like he hadn't eaten much and hadn't been out in the sun for a long time.

"I look out at the world, and I just see a big old ship," he said. "With a full head of steam, making progress all the time. Folks like me and Dixie, we're what the ship throws off when it falls behind schedule or hits bad weather. You know, to lighten the load up and ride higher. To make better time." He pointed his long index finger at the clock on the dash. It was broken, all three of its hands stuck on six. "And we see it, sailing on without us. What could we do for it, anyway?" He laughed, as if an answer had come to him that struck him funny.

"So here we are, Bob, some kind of junk, cast off in deep water. Now there's only two ways to go in that kind of deal. You sink and drown, fast or slow, but still going down, down, down, just the same all the time." He punched his finger toward the floor of the car each time he said "down."

"Or you swim?" I said. I felt like I'd heard this advice before.

"That seems right, doesn't it? Sink or swim, sure. But think on it a minute. Where exactly to? In the middle of the ocean, swimming's just another kind of sinking. Nosir. You dance."

"Dance?" I was so tired it was hard to follow him, but I couldn't quit listening. In the back of my mind, I kept thinking: This is Indiana. It's Thursday. You have two hundred and forty dollars cash.

"You said it same as I did," he said. "The good black book says the son of God walked on water, are you still with me? Well, dance, too. You look up at the sky and forget you're junk and dance. That's what this trip is — Dixie and me love each other, and that's a dance that keeps us on top of the water. It's no more account where the ship is or what the folks on board might say." He paused, his palm up, as if he could almost hear a crowd in the distance.

"I'm just saying what I know here, son, and it's sparse enough, if you tally the years I put in finding it. I'm just telling you so you'll know what's up with Dixie and me and won't think we're loony or feel sorry on us."

I remember hearing the pages of Dixie's magazine turning while he talked and the whistle from a train, and then I was asleep. I had a restless, sitting-up car dream where I was on a tall boat, sailing over meadows and trees, parting them like water. I climbed up flight after flight of stairs to the wheelhouse. At the wheel, Walt stood in his undershirt like a broken-down preacher, talking and talking to Dixie, who was nowhere to be seen.

I woke up only once after that before morning. The car swerved slightly, and I sat up straight.

"Leastways, that's the way I told them," Walt said. I heard Dixie giggle in the backseat, and then I slipped asleep again.

I woke up in Pennsylvania. I'd slept through two of their state-line photo stops, and they showed me the Polaroids to prove it. In the daylight Dixie looked even smaller and Walt looked more thin and washed out, as if the sunlight had shrunk them both, although in different directions.

We stopped at a café for breakfast on the outskirts of a small town. Four big trucks were parked at odd angles in the lot.

"Can I come in this place, Walter?" Dixie asked as we got out.

"You know I don't mind ordering for you," Walt said. "Not one whit. You just read your magazines, and we'll be right back, sweetie."

On the way in I asked him if Dixie always stayed in the car.

"I don't have to tell you Dixie's a looker, Bob," Walt said. "But you'd have no way of knowing the degree to how innocent and trustful she is. She don't understand men and what it is they're always needing to get at. I have to protect her from the wolves of this world."

"She sounds to me like she loves you and only you, Walt," I said. We walked into a small glass foyer with a newspaper stand and a payphone in it.

Walt beamed a big wrinkled grin at me as I held the door open.

"That's kind of you to say so," he said. "But I have a need to be vigilant," he said. "Anyway, truth is, she don't like to go in places much."

We ordered three cinnamon rolls and two black coffees and a milk to go. I said I'd eat in the car with them. While we waited, Walt circulated among the tables, selling ballpoint pens for a quarter apiece. His inside suit coat pockets were full of brand-new pens with company names and slogans on them. He sold enough in just a few minutes to pay for half of the tab.

As we stepped back out into the parking lot, Walt continued talking about Dixie right where he'd left off on the way in.

"I don't mind telling you that's one reason I looked you over so careful, Bob. Last night."

"What do you mean?" I asked. I'd thought I'd been the careful one.

He shook his head and patted me on the shoulder. "It could be you're too young to know," he said, lowering his voice and looking beyond me. "There's just such all kinds of people footloose in the country anymore," he said. "I take care of myself, but Dixie's different altogether. There's times she's just too pure for our world. It's my faith I was put down here on the ground to care for her."

"Well, looks like you're doing just fine by her," I said. We were almost back to the car. He stopped again and pointed at the Cadillac and Dixie in the backseat, reading.

"She's the first woman has ever really loved me," he said. "You know, all the way deep down." He pressed his hand flat against his chest.

Dixie poked her head out the open window.

"Those rolls look real good, Walter," she said.

At a gas stop later, near the middle of the state, we pulled over by a water spigot, and they washed the Cadillac with rags and sponges they kept in a bucket in the trunk. Dixie did the low parts, cleaning the California license plates and the bumpers and fender skirts, and Walt stretched his long arms across the top and the wide hood and back deck. I offered to help, but Dixie said they enjoyed doing it. She kept flipping water on Walt when his back was turned, and he'd look up at the cloudless sky and act amazed. She laughed like a kid with her dad.

At another stop that afternoon, in a crowded station near a large interchange, Walt confessed he was flat out of money, something I'd already figured out. I offered to pay for a tank of gas. He said he might take me up on it yet, but he still had a card or two up his sleeve. He opened the trunk and pulled out three sets of brand-new jumper cables and a used set of expensive-looking walkie-talkies. He went around to the people at the pumps and coming from the restaurant, talking and gesturing like an auctioneer.

While we waited on Walt, I sat on the edge of the backseat with the car door open, talking to Dixie. She showed me pictures from her magazines. She knew exactly how tall every movie star was, male and female, and she got me to admit that I was surprised at a lot of them. She said they used every kind of trick to fool you on the stars' heights in the movies. She said Walter told her she had the face of a movie queen.

I asked her if she'd like me to sit in back for a while so she could sit up front with Walt.

"I can't drive," she said. "My legs won't reach to the pedals." She pulled her skirt up to show me, and I saw her white panties before the shirt settled back on her hips. I looked away.

"Walt's a good driver," I said. "Steady and safe."

"He used to make his living that way," she said. "But that's not why I've rode the whole way in the back, really. Can you keep a secret, Bob?"

"What do you mean?"

"You know. Something you whisper and promise not to tell around. Friends tell them back and forth. Can't you keep one?"

"I suppose I can. Sure."

"There's a special word for what I am. Walt told it to me."

I didn't want to be hearing her secrets, especially about whatever her condition might be. I didn't know how our talking had come to that point. I looked around and saw Walt heading for the car, counting the cash in his hand.

"Virgin," she said. She giggled. "It rhymes with urgin'. Walt says it's best for me to stay in the backseat. He says I make him feel too frisky otherwise. This whole last year we've been saving me until Walter's got a proper job and we're married."

I stood up beside the car. Dixie's skirt was still pulled up high on her hips. her expression turned thoughtful. She picked at the upholstery.

"Bob, would you tell me something?"

"If I can." I saw my shadow broken across the top of the car and the open back door. Dixie squinted up at me.

"Walter says those other times, the ones who made me do it, don't really count. He's not just saying that, is he? They don't count, do they?"

I stared at her and knew she'd had a whole life, one much longer and harder than mine, one I'd never be able to even guess at. Walt was coming closer. I leaned my head into the car, whispering, without really meaning to.

"No. Not at all. Walter's telling the truth."

"So what's going on, Bob?" I turned around. Walt stood next to me. Before I could answer he leaned into the car. "Pull that down, DQ. It doesn't look right."

"Dixie's telling me all about the movie stars," I said. He was staring right into my eyes again. "And how you take such good care of her."

Dixie slid over in the seat and put her small hand on Walt's thin wrist.

"He's our friend, Walter. He's a perfect gentleman."

Walt smiled a little. "That true, Bob?"

"You bet," I said. "Of course." It was probably the most old-fashioned sounding thing anybody'd ever said about me. But I liked hearing it.

"I just knew that," he said. "I just knew I wasn't wrong on you." He slapped me on the back again, the way a father would.

"Well, over there isn't coming any closer sitting over here," he said, pointing down the highway. He closed Dixie's door and walked around the car. I climbed back into the front seat. I felt like I'd been with them too long.

"How'd you make out with the sales?" I asked, wanting to talk about anything besides them or me.

"We're doing fine," he said. "Except I feel kind of shoddy, a little."

"What'd you do, Walter?" Dixie asked.

"Those walkie-talkies is broke," he said. "But I didn't say so. I sold them like they wasn't."

"It's all right," Dixie said. "You did it for our trip. We'll make it up to somebody we meet down there in New York."

At the New Jersey line, near sundown, I took a photo of them, and then we took one with me, too, using the rickety remote device Walt had rigged up with a coat hanger threaded through a plastic tube and the camera propped on the hood of the Cadillac. Dixie stood between us, with her arms reaching upward to hold one of each of our hands. They gave me the picture, and I put it in my back pocket. If you only ever saw that one photo, you'd swear it was of two men, a teenager and a middle-aged man, with a little girl between them, a younger sister or a niece.

After the photo stop, I felt sleepy again, and I drifted in and out, mostly out, but I did hear Walt say he'd driven a cab in Manhattan for almost ten years and was planning on supporting both of them doing that again. He'd bummed around the country for years after that, looking for something but not knowing what it was until he'd found Dixie in Los Angeles about a year ago. She was living in a halfway home for the retarded, he said, and I'd never heard a word said with more bitter regret than the way Walt said "retarded."

"Walter knew I wasn't that other," Dixie said. "I'm just short."

"The best things in the smallest packages," Walt said, and they were off again, laughing and cooing at each other like newlyweds in old movies.

They weren't married, but Walt said they were going to get that way quick once they arrived in Manhattan and he found a job. Right up on top of the Empire State Building, Dixie said. They invited me to come. I kidded them and told them I'd watch the papers for their pictures and announcements. A cool wind blew up and the sky went dark as we crossed New Jersey.

We stopped at a diner, the Go-By Inn, near an exit in Teaneck, just a few miles from the George Washington Bridge into Manhattan. Dixie couldn't stop laughing about the name of the town. Walt went in to get some sandwiches with the last of what he called his swap-meet money. It was dark and he parked the Cadillac near the highway at the edge of the parking lot. I wanted to go in and use the restroom and wash up. Dixie stayed in the backseat, munching on milk balls and starting on a new box of old magazines. Walt locked the car.

Walt ordered, and I heard him asking the waitress if she wanted to buy a ballpoint as I went into the bathroom. I'd pulled a washrag from my duffel, and I washed my face and hands and neck until I felt wider awake than I had all day — ready for my first look at New York City. I pulled a twenty from my shoe. I paid for the three roast beef sandwiches and root beers Walt had ordered. We headed back for the car, juggling the food. Walt promised me a cabbie's tour of Manhattan when we got over the bridge.

But when we got to the Cadillac, I didn't see Dixie. Then I looked in from the passenger side and saw her lying on the floor of the backseat. I yelled at Walt. He dropped his food and unlocked the car. I went around to his side as he turned her over and lifted her up on the seat. It seemed like she only reached halfway across it. Her face was somewhere between blue and red, and yet not purple, something different from purple. Her eyes were wide open, and both the white and the black of them was way too bright — glary, shiny — like she'd seen the true source of eveyone's worst fear and hadn't looked away from it. Saliva streaked all around her mouth, and little brown flakes plastered her chin. In her small white fist the candy box was smashed, and the wax-paper liner squeezed out at both ends. I stood there like a storefront mannequin, a roast beef sandwich and two root beers in my hands, and I wanted to be anywhere but in Teaneck, New Jersey, with Walt and Dixie.

I asked if she was dead, even though I knew she was. He didn't answer me. He kept shaking her and kissing her forehead and cleaning her face with a napkin. But when I headed toward the diner for help, he stopped me, and the next thing I knew, we'd paid a toll and were on a bridge over the Hudson River with a Welcome to New York sign sliding out of sight above the windshield.

I wanted to get away from them, yet I didn't want to abandon Walt. I wondered if the police would believe she'd choked to death, and I was afraid I'd be blamed for something, anything. I wanted to call my father.

As we turned onto the Henry Hudson Parkway, I looked up into the bright thrum of New York City. I heard Walt talking for the first time since we'd gotten back in the car.

"She ain't that far ahead of me." His hands were winding around on the wheel like it was something he could wring out.

"Do you know where there's a hospital or something?" I asked.

"She's still in this car," he said. "I know she is." He seemed to be driving without seeing anything. Our speed was changing all the time. He'd run it up to sixty and then drop back to thirty.

"It's not your fault, Walt," I said.

"It's not your fault, Dixie," he said as he pulled the Cadillac off the expressway, and then we were suddenly at street level in Manhattan.

I didn't know where we were or where we were going. Walt drove like he knew, though, and at every red light, I thought about getting out. My bag was upright behind me, but I didn't want to look at it because I never wanted to see that blue face again.

We parked on a narrow dark street. Walt turned the car off.

"Where is this?" I asked.

"Can I have that?" Walt said, pointing at the root beer I still held. I handed it to him. He reached in a pocket of his suit coat and pulled out a little Bayer aspirin bottle with the label half torn off. He set them both on the dash in front of him. "I did you a favor, stopping for you back there, right, Bob?"

"Of course, sure. Sure you did."

"So you can pay me back now. You're the only one to do this for me. You owe me."

"Anything. I've got some money. I'll help you."

He reached in his coat and pulled out one of the new pens. He opened the glove compartment and grabbed the photo of him and Dixie and the New Jersey sign. He turned it over and handed it and the pen to me. He had my eyes locked up with his, and it felt like he could do that whenever he wanted.

"I don't need money now. If I ever needed it, I don't have no more use for it now. You can write, can't you?"

"What?"

"Just write what I tell you," he said, pointing at the pen and the photo in my hand. I hesitated. "They got to know her name," he yelled. It was the first time he'd raised his voice in the twenty-some hours I'd known him. He lowered it again. "Please," he said. I put the pen against the paper.

"To whatever people who cares," he said. I felt like I'd stumbled into someone else's life at exactly the wrong moment. It had nothing to do with anything I could remember before this one day. I just wrote what he said.

"This little lady is Dixie Margaret Ann Logan. She's thirty-two years old and choked on a milk ball, and I couldn't save her. I spent half my life searching her out, and I'm not going to let her get away now. The best thing if someone can do it would be to put us to rest side by side."

He pulled the photo and pen from my hand. I thought I was going to be sick. I watched him sign his name at the bottom of it.

"Walt, you can't do that," I said. "Come on. No."

"I really appreciate it," he said. "Now you go on. Just keep walking that way," he pointed behind us. "When you come to Eighth Avenue, turn left. Go a few miles. There's plenty of hotels on the cheap there."

"Walt. You're not thinking straight."

"I'd let you have this car but for two things," he said. He looked away, as if ashamed. "It's not really mine, title-wise. And we need it."

"I can't leave you like this," I said.

"You're going to," he said. He reached for the root beer and the pill bottle. "Get your bag and go. This ain't nothing about you. Dignified comes in every different flavor, my friend. This one's mine. You understand?"

"Yes," I said. I didn't move.

He got out and went around and opened both doors on my side. He set my bag on the sidewalk and got in beside Dixie. He set the photo on his lap and opened the pill bottle. I still didn't move.

"You have no right not to let me go with her," he said. "You promise me you won't call anybody to stop me. Promise me."

I got out and slammed the front door, staring right at him.

"I promise."

"Then thank you," he said. He let go of my eyes for the last time. "So long." He closed the door.

I swear I could see that bright white Cadillac from one block, two, three, four blocks away. Almost as if it were glowing, a small moon with four whitewall tires parked on a side street in Manhattan in the night. Finally, when I looked back, I'd lost it.

I walked for hours. I tore and retore the photo of Walt and Dixie and me into confetti and threw the pieces into three different trash barrels. When I couldn't walk another step, I stumbled into the Key Hotel for Men, shoved a few dollars at a cashier behind worn brass bars, took a freight elevator up to a room on the fourth floor, went in and lay down on a metal bed with a two-inch mattress. I kept my hand on my bag next to me. I didn't undress or take my shoes off, and I didn't exactly sleep, but I got through the night.

In the daylight the next morning, it turned out I was only about six blocks from the Empire State Building, but I never went up there or looked for work or did anything else I'd had in my mind. I took a bus from New York to Boston the same day. I had a high-school friend in college there.

As the Greyhound drove me away from Manhattan, I counted my money and put it in my wallet. I still had almost two hundred dollars. It was Friday. I was still nineteen. I didn't know at all what I was feeling, except that I didn't feel alone anymore. Or free. I watched the ships, pushing down the Hudson, silver lines of froth slanting across their hulls, and then the rows of dark waves racing away. I stared at the surface of the water for a long time before I closed my eyes and finally slept. Only sunlight danced upon it.

Peter Fong

Asia Hotel

In Canton the cab drivers pronounce it with three syllables: *A-see-ah.* Until you came, I had never hired a taxi here. Only foreigners and overseas Chinese have the hard currency necessary to pay the fare. Asia Hotel, you said to him in your American voice. The driver nodded, several times, to show that he was willing to understand. You spoke quickly: Asia Hotel. I wrote the street address in Cantonese on the back of your plane ticket. Ah, smiled the driver, A-si-a Hotel. You climbed in and rolled down the window. Meet me there for lunch, you said. It seemed so strange to see your face through a haze of dust. In California I remember the sun, the green of palms, your hand pulling me across an intersection and into a shop that sold only ice cream. I threw one leg over my bicycle, wondered if my luck had changed for the better.

A steady rain dampened the dust. I passed the hours until noon by pedaling around the block, steering nonchalantly with one hand, holding an umbrella in the other. I thought often of your face, reddened with the fatigue of travel, of the drop of rain that traced a slow arc down your cheek in the cab. I spoke aloud my remembered English, gone to rust in the months since I saw you last. It is good to see you, Sue Yin, I said, using the name you had chosen in Chinese for Beginners. You were not the best pupil in my class, but you were the only one to ask questions. Tell me, you said, how do you say, 'Two cold beers, please' ? When my visa expired, you promised to pay me a visit in Canton. Why should you keep that promise? I circled the hotel, testing sentences under the umbrella: How was your flight? Are your accommodations satisfactory? Your hair is a beautiful shade. I hope you have been keeping well.

In the lobby of the Asia Hotel, a tall girl in a kimono posed next to a marble column. She propped her shoulder against the pink stone, pressed her cheek to its curve, bent one leg like a wading bird. The model's eyes followed me as I walked tall in the American clothes you sent from Los Angeles — blue mountaineer's shorts and a canvas shirt with a buttoned-down collar. Her eyes were large and dark, her face empty. Her lips pleaded for a word, almost kissing the air. She could not know that I had lost my job at the grammar school, that I was not a stranger to this city. I kept walking but slowly, turning my head to watch. She folded one leg into the kimono and sank to the floor, silk rustling.

I went into the bar to wait. A girl from Hunan Province with straight bangs and wire-rimmed glasses played "Sewanee River" on the piano. She drawled one note after the other, lingered on 'far, far away.' The tables were full of tourists waiting to check out. As the afternoon wore on they filed away in groups to meet their motor coaches. I thought that I should ask the clerk to ring your room, that perhaps there had been some misunderstanding. Maybe you had meant dinner, not lunch. In that case, I reasoned, I should simply stay on until dinnertime. I did not wish to inconvenience you.

After several hours the bar began to fill again. I sat alone at the rail, listening to the travelers converse in English, offering them an occasional word of advice — the Reclining Buddha is the most pleasant to view, the dim sum best before nine o'clock. I met an old man who used to push nail polish in Hong Kong, and could not defend myself. He called me an Irishman and advised me to marry money. And when that one dies, he said, marry another one. Quick. He had made a mistake, you see. She was young and healthy, and after fifty years she still wasn't dead. I stood up to scan the room for you, for your small face looking down at the cups and saucers. I waited for you to drift in, a lonely fish at the bottom of the tank, and then I wanted a beer. The old man paid.

That killed the evening for me. To hear his talk and not yours. Because he could lift one arthritic finger and point and say, There, there is the scourge of my life. And he knew, he had a name for what he was waiting for, and it was not his own death, but hers. She was on her third pacemaker. He was hopeful.

Peter Fong

Noon Sun, East Bay

Winter's not over, but it feels like heaven, like the day after someone has died—warm when I expected cold, clear when clouds were due. East Bay is iced at least a mile from shore, and I walk out to fish. Old men tend holes, their backs to the big lake that won't freeze. I go until I can see blood on the ice, sleek rows of trout stiffening in the skin of snowmelt that mirrors the sky. Into a hole in the water I drop deep designs. Also my faith in things unseen, a week of bad work, my murderous thoughts. A skater strides easily from blade to blade. I watch her glide away, skirt the edge of open water; I tell myself I wouldn't feel a thing if she were gone. I would not run with a rope to the spot, so small has my life become. All I want is the old age these old men have, backs to the world, hope on the hook, fat trout dreaming, and no death less important than their own. Wouldn't that be heaven—good ice over East Bay, noon sun in March, no God to judge? Into a hole in the water he drops eggshells and canned corn. He says the trout are attracted to the fall, tells about the time he spilled coffee on the ice and the warden asked, Who pissed here? It's illegal you know—a fifty-dollar sin. He'd dipped two fingers in the stained snow and tasted it. He'd said, Not me.

Pete Fromm

The Coyotes' Dark Circle

A week after turning twenty, Pete Fromm dropped out of the wildlife biology program at the University of Montana to spend a winter alone in the Selway-Bitterroot Wilderness. Employed to keep two million of the Idaho Fish and Game's salmon eggs alive, Pete discovered there was much more to the wilderness than fish eggs. This is an excerpt from his book *Indian Creek Chronicles: A Winter in the Bitterroot Wilderness.*

The coyote kills began appearing in late January, splotchy stains in the snow, on the river mostly, which was frozen hard and flat, a highway for any traffic through the mountains. I'd been living alone in the wilderness for nearly four months, and the dark circles marring the featureless white drew my attention as surely as a conversation.

Working together in groups of six or seven, the coyotes drove the deer out of the timber onto the level bed of the river. Tufts of hair would show where the coyotes had nipped, how they'd weakened their prey. Occasionally there'd be tiny sparkling bright drops of blood. I always expected a gradual progression, more hair, more blood, then more, and finally the kill. But it never went like that. Always just a little hair, sometimes no blood, and then, suddenly, the huge trampled circle centered on the rusty brown stain and the greenish pile of stomach contents. Only once did I see a spot where a deer had fallen but regained its feet and run on. Its final circle was yards off.

Shortly after the first appearance of the circles, I came across a hard icy bend of the Selway, a spot the lashing wind had cleared of all but the newest snow. And in that new snow were the tracks of an elk, an elk that had leapt down the last bit of river bank, landing on what looked exactly like more snow. But on the ice all hell had broken loose. The elk's front feet had shot to the left, while his back legs had done the splits. He had held on for what must have been a long time, his feet making outlandish looping patterns on the ice, but then the snow was wiped clean by the big broad side of the elk spinning over the ice.

I grinned, looking at the sign, translating what must have occurred, and wishing I'd been just a few minutes earlier, that I could have seen the mighty elk take such a pratfall.

Walking on though, safe from the wind in the calm of the cedars, I thought of
the thin line separating everything from that dark circle in the snow. If the elk
had broken something, dislocated a hip, there would have been nothing left but
that ring of dirty snow and the pile of stomach grass surrounded by a bewildering
haze of coyote tracks.

I remembered telling my parents about this job, months ago. Since I'd have
no way of communicating with the world, they'd wanted to know what I'd do if I
chopped off my foot with an ax. I told them I'd crawl the sixty miles out, if I had
to. If I'd known, I could have described the way the coyote tracks would flatten
the entire area around the end.

The following morning I woke early, noticing silence had replaced the wisp-
ing, sliding sound of snow shuffling off my tent. I poked my head out, and the
sky was full of stars, not clouds. I was out as soon as I could throw down breakfast.

Beneath the new stuff, the snow was crusted with the cold, hard enough to
support my weight, and I was able to carry my snowshoes on my back. I left before
dawn, happy to be out again, the sliver of moon and the stars giving more than
enough light. I moved quietly through the night's layer of soft new snow, silvered
and shadowed. It was nice to be silent again, after the weeks of every crunching
step on the frozen snow. I went up and down over the old thaw's snowslides, and
two miles slipped by before my dog Boone's hackles suddenly went up. She
stopped and waited for me.

I moved forward with Boone, wondering what could possibly have gotten into
her. The only other time I had seen her hackles up was the frigid night she woke
me with her growling, and I'd flipped the flashlight on in time to see a cow elk
pull her head from the front flap of my tent.

We rounded a bend in the river and came to just another empty snowslide.
The dawn was starting to give enough light to see, and I looked at Boone, but
she was still hanging tight to me. As we started up the slide Boone began to growl.
I slowed, too curious now to stop completely.

At the top of the slide I found a dead mule deer doe. Its flank was split open,
and steam rose from the wound. I remembered Boone's growl, and I glanced
around the shadowed trees surrounding me. I poked around but could find no
other injury. There were no footprints either. Uphill from where the deer lay I
could see a dent in the snow, and then another one a little farther down, with a
slide mark to the body from that. Like a hit, a bounce, and a slide.

I looked at the cliff above me. It would have been a free fall of forty or fifty
feet. But deer don't just fall off cliffs. I thought of the elk falling flat on the ice

and wondered. I looked around again but could find no more clues. Boone had stopped growling when she found the deer. She sniffed at it and sat down.

Circling around one more time, I came up with a drag mark. This was going away from the deer, downhill. It was easier to see on the softer snow off the slide. It was a smooth depression a few inches deep, maybe eight inches wide.

I checked the deer one more time, rolling it over. It was very fresh, the insides still hot. I could think of no reason for a drag mark other than some animal hauling off a piece of the deer. But there was nothing missing. Had there been two deer? I checked again and didn't think so. There wasn't any blood in the drag mark either. None of this made sense, and I glanced again at the dark trees before I started to follow the drag mark.

I turned the first bend, and the drag went straight ahead through the fresh, flat snow and around the next bend. There were no footprints anywhere, just this smooth dent in the snow. I had no idea what I was dealing with. Boone started to act funny again, hackles up, growling. I moved even more slowly.

Soon I was on tiptoes, walking beside the track, thinking I would probably have to come back over all this to study it again. I didn't want to walk over the clues.

We rounded the next bend, and Boone charged. The drag mark led straight to a bobcat sitting in the road. By the time I saw it, it had spun around and was taking a swipe at Boone with a bare-clawed front paw.

Boone reversed her charge a hair short of those claws and came back to my side. The bobcat glared at us then turned back around and started dragging itself down the road. It veered toward the cliff side, making for a snow hollow under a tree.

I was putting two and two together by now. The bobcat and the deer had gone off the cliff together. The deer had been killed, and the bobcat crippled, para-lyzed from about midspine down. I watched it crawl up toward the tree, where its back would be covered and it could make a last stand. But the uphill was tougher going, and it had to stop and rest. It had already dragged itself two hun-dred yards from the deer.

I watched a moment more, too surprised to do anything. The drag mark was left by its hip and leg. Black spotting edged the flank, where the cat's coat switched from the mottled tan and buff of the back to the clear white of the belly. The bottoms of its useless feet were black, with black hair between the toes. Dragging its hindquarters had covered the tracks left by the front paws.

Going up the slight rise to the tree it could only take three or four steps before stopping to rest. Its mouth was open, panting, and I could see a pink edge of tongue. It must be equally broken up inside.

I saw the heaving of the bobcat's sides as it struggled for every breath, the obvious pain of dragging itself along another few feet. Playing the coyote's finishing role, I picked up a large rock from the edge of the river and carried it cocked back in my right hand, ready to come down on the crippled cat's head, wanting to get this over with as quickly as I could.

The cat heard my approach and glanced over its shoulder at me. Then it turned around. To face me. It hissed like a house cat, but louder and meaner. It made a flashing sweep with a front paw, claws out. Then it started to drag itself toward me, its eyes flashing, yellow, malevolent squints. Even mortally injured, it was coming at me, something that towered over it, outweighed it five to one.

Its eyes never wavered, and it was hard to pull mine away from them. But the cat kept coming for me, waving its claws, hissing, spitting. Pretty soon I took a step backward. Boone growled, and the cat really hissed then. It lurched two steps forward, its ears laid back on its head, almost growling itself, like a smaller mountain lion roar.

I dropped my rock and retreated to the river edge. I kicked around until I found a limb of a dead cottonwood about eight feet long and stout, thicker than a baseball bat, but I wouldn't have minded if it was longer. I came back up the bank, and the cat was sitting still, collecting itself.

When it saw me, its ears went flat again, and it started toward me. I lifted my club and stared into those yellow slits of eyes. I had never seen anything so angry or determined.

I tensed just before swinging the club, and the cat stopped. It seemed to know what was coming. Its head dipped toward its shoulders, and I brought the club down as hard as I could possibly swing anything.

It broke across his head, and the cat was finished. I swung once more, making sure, driving the cat's head and shoulders deep into the crusted snow, glad, anyway, that the swing was clean and fast.

I stared at the cat for more than a minute, studying its sides for any trace of a breath, but there was nothing like that. Then, leaving the cat there, I circled around the cliffs, climbing to the top. I picked up the deer's tracks at the edge of the cliff and followed them backward, amazed at the wild turns and twists the trail made. There were no cat tracks, though. Then I found a clump of deer hair. Then another. The cat had been riding the deer through all this, tearing at her.

That went on for about eighty feet. Then I saw the divot in the snow that was the cat's last bound before landing on the deer. There were only two divots, leading to a snow pocket beneath a small pine, where the cat had lain in wait for the deer. The deer had passed within ten feet of the tree, its tracks showing that it was walking slowly, browsing.

The first bound mark of the cat was only a few feet from the deer tracks. Then the deer had leaped, and the cat was after it. There was the final bound and then the mad, twisting, turning dash off the cliff. I looked over the edge at the dead deer and bobcat. I wondered if the deer had seen what was coming or if having the cat snapping and clawing on its back had driven the deer beyond that.

I crawled carefully back down the cliff and picked up the cat. It was surprisingly heavy, probably pushing forty pounds, and I let it back down and sat in the snow beside it. I petted its fur smooth, never having imagined such a death.

I carried the cat home with me and set to work skinning it, curious to see what I would find, not quite able to leave the fur to be torn to shreds by the coyotes. As the skin came off, huge areas of blood-shocked meat were exposed, giant bruises over the left hip and the center of the spine. The spine was broken, as was the hip and the leg. I wondered if the cat had been caught under the deer when it hit. It certainly hadn't landed on its feet.

I checked the teeth. The canines were split and broken, not from the fall, but from age. Not one was intact. They were about one quarter their healthy length and dull and flat rather than sharp. That furious charge hadn't had a chance with no teeth to finish the deer.

Over the next several days I visited the dead deer again and again, wondering when the coyotes would find it, wanting to see just how soon that stain in the snow would form.

But before the coyotes came the ravens, and even an immature bald eagle. I'd been here four months without seeing an eagle. Where had it come from? How had it known there was meat available?

I discovered that the ravens set out guard birds, one upstream and one downstream of the carcass. If I walked down the river I would see a raven launch from a tree several hundred yards before I got to the kill. Then I would hear it cawing, and by the time I was within sight of the kill there would be nothing there but raven tracks. The eagle would flee with the ravens. Its tracks stood out clearly in the chaos of the raven prints, as long as my hand. I could barely believe how big the eagle really was.

I began to play games with the ravens, sneaking around through the trees, trying to take them by surprise. They always caught me if I followed the river, and I tried circling wide, going up on top of the cliff and peeking my head over the edge. Then I had them, fifteen ravens working on the deer. I laughed and they erupted, quick black shadows flitting through the trees, fleeing danger. They never did figure out the high approach, and I'd often catch them working on the deer, or, if the eagle was on the carcass, they would be standing all around, ready to move in as soon as the eagle left.

Four days passed before the coyotes finally arrived. Their tracks pounded the area flat. There was a little splotch of greenery and a pinkish stain in the snow. Same as ever.

I followed their tracks into the kill, six of them coming in from across the river. They dragged the deer all over the place, and it was hard to follow. But I saw the scuffs around the one hole in the river ice, the water running black three feet below the snow and ice covering it. At the downstream edge of the hole I could just make out an inch of leg and the deer's split toes, six inches underwater. The ice hid everything else, and I wondered if they'd lost the whole deer or if I was only seeing a broken scrap of leg.

Even picturing the frenzied tearing, the yanking this way and that, I grinned, imagining the sudden slip and splash, six coyote faces staring down into the black water, suddenly quiet. I let my face go all stupefied, imitating the coyotes I pictured, and I said, "Whoops."

I laughed out loud. That was the last trace of the bobcat and the deer, the eagle and the ravens. But the coyotes would leave other splotches, picking off whatever could not make it through one more winter, whatever, like the old bobcat, could not endure another stretch of hard times before the easy days of spring.

The spring would come eventually, and the snow would melt, hiding the evidence of the coyotes' work. The winter, I knew, was a hard time for the coyotes too, but I never found them at the center of the dark circles in the snow. Winter dropped them, when they could no longer make it through to the long, warm days, in places more private.

Lowell Jaeger

How This Very Rocking Chair You're Sitting in Came to Be

The left rocker you lifted from inside a sagebrush
where someone had stabbed it upright to mark
the trail. You'd have pitched it aside after rubbing
the raised grain of weathered oak in your palm, testing
the strength of its curve against your thigh,
but spied the right rocker and some cross-members
under a giant saguaro a hundred paces farther on.
You were out of water, didn't know your way back,
and didn't know where your way forward would lead.

And the woman with you would soon be your wife,
though neither of you knew that. She trusted you
as much as she could — which wasn't much —
and the reason she kept asking as if the answer
should change: "Are you sure? Are you sure?"
If you'd been old as now you would have turned,
said simply, "Hell no, I'm lost as anybody else."
But you were young enough to nod, jut your chin,
puff your chest while your knees trembled beneath
your true heart's boom like a doomsday drum.

You scooped up pieces of that chair — rockers, hand-
turned cross-members — and carried them with you as proof
you gambled on living by gumption to reconstruct
this ruined rocking chair some busted pioneer
must have once upon a bad day abandoned there.

Ah — a few crazy dance steps to the left and right —
two tall poles to form the back of the rocker, six

slats. Elbow rest here, there. Better than an armload.
And she refused to help with a single stick of it,
even though you weren't on the trail you thought,
but one something like it, so you both survived.
Married less than a year later. All those pieces
you assembled in the basement back home,
sanding, gluing, varnishing. Learned to cane
the seat — sent away for instructions — softened
the bands of cane in the tub, one by one wrapped
the cross-members, stitching each loop with thread
to hold them snug as long as they might last.

They lasted longer than your marriage. You still
own that rocker. Your wife went to pieces
eventually. You've vowed — an older, wiser you —
should you stumble on her scattered remains,
you'll leave them bleaching where they lay.
"Hell," you'll shout into a hot blast out of nowhere,
"Nothing's much for sure." Then you'll march on
the way you've always been headed, even so.

Ruth Rudner

The Big Drive

On a hot, dry September day, after a hundred years of Montana statehood, five thousand people gathered a short way from the town of Roundup for the start of the Great Centennial Cattle Drive. Horse trailers, trucks, and covered wagons lined the staging ground parking area from one end to the other. Beyond the parking area, tents and tipis filled the hollows of a rolling landscape. Draft horses — huge, calm, magnificent — stood tethered to the wagons circling the tents. On the rolling hills behind the camp, riders exercised horses hauled long miles and hours in trailers. On a slight rise, the Montana Memorial Detachment, 7th Cavalry, Company K had pitched its tent. Company K was Major Reno's company, the one that got away from Custer's last stand. A thirty-five-star flag flew over the cavalry tent. Cavalry officers paraded on their sorrel horses. In the dusty corral across the road, the lead herd of cattle, all of them Longhorns, waited for morning, and the start of The Big Drive of '89.

For the six days of the Drive, this camp — the eighth largest town in Montana — would be packed up every morning, move on, settle in to the next site every afternoon. Each day's town evolved almost instantaneously, complete with a proper frontier bustle to its main street where horseback riders threaded their way among pedestrians — cowboys in long, sweeping dusters or leather vests, women in long calico dresses, small children in sunbonnets, a nun, a mountain man or two. There were musicians, poets, and storytellers who looked like all the other cowboys but held a different magic in their souls, or, perhaps, just a different — a more public — access to the same magic. The dusty street built in an hour held both a history and a present. At each camp a huge red-and-white striped tent erected by Budweiser functioned as saloon, dance hall, community center, and opera house. The town had its own medical facilities and a daily newspaper printed on an 1840s press. Nighttime campfires in each wagon circle softened the hard, wide darkness of the prairie night, quieted down this monumental carnival bursting with its hundred years of energy and myth and eagerness for the West. No one is so eager for the West as the westerner. He indulges in it as if it were some freeing masquerade, and yet it is his own.

I was on the drive to write a story. I was really on the drive because I love cowboys. I have ever since childhood when my father, taking me to the western films he loved, thrust into my growing up a vision of that heroic, lonely landscape in which the cowboy rides forever into the sunset. Tall, lean, scarf knotted around his throat, big hat on his head, dusty boots, jeans worn from the saddle, mellow old leather chaps worn from the years, eyes mirroring a universal loneliness back there behind the permanent squint — he rides out on his good horse into eternal sunset.

I had always wanted to do it — to ride off into the sunset, tall and lean and weathered and tough and alone. I wanted to be that cowboy I loved. I wanted to understand aloneness to the depths of my being. I wanted to feel loneliness so hard that it would be like lying on the baked summer Montana earth or leaning against the rock of mountains. I wanted the solitude of hermits and of saints, . . . but according to my own myths, the myths my father gave me. I could see myself riding into the sunset. I could feel it.

There was only one problem. I didn't know how to ride a horse. Actually, the problem was deeper. I was terrified of horses. When my father tried to teach me to ride at the age of two, the horse seemed so large, I so small, the distance to the ground so far. My father didn't press it. I grew up afraid of horses and longing for them. When I moved to Montana forty years later, it was clear that learning to ride was now or never. After that horse packing trip in the Bob Marshall Wilderness Area, I registered for Beginning Equitation at Montana State University.

The horses ran kicking and bucking into the school arena. My stomach did the same thing, but it was too late to turn back. If I left the class now, I would never ride a horse. I told the instructor about my fear, and he assigned me Babs Barmaid, a wonderful mare who is sort of a special for cowards. Babs did all she could to help me. While the rest of the class chased their horses across the arena to catch them, Babs walked up to me. She practically put the bit in her mouth herself. Anything she could do to help, she did. Allowing me to believe I was in control, she taught me control was possible.

Before the Great Montana Centennial Cattle Drive, I had had time to take the beginning class a second time, the intermediate class once, and go on a couple of pack trips through Yellowstone. I had been on a few horses besides Babs, and I believed absolutely that anything you wanted to do as much as I wanted to go on the cattle drive had to be possible. I forgot I was scared of horses.

I borrowed a horse named Tess from some people in Kalispell and drove up there a couple of times before the Drive to ride her, then arranged to meet her — and her owners, Jan and Jim, at the staging ground.

The first evening in camp I saddled Tess, Jan saddled her horse, and we rode out beyond camp. All around us men and women loped their horses across the hills so that riders and horses and hills all seemed part of the same thing, some absolute moment of life and movement and endless time. Here, in a great group fantasy, was the white history of the West, the present reestablished in a past that belonged to us all.

Suddenly I realized where I was and what I was doing, and I got scared. Here were five thousand people obviously born in the saddle. Four thousand nine hundred and ninety-nine. How could I have imagined I could do this? What if I did some stupid thing and fell off my horse in front of them all, got trampled out of stupidity. I do not want to die out of stupidity. I wasn't really worried (for the first time) about getting injured or killed. I just didn't want to be embarrassed. But there was nothing I could do about it now. Except ride.

The first dawn was clear, and already hot. My fear hadn't lessened, but now there was an excitement curling around it, holding it the way a mother holds a baby, or a lover the beloved. If the fear was me, I felt protected by the excitement, and, for the moment, distracted by the movement of the camp. Jan and I sat on our horses at the fence, near the gate through which the train would roll. Across the road, a few of the 105 cowboys there to drive the cattle herd waited with the lead herd. When the corral gate was opened, the cattle surged through onto the narrow road, cowboys flanking them and behind them. The cavalry, its thirty-five-star flag hoisted at the front, followed — off to a far surer victory than it had probably ever known out here. The wagon master shouted, "Wagons . . . Ho!!" and they began pouring out of the gate — covered wagons, buckboards, surreys, one after another after another, their proud, beautiful teams swirling up the soft Montana dust in this immense moment of absolute belief in the hope and possibility of the American West. Three thousand three hundred and thirty-seven riders followed the wagons. The rest of the 105 cowboys drove the main herd over a different route than we would travel, but would end up near the wagon train camp. Twenty million people could be fed by the trail herd if it was converted to hamburger, I was told.

We entered Roundup. Thousands of spectators lined the street, shouting out their excitement, their pride and support. I felt them riding with us, but I also felt immense to be riding, as if I, myself, had suddenly become bigger than life. I hadn't thought about that, about being a part of the parade, about what it would feel like to ride a horse down a corridor lined with thousands of cheering people.

Out of Roundup the wagons settled in to some rhythm of the road, riders to the heat and the crowds, horses into the hot ride surrounded by thousands of strange horses, shying from time to time when they got too near a wagon. Odd, these horses would all have been comfortable around a motorized vehicle, but most of them had never seen a wagon before.

At the first camp I met The Cowboy. He was holding a press conference to answer questions the accompanying reporters had after the first day's ride. I stood at the back of the group of journalists circled around him. He was tall and easy and used to being handsome. Engaging with each person who asked a question — about the logistics of setting up camp, securing the horses, providing water enough for so many people and animals, maintaining medical facilities, law and order, entertainment — he really looked at them. He listened. He didn't rush. He had a kind of time about him. None of the questions the journalists asked had occurred to me. I just wanted to ride my horse and smell the dust. On the other hand, I looked at that man's eyes and knew I had to ask a question. Any question. The conference seemed to be over. The journalists began to drift off.

"What do you think of the drive so far?" I asked.

"It's a miracle that a place like Montana exists where something like this can happen," he said, looking fully at me now. Dark brown hair curled out from under a tall brown hat. He smiled. His blue eyes laughed. The creases in his face emphasized his ruggedness.

"Tell me about Montana," I said.

"This drive will let the world know Montana exists," he said, "and let Montanans know they matter," he added, referring, I supposed, to the fact that somewhere along the way the drive organizers had decided this was too big for Montanans to handle and brought in an out-of-stater to run the organization. It was an act not uncommon in Montana, where people think that if a Montanan does it, it won't be as good as if someone from somewhere else does it. The result of bringing in the outsider was that the Cattle Drive almost didn't happen. The man probably knew about organizing political campaigns — that was his background — but he knew a good deal less about horses than I did, had probably never seen a Longhorn cow, a covered wagon, a cowboy who wasn't in a movie. He had never ridden or walked across this land of sagebrush and cactus, of rolling dry earth. He could have been anywhere, for all he knew. You can't come to Montana like that. In Montana you have to know where you are. You have to know you are in Montana.

At the last moment the man was dumped, and the floundering drive was taken over by Montanans who pulled it together with the sheer force of their immense energy and will. The Cowboy, one of the original organizers of the drive, had opted out when the outsider was brought in. With the outsider out, he came back. He was, in fact, not a cowboy, but a cartoonist, one of two cartoonists who had put the whole thing together. That seemed right to me. There was a way in which this whole thing was one huge comic strip where whatever role any of us assumed had its place — humor, adventure, romance, pathos — something clearly drawn that could be played out across the course of years, something one could depend on, something that, one way or another, was part of all our lives.

There was nothing more to say. I introduced myself and held out my hand to him. He held it a long time.

One day and night on the trail was all it took to make us feel the drive as a way of life. By the following morning it seemed as if we had been travelling like this forever. How quickly one gets into routine, providing it is the right routine, the routine natural to one's temperament and one's soul. It suited me — walking across camp in the early mornings, watching the camp wake, a few horses being exercised in the soft mist, dry dust rising up to mingle with mist. A cowboy walking down the camp road, his long duster sweeping back behind him, appears like a vision out of the mist. The sounds from the chuck wagon tent lure him in. The earliest risers sit on bales of hay outside the tent, mugs of steaming coffee in their hands against the early morning cold. Sun filters through mist, through dust. The quick heat of day spreads over the camp, moving now, with tents being razed, wagons loaded, corrals broken down to be piled on the flatbed truck that will take them to the next camp. Horses whinny to one another. A man, seated on the edge of time, plays a harmonica. It is full day, and the train is on the trail. Thousands of horses are on the trail. The rolling sagebrush country is alive with riders and horses and cattle and wagons and a hundred years of dreams. This dream we are having is no different from the early dreams. We are no different from the early dreamers. No matter who tells us otherwise.

When, at the very end, the routine changed, all of life changed. On the last night, at camp not far from Billings — Montana's largest city — the camp was opened to people not on the Drive. They came by the thousands to have a piece of it, and to watch the big country/western show planned as a finale. The headlights of cars from Billings and probably half the other towns in Montana formed a chain that ran for miles, as far out along the road as you could see. These crowds would not see the real life of the Drive. Their appearance cancelled it. The line of headlights cancelled it. The rows of parked vehicles, the big stage with its spotlights and loudspeakers, the aura of fairgrounds cancelled it. You couldn't blame the visitors for wanting in. And you couldn't blame the drive organizers for having planned the event. After all, the drive was for Montana, not just for the few thousand people who had participated the whole way. The few thousand people were for Montana too. It was just that we were somehow surprised by being thrust so adamantly into the present. It was as if we were blinded by the lights so that all that had been our lives for the days of the Drive faded into some darkness where we could not see. We knew the Drive would end. Yet its ending caught us off guard. Many of us stayed to ourselves, back, away from the lights, clinging to the last to the time that was ours. But you cannot keep endings from happening. They happen. If you cling, you cling to what is already gone.

In the early morning, horses, riders, and wagons lined up for the parade into Billings, the grand finale. In a sense though, we had already had our ending, already left the days of the Drive, the intensity of history. The Cowboy stood near the gate to the road, holding out his hand to those who passed. "Thanks for coming," he said and smiled, the warmth of his smile making each person feel as if he or she, personally, had been of utmost importance to the Drive, to The Cowboy, to the history of Montana. "Thanks for coming," he said to me, as he held my hand, again, a little too long. Not long enough. I rode on through the gate next to Jan.

It was a short ride to town, where spectators, standing on curbs, on vehicles, on top of trailers, on top of roofs, lined the route. They shouted their greetings, their triumph. Signs in shop windows, hoisted onto roofs, draped across vehicles welcomed us, and we rode in as if it were a triumph; as if we had been coming a long time, across a great distance.

For me, it was a great distance. I had ridden fear two thousand miles across America in order to come to this place where I could ride Tess into Billings. It had taken me more than forty years to do it. It was worth every mile, every minute of the time. After all, I was heading into the sunset all the way.

Stopping near the stockyards, we sat on our horses and watched the cowboys bring the herd in, keeping them within the confines of the roadway. They came like a river, a river of Longhorns, relentless and without end. They, too, had come a long way, ushered in to the end of the twentieth century after a hundred years coming across the plains. The cowboys had not changed in all that time. The cattle had not changed. We had not changed. Billings had changed. The road was paved, and people who lived there had cars and trucks and television sets, and special arrangements had to be made to close the streets so the cattle and wagons and riders could come through. We stood and watched, our watching our good-bye to the huge beautiful fantasy the Drive had been. The wagons, the camps, the horses, the cowboys, The Cowboy, the poets, the dust — all a dream, all gone now, all eternally present. In ending, the dream became fuller than ever. What endings do is let you know the thing itself was possible.

With the last of the cattle past, traffic resumed on the street. We turned and rode back out to camp, where the horse trailer would pick up the horses. We rode with the traffic, to the side of the road. The road was no longer ours. We had become peripheral. We stopped for red lights. We crossed the parade route and rode up the country road back to camp. There were other riders along with us and some going the opposite direction. An occasional vehicle passed on the country road. The Drive was over. I had done it. I had not fallen off my horse. I had forgotten I was afraid. I had entered that childhood my father gave me.

Nevada

Last week I was in a Las Vegas High School with chain-link fence from cement to ceiling. Above that barbed wire. An armed guard welcomed me, gave me my badge (which I had to surrender to leave the campus), and I was escorted to the library for a reading. Not one student had ever seen a poet, not one. Few, if any, knew there were poets like Gary Soto or Lucille Clifton writing about their lives — in language that moved them to tears. But they do now, and they will not forget the moment they learned that poetry is about real things like cancer and birth and love at twelve years old. They knew the New England fence of Frost, but they did not know it was part of their lives like the fence that surrounded their school.

SHAUN T. GRIFFIN

Shaun T. Griffin

Madonna in Traffic

Your eyes, shunted away in dark
amniotic fluid, what do you see
staring onto Boulder Highway,
mother straddling the island with cars
slipping either side of her waist,
what face do you look upon
stringing headlight to tail with the
unknown family at the intersection?

Her sign is finger-painted with magenta
letters but you cannot read the words
Hungry. Pregnant. Need Work. Help Please.
You must not know her ringless stranger
as she coughs the cardboard high into the air
then stills your limbs, swinging into the flesh
you now gather. For seven months
you have trailed jobs to cities hot and broken

and once there, the old streets and soda crackers
came easy but inside the cotton dress
that blows toward Lake Mead, you wonder
if the next exit will find the hot meal
promised in long-ago Kansas, or shots
mother missed hitching out here. This road
has grown like a child and nothing, not traffic,
not plain people will shade the world outside

but this small face that crowds her skin,
this membrane she touches
with stomach to sign may as well be
her breathing room where it's calm and smooth

and that's how you feed the fetal drum
looking out on this six-lane highway
with all Las Vegas glowing in the mirror
of every timid glance driving home from work.

Stephen Shu-Ning Liu

Midnight Cries

For Chi Ch'ing

It's not time to go, Chi Ch'ing, my sister. Tell me about
the teetering swallows the kite-tattooed March sky
the first fireflies the owl's hooting behind the house
the jasmine-picking at dawn and all the village cocks
the Dragon Boats in May the cake-breaking in August
the Broom-Tail Star the jade towers in Mom's moon
the bamboo stilts the handkerchief-dropping by the pond
the September hiking the temple bells in evening mist
the orchard teeming with oranges and plums and grapes
the reapers' loud singing the stout carps from the river
the word-march games after supper Dad's sudden laughter
the fox-spirit tales Grandma's heavy walks on the stairway
the shouting at the snowfall the New Year's Eve fireworks
the candle-lit family shrine Grandpa's earnest smile
and his murmuring blessings his old sayings his poems . . .

Preserve yourself in these memories and trust Heaven that
we may meet again but don't sigh don't turn away
the moon's down the woodland's dark stay awhile I would
not wake to hear the cannons ah my sister let me not see
the Pacific reversing its flows in grief stay ah Chi Ch'ing
it's not time to go the moon's down the woodland's dark . . .

Stephen Shu-Ning Liu

A Mid-July Invitation

The energy crisis is over. Lights are back on the Strip.
Name the place: Sahara, Caesar's Palace, Casino de Paris.
This way, please. Come, my people; drink on the house.
You, Great-grandpa, dice-thrower from Sichuan, casting away
one hundred acres of our land overnight, be of good cheer,
this satchel of gold will last you a long while;
and you, Uncle Lu, widower and recluse of Fu Ling, accost
this Dixie belle, dare what you've never dared before:
this bottle will make you bold; and you, Da Shing, you
longed for a journey, you read by midnight lamps and drained
your blood between Confucius' pages and Newton's first law
of motion. Don't despair, little brother. I'll see you
enter a college this fall. And you, ah Shu Ying, how your
windows framed those lonely mountains. How winter light cast
pallor on your skin and bones. How you withered in spring wind.
Like our lily pond, your eyes had never reflected a stranger's
face. Come to the party, my sister. I'll teach you to dance.

Let me hear your moans, let me feel your bony hand.
Come, I know you all. Come, away from the Yellow Springs.
It's mid-July: clouds cross the moon, the earth shudders,
and the mice must not catch you sleeping under the wormwood.

Gailmarie Pahmeier

Sometimes Our Gifts Are Small and Fast

Emma learned to drive at eighteen —
sometimes schooled by country boys in denim jackets
down endless dirt roads going nowhere but away,
sometimes taught by college boys in sweaters and long cars —
but always by boys whose passion
far outdistanced their patience.

Learning to drive meant learning to live.
Tall plastic glass of sugared tea
held snug between her legs,
radio full of Peggy Lee, weather reports, baseball.
Seventy miles an hour and an afternoon
brought thoughts of him, their car.

Her father lies on his back, knees up,
arms extended. Emma wants to go
downtown, wants to drive to the river,
ride around, watch some lights.
She sits on his knees, takes his left hand
as steering wheel, his right as stick shift.
Her father makes the engine sound, eyes closed.
Emma drives hard, all her windows down.
When her mother calls for dinner, tires squeal.
His legs open — a telephone pole or highway divider —
and Emma crashes into her father's embrace.
She is seven and she knows this road.

Now an atlas away from that living room,
she drives and drives faster
to meet a young man whose hands are large.
He promises to hold her, keep her safe and full and free.
He doesn't know how little she needs.
Emma's already got a car, a memory, and a place to go.

Gailmarie Pahmeier

Telephone Call

When Emma heard him say he didn't love her,
she thought of spring,
she thought of a spring without baseball,
what it would be like if boys who lived in towns
with names like Idabel, Osceola, or Tonopah
held smooth round rocks in their hands
without knowing how such a small dream
can send a boy to a city
of lights and noise and grateful women,
or what it would be like if the girls
who loved them never knew the hard bleachers,
or the anxious taste of chewed pencils,
never kissed a boy who left the dust
from a slide on their skin,
or what it would be like if fathers never knew
how old they were because their arms
didn't weaken, their shoulders, backs never slipped,
their sons earned pride or sadness or shame
in some less simple way,
or what it would be like if mothers
didn't stand at kitchen windows and see
their boys learn that women watch,
that a good woman will ride
all the way across the state
with a game on and never
ask for music.
When Emma heard him say he didn't love her,
she thought of dresses she had never worn.

Kirk Robertson

Music

For Valerie & for Jack Fulton

Dave saved up his money and bought a bar. He liked classical music, and since the bar was in the middle of the Great Basin night miles from the likelihood to hear any such thing, he decided what the hell, called it the Mozart Club. He really couldn't remember whether it was Chopin, Satie, Mozart, or Mendelssohn that had moved him so, but he like the sound of Mozart. He painted a big skeleton on the side of the bar emblazoned with the legend This Guy Drank Water. A lot of local folks thought that was pretty funny and began to call the watering hole home.

Every month or so Dave and this painter friend of his would make the daylong drive to Reno on a supply run. They were at the Santa Fe and had consumed way too many picóns and that great Friday night Basque steak dinner. They were standing around the bar drinking Winnemucca coffees, debating whether they should head back or not, and if they did who, given all the picóns, was the most qualified to drive, when she walked in.

She was the most drop-dead beautiful woman you'd ever seen. She could have been northern Italian or English or Irish, what with that stunning mane of red hair and those amazing legs. But she was, in fact, Austrian. After a quick look around she walked to the end of the bar and sat on a stool, crossing her legs high. Dave, and everyone else in the bar, was speechless. She had silenced that rowdy Friday night crowd just by walking in like the way, sometimes, the sun going down can stop a wind that's been howling all day across the desert's face.

Dave watched his heart tumble out of his chest and flop around on the bar like some fish sensing that it was, after all, the seventh year of a drought and this just might be it.

"Would you like a drink?" he suddenly blurted out.

Their eyes locked and that was it. They spent the next three hours drinking at a small table in the back. Dave kept feeding her small slices of lime from the palm of his hand, and she'd laugh, oh how she'd laugh. She'd get up every so often to go and call someone, and Dave would watch her walk to the phone and back, wondering, wondering. . . . He even reached under the table once and squeezed her leg, thinking, oh my God, what a stupid thing to do, now she'll walk out, and I'll never see her again.

But she stayed and talked and drank, and they both felt some kind of furnace burning within them like never before until, finally, she said, "I have to go. My brother's coming to pick me up."

She left with her brother. Dave left with his painter friend, and they all ended up standing in the parking lot, Dave and her just staring at each other, neither wanting to break the connection. "Jeezus Christ, Dave," the painter said. "Put your goddamn eyes back in your head and open the goddamn door."

Who's to say what happened next or how it happened, but Dave hung around until he saw her again, and that's all it took. A done deal. Never a question. She came back to the Mozart Club with him. That's when the music really began. And from then on everyone kept commenting on how amazing it all was, how right it all seemed, how good they looked together, how glad they were for Dave.

This is it, Dave thought. At last. And he began to think of waltzing toward the millennium on a sea of melodious light. But then there's always life. It goes on, as they say. And it does. But it also can just suddenly stop.

He went down to the bar one day and came home to find her gone. No note. No word. Nothing. Her clothes, her shoes, everything but her still there. Dave looked and looked, went back up to Reno, but nothing. Not a trace. No one even knew her.

It was as if she had never existed, as if it had all never happened. But Dave knew it had, and he tried to forget but couldn't because he didn't really want to. He never did look at another woman, and he drank more than a bit, and it was worse than fightin' the weather, all that thinkin' about it, wonderin' what had happened, why there were all these years of nights they might have been together but weren't.

It was thirty years later, almost to the day, when this gorgeous redhead walked into the Mozart Club. Everyone was stumblin' over themselves, hittin' on her, trying to buy her a drink, everyone, that is, but Dave, who just sat at the end of the bar nursing his drink. But she wasn't interested in all the attention and wanted only one thing.

"Is there anyone here named Dave?" she asked.

"Down there, end of the bar," Dave's painter friend said.

She walked down to the end of the bar, everyone watching her every move. "Dave?" she asked.

"Yeah?" he said, looking up from his drink, his bloodshot blues meeting her amber ones. "Whatya want?"

"I'm your daughter," she said.

And so the story was told. How her mother was from a very wealthy Austrian family; how she had come to the States on vacation with her brother; how her mother had walked into a bar in Reno one Friday night and fallen head over heels in love with the piercing blue eyes of a guy named Dave who owned a bar; how her grandmother had disowned her mother for having the audacity to do that; how after that it didn't seem to matter until her grandmother fell ill and wanted her daughter back home before she died; how her grandmother had sent her son back to the States to kidnap her daughter; how her mother was in a car accident and they were able to save the baby, but not her; how her grandmother recovered, raised her, and never mentioned any of it; how her uncle told her all about it only after her grandmother finally died.

Gary Short

Wovoka

For Carole Maso & Duane Slick

At his grave I find offerings —
a horseshoe, some oddly shaped blue pebbles,
& the thin bones & skull of a crow.

The horseshoe will sink into
its own impression, settle finally
into the dirt until only the idea
of the horseshoe will remain.

A living crow
is perched on a moon-colored stone.
It lifts, a shadow unfolding
over seven bleached hills of dust
toward Walker River. The bird's wings
are black prisms.

My fingers worry the blue pebbles
worn smooth by the affection of water, worn down
to the river's old truth.
I let the pebbles drop as measures

at the grave of Wovoka,
who dreamed the Ghost Dance & believed
if his people danced long & hard enough
the dead would live again.

When men from other tribes came to him,
they asked for proof of his vision.
Wovoka took off his hat

& invited them to look inside it.
Some saw only darkness
inside an empty hat, but some saw
the whole spirit world.

I stand & turn
in the four directions of this world,
as though purpose
supposes what ought to be seen.
One man's dream in the bowl of a hat.

The vision I want to see is in the distance
that does not end.
I have come to haunt the dead.

Gary Short

One Summer

Mother returns from the orchard.
She's made a basket of her blue
& white checked apron
full of apples streaked with color
like the dusk sky, & sweet.
Each with a short stem
to twist & make a wish on
the first letter of a girl's name.

A wish. The girl is from the city,
visiting her aunt & uncle down the road.
On hot days we float a makeshift raft,
made of lashed boards,
out to the middle of the lake.
Late July her shoulders ache with sunburn.
I rub lotion into her peeling skin
& move close to let my lips graze her neck.
She'll be going home soon.

On a muggy evening my father gets drunk
& staggers past the hissy geese
to feed the two pigs.
He throws them eggshells, rinds of melon,
curled & rusted apple skins.
The pigs grow huge with our refuse.
They will be slaughtered in September.
My father strokes their pink ears. He tells them,
"You're the only ones who understand."

I am sixteen.
I don't understand

anything. The taste of the girl's kisses
are sweet & deep but not like apples.
In the backseat
under a leaf of moon,
she takes my hand
to her belly & makes me trace
the scar of the C-section
where seven months before
the boy was slipped out — one first & last look
at the baby, shining with birth-slick,
before they took him away.

New Mexico

As for anecdotes about TumbleWords experiences, two incidents come to mind: The first occurred at Humphrey House, a group home for troubled teens in Hobbs, New Mexico. When I arrived, a caseworker unlocked the heavy front door and invited me in. After I stepped inside, she double-locked the door behind me. I tightened my grip on my manuscripts and followed her to a common area where more than a dozen students waited. Some of these teens, I'd been told, were runaways and orphans, victims of abuse and abandonment. Several had had brushes with the law. Suddenly I lost confidence in my presentation. Reading and writing fiction seemed like such a luxury when taken in the context of these troubled young lives. I felt embarrassed to have spent so much time imagining plots and characters while these children had been forced to face the more basic problems of shelter, food, and safety. What could I say to them?

"What do you like to read?" I asked at last.

"Science fiction," one boy answered.

"Mysteries," said another.

And soon we were into a lively discussion. Everyone talked about their favorite books and authors. After some minutes, there was a lull in the discussion, and a young girl said, "I like fiction because it teaches me about life."

Her quiet statement stopped me. "Tell me what you mean," I said.

She squirmed in her chair. "When I read a story, I get inside the character and see how she solves her problems. Sometimes it helps with my own problems."

I took a long breath and relaxed for the first time since I had arrived. "It's wonderful you understand that," I said. "You're absolutely right."

The tables had turned. I wanted to teach these kids something important about fiction. But now I had become the student, and the teacher was a young girl who taught me what I had forgotten — that fiction teaches us the lessons of life.

The second incident occurred in Shiprock, New Mexico, where I read excerpts from my newspaper columns, "Reflections from a Country Store." The columns tell about my life as a small-town storekeeper, and I'm continually astonished that readers find my ordinary life interesting.

After the reading, a Navaho woman told me she would like to write about her ordinary life too. "Do it," I said. "Some people would think your life on the Navaho reservation is terribly interesting — maybe even exotic."

"Oh no," she said with a wry smile. "My life is almost as boring as yours, but you've shown me how to write about it anyway."

— JEAN BLACKMON

Heather Ahtone

Cry

in a quiet way i made it to the bathroom
no   it was not the movie
but the dark isolation
that crept in after the credits   before the lights came up
that prevented the cushions from offering comfort
that silenced my outrage at the story of my nonhistory
that caught my throat when the woman was silenced
that closed my eyes when the child was touched
where no child should be touched
how no child should be touched
in the movie i paid six dollars to enjoy
in the company of a man i couldn't love
watching the reels of film rotate in my head
around the screen to the corner store and the twelve-year-old
standing in a tight gold dress and heels too high for me
earning an existence worthy of no one
No One
they called her when money spoke their desires
to her innocent ears and profane mouth kissing a leather
wallet of testicle tissue in his back front pocket
pulling her newborn hair with rotted teeth he smiles a tequila-stained not smile
he kicks her out of black beat-up bmw and rolls on around the corner
to the theater and we hold hands
as the credits roll and the lights come up

Heather Ahtone

Two Eagles

My uncle said he saw the eagles — two — fly overhead as he prayed to the
   Creator. I
didn't see them — but then I wasn't looking up. I could only see the blood
   tracing
stains on the breasts of the dancers — eyes closed to the sun. My hands
   trembled
against the stillness of my thousand-year-old will passed down by the ghosts of
my ancestors to this moment — two years ago.

My urbanized eyes — so used to the bloodshed common in the city of angels —
begged me to turn away. But were held in place by a spirit — surfacing at the
   call
of the drum. Blood pulsating from pride kept rhythm with the left step.
Dancers whistled their visions to a sky listening with a clear face.

The holy man approached — I wanted him to stop — recognize me from a battle
fought before the white men came. Holding my head high with soft eyes, I
watched him pass by without a glance. My eyes dropped unable to look at the
dancers with prayers on their lips. Prayers for their families and the children
waiting for birth. Prayers for the elders who could no longer dance for
themselves. I raised my eyes to the sun and offered a prayer. I found myself
speaking openly with a voice I did not recognize as my own.

I looked in time to see the ropes snap and my uncle fall to the ground. A breath
escaped as a rush of humility engulfed me. I stepped away from the arbor and
walked to the nearby field of sage. These were my people and I was one
   learning
to speak to our Creator for the first time. I looked on the horizon with fresh
eyes and a fresh spirit and there they were — two eagles — dancing.

Leon Autrey

Young Banker

It was late morning,
when this young banker drove up,
We welcomed him in
to have a cup.

He had styled hair,
his fingernails were clean,
his face was oily,
his dress shirt was green.

He wore odd-cut britches,
with a crease down the front.
rings on his fingers
and his eyes were sunk.

He said, "I've come to count your cattle
and observe the range.
You need more cash flow,
The bank's made a change."

My wife cooked lunch,
biscuits, gravy and meat.
He said fresh fruits and veggies
was all he would eat.

I shrugged my shoulders,
and replied, "Okay.
But it could turn into
a very long day."

We went to the horse corral.
I caught him Old Soap
just hoping
that Soap wouldn't goat.

As we were riding off,
I heard this bean sound.
I looked back,
this banker's on the ground.

He had reached down,
on Old Soap's right side.
"My foot wouldn't go in the stirrup,"
he cried.

His styled hair
looked really sad,
What hung on the fence
sure looked bad.

When we got 'im to the house,
it started to rain.
The canyons got up,
He's having great pain.

The roads all washed out,
He had to stay.
For four days, he had to live,
a brand-new way.

For two days,
this young banker wouldn't eat.
The third day he pigged out
on BISCUITS, GRAVY AND MEAT.

Jean Blackmon

Rescue

On Saturday morning Lester sat with his foot in his lap, clipping his toenails. He scowled at Winnie's wooden sign that lay on the coffee table. It read Historic Adobe House. Tours $1.00. Lester figured his wife, who now called herself "Winn," was having a midlife crisis. She was entitled to some turmoil in her forty-eighth year, but her passion for business was getting out of hand. To Lester, parading tourists through their home at a dollar a head was proof positive that Winnie had gone haywire.

Already Lester had given up his den. He'd been sucked out of it like a spider down a drainpipe. Before he knew he was in trouble, he was somewhere else — banished to the back of the big old kitchen where he sat now, looking into the gallery, his former den. He hoped no customers would arrive before Winnie finished her shower. If they did, they could watch him trim toenails. He switched feet and dropped clippings into a tidy pile on the coffee table.

Near as he could pinpoint, Winnie's crisis started after Tom, their youngest, joined the army. That's when Winnie started making doodads. She carved pot-bellied wooden cowboys, roadrunners, and mustachioed prospectors. Later she made a sign to hang outside the den door that said Winn's Gallery. Come In.

Situated as they were on the interstate next to Lucky's tourist shop, motorists (strangers!) wandered through Lester's den. They'd admire the old adobe house Lester's great-grandfather had built, then buy a knickknack and be gone.

One night when tourists interrupted a Broncos game, Lester asked a teenager in lizard boots to kindly lift the other end of the couch, and the two of them moved Lester's couch, TV, and six-pack to the back corner of the kitchen.

When the tourists drove away leaving nineteen dollars in the till, Lester had lost ground, surrendered real estate, vacated his den. Without a kiss good-bye, he was exiled to new territory.

"Thank you, honey," Winnie said. "Running a business makes me feel like I'm finally doing something important."

Lester couldn't believe it. She raised three sons. Wasn't that important? And what about spending thirty years as wife to a man who tended the plumbing and septic needs of an entire county? Wasn't that important?

In the weeks that followed, Winnie moved the refrigerator into the den and increased inventory to include canned pop, string cheese, and Saran-wrapped sandwiches. A hairsprayed ladies' man who worked Interstate 40 delivered chips and beef jerky. For an introductory offer, he brought Godiva chocolates that sat in a dish on the coffee table. Lester popped one into his mouth. Godiva? What was this guy selling? Lester should warn Winnie about guys like that.

In fact, Lester should warn her about this whole business. He didn't want strangers traipsing through. But he'd discuss it later. Today he had to pump Hansen's septic tank.

The phone rang.

"Hello."

"Is Winn handy?" It was the lacquer-head salesman who had brought chocolates then set a spinner rack of beef jerky where Lester's couch had been.

"No." Lester's voice cracked.

"This is Buck from Statewide. I'm at the Holiday, room 218. We have a new line of cracker snacks. If she'll give me a jingle, I'll share the prices with her."

Salesman jargon. Winnie should give this guy a "jingle" so they could "share" the price of cracker snacks? Lester scribbled the phone number, wadded it into his pocket, and hung up.

Winnie came in wearing Lester's bathrobe, her head wrapped in a brown towel, the color of her hair before it turned grey.

"Who was on the phone?"

"The jerky salesman," Lester said with a slight curl of his lip.

Winnie kissed Lester's thinning hair.

He picked up the sign offering house tours. "Don't do this," he said.

Winnie massaged his neck. "Well, Lester, it's only for daytime when you're working."

The massage felt wonderful.

"Who'd want to see this old house anyway?"

"Lots of folks, Lester. Here, eat a chocolate before I give them to customers." She nudged the candy toward him. "Folks deserve to see an authentic old adobe."

Wasn't that just like Winnie? Thinking she owed something to strangers. Lester scooped the little heap of toenails into his palm. He wanted to sprinkle them over the chocolates, a topping for customers, but Winnie held out her hand. He gave her his toenails, and she dropped them in the trash.

Lester pulled on socks and boots. "I'm headed to Hansen's. Watch out for this jerky guy." He tossed her the message. "Give him a jingle."

The ride to Hansen's was long. Lester's pump truck has to be babied uphill, and all the way Lester stewed. Forty-eight was tough, he knew. He'd been there. He'd had a crisis of his own with the blonde cashier at the Conoco station. Winnie never suspected anything. The cashier never suspected anything either because Lester's hormonal turmoil occurred entirely within his own imagination. Inside there had broiled a lusty cauldron worthy of a teenager, but outside, his fling consisted of daily stops to buy peanuts. He leaned against the 10w-30 motor oil, munched nuts, and spun yarns about the hot parties and fast cars of his youth.

The miniskirted cashier perched on a stool crossing and recrossing her legs. But Lester controlled himself. If that was his midlife crisis, it hadn't bothered anyone. He'd like to say the same for Winnie.

When Lester stopped at Hansen's, a rotund old setter lumbered out to meet him. The dog stopped while Lester scratched his ears; then, like a gourmet whiffing a banquet, he waddled on to sniff the truck.

Joe Hansen emerged from the house. "Hi," he said. "Red hasn't moved that fast since last time you came."

Lester put on gloves and stretched the hose toward the septic tank. Red led the way. Lester and Joe lifted off the concrete lid exposing a hole eighteen inches wide. The odor of raw sewage rose up like a nightmare.

Both men backed away.

Red bounced around the hole like a puppy, salivating, whining, sniffing closer, backing up. Finally he dropped to his stomach and looked from Joe to Lester and back again, his tail wagging, his lip quivering.

Lester laughed. "Old Red sure knows how to smell the roses." He dropped the hose into the tank and went to turn on the pump.

When he came back Red was scrambling in the dirt for a foothold. He had stepped too close, and before Lester reached him, Red tumbled into the septic tank. He came up blinded with muck and swimming for his life. Joe was nowhere in sight.

Lester couldn't grab Red because the dog, in his panic, paddled away from the hole.

Lester ran to turn off the pump. He heard Red swimming, probably holding his head in six inches of air space between the sludge and the top of the tank. Lester laid across the opening and reached for the dog. He dipped his hand into the slime, searching.

"Here, boy," he called, gasping through the stench. "Here, boy."

Then he yelled for Joe. "Where the hell are you, Joe? Get out here." All he heard was the slap, slap, slap of the old dog swimming.

Then Lester had him — a good grip on Red's collar, and the dog's head popped up like a bull's-eye.

Holding the collar, Lester braced his feet against the opposite side of the hole. He laid back and dragged Red out on top of him. Though heavy, Red skidded along Lester's thighs like he'd been greased. When he reached Lester's midsection, Red wiggled like a pig in a wallow, gained a foothold, and shook himself.

Joe came out of the house carrying two beers. "The phone rang," he said. "Have a beer."

The men hosed Red down, and the old dog fell asleep on the porch.

Driving home, Lester chuckled. He was a clean man, finicky even, for a guy in his business. But here he sat, filthy, driving with the window open just to stand himself. He lifted his nose and sniffed, imitating Old Red, then closed his window, took a long, deep, satisfying breath, and laughed.

When Lester arrived home he parked out back. He stepped onto the enclosed porch and undressed, dropping his rank clothing outside the door. Naked, he entered the kitchen and headed for the shower. The odor hung around him like a dark cloud, but he felt lighthearted. He wanted to tell Winnie about Red.

Then strange voices stopped him short. He froze in the hallway to listen. Winnie was leading a tour. He peered around the corner and saw two women studying the grooves along the bedroom windowsill where Lester's great-grandfather had sighted his gun during Indian raids. Lester dashed back through the kitchen to the porch and pulled on his dirty jeans. Lord have mercy, wouldn't that have been a tour?

The three women moved into the kitchen, and Lester peeked around the doorjamb. The strangers were older than Winnie. One wore a silky red jumpsuit, and the other, a shorter woman, sported a pink Day-Glo sun hat.

The tall one said, "When my kids left, I travelled to keep from rattling around an empty house."

"Well, Lester's here," Winnie said. "But he's got his job and all."

The woman nodded, all sympathy. "Well, it's different for men," the tall one said.

Lester stiffened. He never understood how Winnie could get so personal with absolute strangers.

When the women settled around the kitchen table, he rolled his eyes. What now? A barefoot trek through stickers to the side door didn't appeal to him. Neither did walking through polite company wearing the Hansen sewage. He'd sooner walk through naked.

"I was so lonesome," Winnie said, "I almost hung a sign saying Free coffee. Come in."

Lester heard the catch in her voice that signalled tears. She was lonesome? Why didn't she tell *him*? It would have done more good than telling some stranger off Route 40. Why, he felt lonesome the whole time he was at the Conoco, the whole time she was carving cowboys.

"I'll get ice for your soda," Winnie said.

"I'll get it," Lester said, surprising himself, stepping through the door. Then he was through the kitchen and into the den opening the refrigerator. He returned with two hands full of ice.

"Lester, when did you get home?" Winnie stepped between him and her guests, but he dodged and held out a handful of ice to each woman.

"No thanks," said the tall one, covering her drink with a well-manicured hand.

"None for me," said the short one, raising a napkin to her nose.

"Lester, you're filthy. Where's your shirt?" Winnie was chuckling now, Lester knew by the tuck in her cheek. Her amusement inspired him. He dropped the ice into the sink.

"I'm Lester," he said, wiping wet hands on his jeans. If one of the women had offered a hand to shake, he would have kissed it.

"Did Winnie offer you chocolates?" He held out the candy dish. They declined, so he pulled up a chair and sat down.

"I've had a hard day pulling an old dog out of a septic tank," he said. "The dog is fine. The problem is, I hate to wear these clothes into the bedroom. So I'm stepping out that door," he pointed, "and taking off my pants. Then I'll walk through naked. You're welcome to stay, but it'll cost a dollar."

He winked at Winnie. "I'm kidding about the dollar," he said. "But I'm dead serious when I say I promise to close my eyes in order to protect your modesty." Lester stood, lifted an imaginary hat, and bowed.

The women laughed, clutched their purses, and moved toward the gallery.

"I'll pay a dollar," said the woman in the Day-Glo hat. But to Lester's relief, she didn't. When he walked through, there was only Winnie, elbows on the table, chin in her hands, smiling.

Arsenio Córdova

The Captives

"Your son will remain a captive as long as my son is a captive." With those words Josefa Martinez removed the statue of the Child Jesus from a Catholic church in the Taos Valley (Arroyo Seco).

It was a long trek to the mountains and to the waterfall known to the villagers as El Salto, but Josefa had to hurry before anyone would see her or became suspicious or discover that the statue was missing.

Taking the infant Jesus was an act of desperation, an effort to force a miracle by the Almighty.

Josefa's son Manuel, a few months earlier, had been taken captive by the Mescalero Apaches in the Mora Valley. Josefa suffered a breakdown, and her husband, Julian, in an effort to save her sanity, decided to move his family to the Taos Valley. With the couple came their two daughters, Josefita and Maria de las Nieves.

Josefa knew that she had completely ignored her husband and two daughters since the abduction.

Manuel de Atocha Martinez, as her son was named, was her pride and joy. On that fateful day in August 1867, Manuel, age seven, and another child, Bernardino, were playing in the field by the house. The quiet of the day was broken only by the occasional bleating of the family sheep, which Manuel and Bernardino were watching.

Before the two boys realized it, they were surrounded by a band of Indians and taken captive. The Mescalero Apaches had been known to take captives and raid homesteads in all these northern New Mexico communities. By the time Julian and Josefa realized what had happened to their son, the Indians and the children were gone.

Now, as she worked her way up to El Salto, Josefa blamed herself for not taking better care for the safety of her son. Why did she allow him to wander off so far from the house?

At least she knew he wasn't dead. There was hope, and now, if the Blessed Mother listened to her prayers, Manuel would be returned.

The path to El Salto got a little steeper as she approached the clifflike formation where water ran abundantly. There, on a side of the cliff, she saw a small opening. There is where she would place the statue! Careful not to forget the spot, she dug a bit in order to make the child Jesus fit comfortably. "I must remember the exact spot so that I might retrieve my Child Jesus when Manuel returns." Covering her tracks, Josefa returned to her home, confident that it would only be a matter of time before Manuel returned safely.

Arsenio Córdova

Raíces

Órale, ese ¿ Que pasó?
Te fuiste al college
Y volviste talking English only.

Don't forget where you came from *ese!*
Tu cultura y tradición run in your blood.
You can forget about them.
Pero la sangre India corre en tus venas.

Tú eres La Raza nueva, ese,
Hispano, Mejicano, Mestizo, Chicano, Indio.
La nueva España te produjo.
You are a beautiful race.
Be proud, walk tall,
For you are the creation of a new world.

Oye, Raza, canta tu canción,
Dádsela a tus hijos.
Díles de tus antepasados
Y de su historia.

Oh, by the way *ese,*
The word is *atole,*
Not *Tolo.*

Larry Goodell

Thatsapoem

How do you write a poem. Poem on a napkin.
Think about the size of the paper you're writing on.
If you're doing it in your brain only, there's no limit to
      the length of the line you're going for
But on this here napkin they gave me at the Thatsaburger
I've got about 5 inches from left to right.
5 inches to write what my brain thinks &
      translates from brain languages into American English
         and if my brain thots keep going in a long
            sentence I've got to wrap the writing of it
               back to the left margin, indenting
                  each time so I have a stepped
                     stack of words, diagonal
                        in until I've just
                          about run out of
                             space!

So I've got to wonder if this is a poem or not
What would any other language have for the word *poem*
or would there be no word at all in some tongues
for *poem!*
And *then* how would you write one: I guess you
      wdnt bother.
So why write a whatever it is.
      Well
I've got this napkin and I've got this Bic Micro Metal
      ballpoint pen
And I've been called a poet for so damn long
I don't know what else to do in a situation like this.

I've finished my ham, egg, cheese on whole wheat toast
      sandwich,

2nd napkin!
By the way if you write on a napkin, put another napkin
         under it because the ink bleeds through the one
         you're writing on.
And I've finished a couple cups of coffee, refills free!
Got a little container of milk so I can have that in my coffee
instead of that damned nondairy creamer.

And I must say two thirds the way through my breakfast sandwich
it was so good and the light was so clear
and the place seemed so open & spacious with its
         blue & white tile floors
         and the Navajo guys & gals & that little baby
         were all so enjoying their breakfast
         the infant was just sleeping
that somehow I felt like I was in heaven.
How could there be any more in life than
sitting here in perfect contentment.
But what is perfect
and is there any such thing as heaven & can it be attained
right here in this corner booth at the Thatsaburger
in Shiprock New Mexico.
If you want to know the truth the astounding presence
         of that gigantic volcanic core spectacular rock
         Shiprock, *rock-with-wings,*
         is so present in my thots tho I can't see it directly
         from where I sit
that I must get up: it is so overwhelmingly there.
I want to see it.
Is there perfection, is there any kind of heaven.
There is a kind of perfection, there is a kind of heaven.
I just experienced it.

3rd & final napkin!
But is there a poem. What is this thing.
Why did I write it.
         Well

maybe it's just a letter
like my Grandma Goodell used to write
to all her brothers & sisters
maybe it's just a way to bridge
the gap from me to you.

Kendall McCook

Comin' Home

Antioch, Moses, Clapham, Sedan, Seneca, Grenville, Mount Dora, Folsom, Otto . . . Deserted . . . Abandoned . . . Hidden under mounds of blown dust. Sound the names aloud and you give breath to the dead places. Lonely, faded red gasoline pumps lean into the dry wing, hunched over the cracked glass and concrete slabs, like the bent old men in Clayton who teeter on wooden canes and remember. In the dying towns, the voices rattle against the quiet. The strong men are gone, and the walls they raised have fallen.

In the empty hotels, where the railroad once streamed its life's blood, the voices now come in the dark. They sit at the tables and shout with forlorn spirits filling the night with dreams that will end with the day, the light burning away the cold shadows.

In the morning, it is still. Outside, the highway carries cars that hurry by. On the rails, the long trains roll on, but they do not stop here. There are no rough men stepping down to gather before the high dinner table, and the old hotel stares with paneless eyes.

Through the main streets always travels the railroad; the steel runners pierced the land, and on their shoulders the people rode, huddling in family-chartered boxcars, bringing themselves to this new land where they would live out their lives. Corroded tracks stretch in broken lines to cross the pastures that separate this apparition from the next ones twenty miles down the line.

These dust-piled community graveyards were towns once. Thirty, forty years in the past, there were people — wives, husbands, their children, lives lived, forgotten. Soapweed and thistle, brown-stemmed buffalo grass, packed swells of the soil that buried them, cover the humps and depressions of fools' foundations.

Seneca has a post office. Just off the highway. Old man Barton keeps the flag hoisted from his combination grocery store and mail station. It is a gray, two-room building, the sole utilitarian remains of the Seneca community. The unwaxed wooden floor allows its dust to be shifted when an occasional customer sees fit to intrude. On the shelves, unpainted and wobbly, Barton has arranged various unperishables for those few who eschew the thirteen miles' drive to Clayton. Several bottles of bluing, mousetraps, sundry canned goods, detergents, all obdurate to change, wait patiently for use. Beside them, to the right and near the door, a dozen short rows of library books take their places against the wall. Zane Gray's *Nevada*, *Riders of the Purple Sage*, and others. No one much bothers them anymore. The people who lived here and squinted at the yellow pages in dimly lit farmhouses have moved, and in the cities where new children of other generations and other times have been born, and will be born, there are televisions with brightened screens and talking heroes who will forever dull the faint impression of this place as fact or even memory. In the books the words remain, but they will not be read, nor will the people who left them there return, for these are of the past and cannot, will not, be retrieved.

Behind the post office and two hundred yards to the south, there is a school. In the pasture, three long buildings and one vast cubic structure protrude. Classroom windows, waist-high to the walls, broken, cracked, feel no daydreaming eyes watching the trees, longing for the school day's end. Cans and trash cover the floors, the blackboard scrawled with the profane markings of the last two revelers who drank their beer and let water on the walls. The heavy stucco frame stubbornly resists the crumbling that will come. It is no longer of use, this abandoned assemblage of rooms. And the gaping gymnasium alongside will fall. The last game has been played, the hardwood is warped and twisted. Time . . . Shattered glass . . . Empty . . .

A mile south of the school, there is a farmhouse. Fenced in, a hundred and sixty acres of low, brown-burned grass pasture surrounds it. Corn . . . and beans . . . Maize . . . Dust and scarred rows filled with swirls of sand. A dried, eroded wash cuts its deepening path across the land. A half-dozen weary cows lower sagging heads to sniff the dust and chomp despairingly at the shrivelled grass tufts to feed their distended bellies.

A tired old man watches. His denim-covered arms, small and withered, fold themselves loosely over a wooden corral. The lowered head cups itself in the valley of crossed forearms. Gray, clear eyes, almost hidden within deeply wrinkled lids, watch the land. The glowing sun has moved across the sky leaving the shadows to soften the heat. In the west, where the brightness lingers and hesitates before passing into the night, there is a last full display of red. It is here, between the colors of the day's leaving and the cool dark of the summer night's coming, that the old man pauses. It has been this way with him for a long time, as it must have been with his father before him. He is tired with the weariness only one who has lived out his days walking dry fields can feel. He is old now, and there are no plows to follow. There is grass where the rows of crops struggled in the heat and gave up to the wind. Blinking, he stares into the dusk. Thinking . . .

The people . . . Where are the people? George . . . and Frank . . . Dead. Their farms . . . Beans . . . Millet the size of your index finger . . . Time was . . . No one left. . . . Nine on the route this month . . . Carl Johnson a mailman . . . Drive a pickup . . . Bits of paper . . . Bills and letters, magazines . . . Milk cows and hogs . . . Gettin' by . . . Holdin' on. Keepin' the land . . . Families . . . Was more than eighty on the river . . . A hundred in Otto . . . Bought for taxes, mortgages . . . Ranches . . . Lorenzo owns most of the river; Keyes, the banker, has Otto . . .

Nineteen-thirty-three. Borrow a mule. Get a loan for seed. Hell, it'll pass. . . . Rain's been late before. It'll come. Three families packed up, gone to Texas. . . . George and Frank in Seymour . . . Pickin' cotton . . . Bustin' up . . . Losin' hold . . . Got to get by . . . Can't quit now . . . Been too long . . . Otto school's closed. . . . Seems like this damn hot wind don't never stop blowin'.

"'Member when we first come here, Carl?"

"First day of December 1913."

"Me and sister Julie, built a dugout, carved a hole in the ground and covered it with mud. Planted the crop and waited for rain. Got so damn wet by fall thought we'd never get the beans in. Built this house . . . Bought a car in '28. Raised twelve kids, buried two."

"What the hell, things'll settle. Seen hard times before."

"Can't get no worse. Plowin' dust now . . . Can't recall it ever bein' this bad."

"Two bad drys in a row . . . "

"Never could figure 'em givin' us land like they done."

"Pay the taxes or they'll get it back. Your house, too . . . "

"Got to pay taxes."

"Got to eat."

Before the black clouds of silt forever choked away their still breathings, there were families. Coming together on the Sundays they saved, they met in the churches, and along the creeks, and in the houses. In the beginning only a few came, but the units that were apart gave birth to children, and in the schools they built for them, the new lives had no memory of what had been. The wandering despair of farming the owner's land, the panic of leaving, the fear of having no place to go. In this place, they would stay; the farm, the homestead became for them the symbol of their hope, the connection that brought peace into their lives. In the voices there was a calm. On the long table there was food. The men smoked carefully rolled cigarettes and talked of the week that had passed and the one that would come.

The Thompson house, two-story rock, hardwood floors, evidence that the dream was real. Running water, electricity, warmth and permanence, bounty from the hard-crusted land broken by their plow. White tablecloth freshly ironed. The neighbors here, the Sunday afternoon meal working itself into the communion of the day's passing, the people steeling themselves against the lonely darkness and hollow dread of seeing these things slip away.

"See anybody in town yesterday?"

"Not many goes to town anymore."

"Beans down to nothin'. Nobody's buyin'."

"Saw Tom Jackson from Sofia. Said they quit layin' track to Colmer."

"Oldest boy joined up. Navy."

"Heard they was work in Amarillo."

New Mexico. Land of enchantment. Read the license plates. Settled by land grants, ranches, and homesteads. Immigrants walking over the dry plains. Sharecroppers and tenants lost and frightened, following the dream across Texas, leaving traces in the graveyards of Carthage, Itasca, and Morgan Mill, the westward drift of years moving on. The land opened by the railroads to bring in the people, commerce, profit to be made. Thousands of them on the prairies claiming the land, dugouts shaped with working hands. Turned the pastures of high grass under, fenced in the homesteads, waited for rain, prayed earnest Protestant prayers, and the mountains moved. In the forty years they salvaged from the dry winds, the miracles blended into their lives, became for them an affirmation of truth's struggle.

And then it was suddenly over. They had lied. The hot August wind withered the green stalks in the sun like gnarled pieces of wood. It spread through the furrows and scattered topsoil, picked up the fine brown sand and carried it into blowing whirlwinds. Skies darkened with it. Lungs grew heavy with the ever present breath of it.

The people . . . fools . . . believed in the fact of their salvation, had seen it with their own eyes, had themselves tasted of the loaves and the fishes. . . . Patient Jobs penitently enduring the test. Waiting for the Hand of God to reach down and turn back the wind. Without escape, they were inextricably tied to the America that had blessed them, and they whispered, "It'll pass."

Looking for a loan, the testimony of faith. Federal Land Bank. Mortgage the farm. One more year. But the rains never came, the dust shifted into a dry ocean, and the seeds burned in the sand. Taxes came due and were forgotten. Suddenly and without notice, it was over. In the people was a sorrow, a dead remembering of the days without hope. In the wagons they loaded the families, and on the patches of ground, the houses they built were as cold and empty as the gray night that filled the hollow shells.

Into California, Texas, Oklahoma the people drew back, and the memory became an illusion clouded by the slow stepping of time. The physical fact of their going lingered in the shadows of the walls. The communities . . . their schools, churches, homes . . . settled in the dust. Skeletons, lifeless bones, rattled in the wind, marking the places where the people had been.

A few held on, moved to town to become policemen, mailmen, clerks, and laborers. W.P.A., the handle to grab, holding with white-gripping hands, keeping the faint dream alive.

Lowering his eyes to the ground, the old man turns from the corral. A greasy, brown-stained cap partially shades his vision. When he shuffles his small boot-clad feet, Carl Johnson wearily trudges toward the house. The wrinkled tan of his face is tracked with the lines of an omnipresent worry. *Forty years . . . Been a long time.*

Picking up the keys from the kitchen table, he calls to his wife, "I'm goin' into town, Ma. Be back in a couple hours."

Opening the screened door, he steps out onto the cement porch. His eyes catch the outline of the old Willys. Its torn, green rusted sides are heaved as if some muffled explosion has forced them outward. Worrying his gums, the old man stops. He turns, pulls back the cap, touches the thin hair, wipes a nervous hand over the sweating strands, and regards the still figure of the woman who stands at the door waiting for him to leave.

Old woman, fat and tired . . . Lonely out here. Because of me. Married forty years. Hard life and her not knowing why. Kids moved off and gone. In Pueblo and Denver and Albuquerque. Damn wind . . . Wish to hell it'd rain. Don't make a damn . . . Can't even milk . . . Damn withered hands.

It's almost fifteen miles from Seneca to Clayton. Highway 18, farm-to-market road paved all the way. Follow it north fifty miles to Oklahoma, south twenty to Texas. Not many travel it these days; the farms are gone, and only the feedlot nine miles north of town gives any signs of activity. The rattle of a truck or the quiet hum of a passenger car seldom disturbs the solitude.

The faded green form of a pickup edges slowly along the yellow dashes, barely straying in stretches across to the other side. It does not matter, for there are no other people this morning, and Carl Johnson is alone. The steering wheel twists crazily, the black tape passing smoothly through his weak grasp. The burning brown end of a freshly rolled cigarette extends from his dry lips. He inhales the smoke slowly and stares blankly through the lines of a broken windshield. Watching the land. Feeling it move beneath him. Like the walls of a familiar room, it closes in on him. Scattered growths of yucca quiver in the stirring dust. Prickly pear and cholla cactus choke back the prairie grasses.

A tabletop mesa invades the old man's gaze. In the distorted weariness of his longing, he views not the illimitable expanse of unbroken pasture, but regular divisions of ordered farms. Turner place there at the base of that sloping hill. Straight rows full with heavy burden of grain. Good farmer, Turner, furrows to be proud of. To the west and adjacent to these, the Lewises' one hundred and sixty acres. Corn slow in coming up but catching hold. In every direction the witness of labor, fields full with promise and plenty.

Rubbing his eyes, feeling the confusion, Johnson approaches the junction that separates east and west. Turning, he squints into the sun and drives toward town, passes the Santa Fe Trail marker, rolls reluctantly by the village limits sign (Altitude 5200 feet), into the streets and houses of Clayton. Moving cautiously over the strategically placed deep dips in the highway, the pickup eases down Main Street.

The Iverson Mansion, white paint flaking, loosened boards like broken arms hanging from the sides. City National Bank, clean-bricked and new. Bronco Bowling Alley, doors nailed, permanently closed. Eklund Hotel, yellow sandstone monument to Wild West days . . . Luna Theater, Farmer's Feed and Seed. *Better pick up some cake. Cows need somethin'.*

Reaching the high curb he pulls close, away from the wide street. Stepping hesitantly down from the peeled rubber running board, Carl Johnson gives the door a faint shove and looks up at the same sign, faded with age, and the well-formed words he has recognized for forty years. Farmer's Feed and Seed Your Neighbor and Friend.

As he pushes open the heavy wooden door, Johnson warms to familiar feelings. The musty odor of stacked rows of feed, the ever-perking pot of coffee burning through the stale air.

"Mornin' Jim."

"How ya been, Carl? Ain't seen you the last few days. Everything all right?"

"Gettin' on pretty good, all things considered. Can't complain. It don't take much feed for ten calves, that's all. Need a sack of cake for the cows, though; have Tom put it in the back of the truck, will ya?"

"Sure, Carl. Think one'll be enough? We got plenty."

"Yeah. Thanks, one oughta do."

"Put this on your bill? Say, how's Laura been?"

"Doin' good as can be expected, I guess. At least she don't complain if she ain't."

"She workin' at the school cafeteria again this year?"

"Well, I reckon so. Need money to pay all these damn bills, and I'm gettin' too old to steal."

Jim Marshall laughs lightly, a soft, unself-conscious, easy gesture. Spreading past middle age with a noticeable paunch, he rings the cash register, lifts the tray, and deposits the charge ticket. He enjoys the drift of conversation among people he knows. It is a part of business, and he understands the need for talk. Born and raised in Union County, Jim helped farm his father's homestead until they went under. People like him, and they come to Farmer's Feed and Seed as much for talk as buying feed. There's another feed store in Clayton. It's chain-operated; prices run a little less, but Carl Johnson never bought from Worley. He's known Jim since his dad homesteaded in Otto sixty years ago. Like most of the rest, they lost the farm in the thirties, and Jim's worked at Farmer's since he got back from the war. He's manager now, a good job in a town this size.

"Goin' to drive in this year, or try to find a place in town?" Jim asks.

Sipping from a freshly poured cup of black coffee, Johnson leans an elbow on the counter. The hot liquid warms his throat, and he measures his words.

"Well . . . I tell ya . . . We thought for a while maybe this last year would be the one to get us out of the country. The mail route don't even hardly make expenses, what with gas and all. Seemed like that damned old cold weather would never let up. I swear it gets worse ever' year. And . . . now that I get that Social Security check regular every month, we thought movin' in would prob'ly be the best thing . . . kicked the idea around till it warmed up, then guessed we'd just stick her out another year."

"You ain't gettin' any younger, Carl. Better think her over good. Be cold weather 'fore too long."

"Yeah—maybe you're right. Say, Jim, if that feed's loaded, I'll be gettin' on. Thought I'd stop by the home and see how Bob Walker's feelin'."

"How's he been anyway? Haven't heard you mention him lately."

Johnson stops his movement toward the door then considers the usual query about Walker.

"He don't act like he's doin' too good. Can't get around much outside of bein' rolled around in that wheelchair. He's got to where his mind sorta comes and goes. Don't pay attention half the time to what you're sayin'. Just sorta nods his head and looks off."

"Ain't been the same since they put him in the home, has he, Carl?"

"Old man got nobody to look after him. Had to do somethin'. Him out on that farm, fumblin' with a kerosene stove and livin' filthy. Too old and feeble to take care of hisself."

Jim thinks. Bob Walker in a rest home. Had a good farm, don't seem like that long ago. Hell, he used to run through life, first to plant and get crops in. Never slowed down. Did more work in a day than most now do in a week. Not five years ago. That first stroke. Oh, what the hell, everybody's got to get old. Damn shame. Nothin' left. Work all those years to build somethin', then get to where you can't take care of it.

"Most of the old-timers have moved to town," Jim observes. "Buster Ankley from up on the Cimarron was in yesterday. Said he bought a place over on Oak Street; his old lady's not able to get around too good after her last spell. Needs to be close to the doctor in case her heart flares up again. Sold out to some Texas outfit."

"Heard about it. They're buying up a lot of land on the river. Don't see how they can pay those prices. Nothin' but yearlings, they tell me."

"And hired help," Jim answers. "Well, say hello to Bob for me. Tell him I've been meaning to get around to seein' him. First chance I get, I'll drop by."

"Sure. I'll tell him. See you, Jim."

He walks down the cement steps away from the store. The small bent figure moves slowly, steps down from the curb and pulls itself up to slide onto the torn, ragged pickup seat.

Clayton Convalescent Home. Built three years ago, its modern brick architecture exemplifies the progress that has come to Clayton. Spread in a low, well-ordered line, the rooms combine to give the appearance of streamlined excellence. A large asphalt parking lot welcomes the few visitors who sometimes come to console and comfort the home's inhabitants. The close-cropped, well-manicured grass lawn softens the approach of relatives and friends. Inside the large, swinging glass doors, antiseptic walls are broken by functional, compact

individual rooms that are home to the loose-skinned, hollow-eyed forms who occupy them. There are fifty of these efficient cells, and each has all the necessary
conveniences that senility requires for existence.

Turning the key, Johnson shuts off the engine, reaches for the door handle,
pulls down, and eases out of the pickup. Feeling the crunch of gravel beneath
his feet, he hesitates as he moves toward the lawn. Catching a glimpse of the row
of aluminum lawn chairs, his eyes avert the vacant glances of several sallow faces.
The hot sun filters through passing clouds, burning the several gray heads that
tilt forward in the chairs. Their rumpled hair glistens with drops of moisture
beaded by the summer's heat. One nodding visage weakly raises, questioning
Johnson as he passes.

"Carl?" the thin frame whispers.

"Uh . . . Oh, hello, Mr. Jenson. Didn't recognize you sittin' there. Sun's sure
hot, ain't it."

"Aw, heat don't bother me none. Feels good to me just bein' outside. Lookin'
for Mr. Walker?"

"Yeah, wanted to let him know how things is comin' on his place. Better go in
and see if he can have visitors today. See ya, Bert."

Jenson's glassy eyes follow Carl Johnson's back as he pushes open the door and
walks inside. The dull eyes linger then return to their earlier focus. He fastens
on the crawling ants that meander among the thick blades of grass. His loose skin
tautens. Raising the iron base of his chair, he struggles to set down the runner
on several helpless creatures that writhe beneath the crush.

Inhaling the sweet nursing home smell, Johnson shudders. Death hospital.
Keeps 'em out of the way. Pay somebody to keep 'em from bein' underfoot. Re-
moving the cotton cap, he walks up to the carefully polished brown Formica
reception counter. Clearing his throat, he murmurs, "I'd like to see Mr. Walker,
if I can, miss."

Looking up from her work, the receptionist brightly answers, the cheery tone
in her fresh voice shrill and gaily inappropriate.

"Well, hi there, Mr. Johnson. Bet you're here to help Mr. Walker with his
lunch, aren't you?"

White-clad and pleasant in youthful self-assurance, she straightens her skirt
and scoots forward in the chair.

Looking at the shiny silver watch he retrieves from its pocket, Johnson hesitates.

"No, ma'am. Thanks just the same. Hadn't noticed the time." He pictures the last visit, Mr. Walker propped up like a helpless old doll, his white cotton bib spattered with the slaver that oozed uncontrolled from the paralyzed crevice of his stroke-frozen face.

"Has he been feelin' well lately? Haven't been by in a while. Wanted to check on how he was doin'."

"Oh, he's just doin' great," the girlish face answers. "He's quite a card, that Mr. Walker. We all sure get a kick out of him around here. Laughin' and jokin' all the time."

Johnson doesn't hear the flood of her reply. He considers leaving; confused, he falters.

"Maybe I'll just sit here and wait until he's finished eating. You'll let me know, won't you?"

"Oh, my yes, Mr. Johnson, you sit over there on that nice, comfortable couch, and we'll tell you the minute he's through."

Letting himself down onto the soft pillow of heavy vinyl cushion, Carl Johnson settles into an uncomfortable heap. Straining, he struggles forward to rescue a standing ashtray that totters from his brushing against it. Nervously lighting a cigarette in the dim orange light of the hanging pole lamp, Johnson absently thumbs through a disarranged pile of magazines on the low table before him. Picking up a recent issue of the *Farm Journal*, he distractedly glances through the pages. Swather. Farmhand loader . . . Air-conditioned, power steering tractor with radio . . . Hell, farmin's got to be quite the picnic. How'd you ever pay for all that fancy equipment? Guess folks nowadays got better sense than it takes to follow a team of stubborn mules all day in the hot sun. Placing the magazine back on the table, he shifts his weight impatiently. He becomes suddenly aware of his growing discomfort, extricates himself from the couch, stuffs the burning cigarette butt into the ashtray, and returns to the receptionist.

"Uh . . . excuse me, miss. Would you tell Mr. Walker I come by and will try to see him another time? I got some things need taken care of this afternoon."

"I'll tell him for you, Mr. Johnson. But he shouldn't be long now. I'll give him your message if you just have to be goin' though. Seems a shame." She calls to his disappearing figure, "He does so look forward to your visits."

With a full breath of relief, Johnson passes from the home into the now darkening skies of the summer's day. The electric air is charged with the approach of an August burst of rain. There is in him the same alert awakening of the senses that has always come with the gathering clouds of a summer rain. Walking by the now empty row of lawn chairs, Johnson steps onto the parking lot.

The worn vehicle sputters to life and again jumps forward, leaving the home and moving past the recognized houses of Clayton's west edge; the two escape the last fringes of town. Turning west onto the Springer highway, Johnson lifts an automatic wave to a rotund, lounging form that signals from his perch on the wooden bench in front of Hudson's store. Scattering gravel in a light spray, the Willys gathers speed on pavement. In a throw of rattling spasms, the green form bounces in a continuous series of jolts and shifts of grinding gears.

Several miles west of town, a deserted dirt road divides north. Slowing, Johnson raises his left arm high to signal the turn then heads through a swirl of dust that swells behind him. How long since I been down this road? At least a year — no — longer than that. Christmas a year ago.

Johnson lowers the pickup window, and his right foot moves in automatic re-lease of the gas pedal. In the cooling air he feels a soothing calm. Outside, be-yond the enclosure of the old pickup, images from the past focus from a blur. Distinctly, he sees the details of the land, the acres of green soapweed etched against the gray-becoming sky. In the near distance, Johnson places the outline of each windmill and clump of trees into position in his mind. The names of the families whose homes these were roll easily off his tongue. In his chest there is a loosening, and a weariness in his eyes softens. Here, where only the memory can give life, he is coming home. Fastening on one isolated grove of trees and the whirling fan of a lone windmill spinning against the dark clouds, the old man's eyes rest on a decaying three-walled structure. Crossing over a sunken tin culvert, Johnson comes to a stop. He leans back against the seat and sits quietly for one long moment.

Stumbling over the scattered rock fragments of wall, Johnson steps into the gaping hole that is formed from the crumbled stone beneath him. Unnoticed, their heads lifted curiously upward, several grazing cattle pause briefly to con-sider the intruder who stands with arms folded inside the Otto school. Listening, his head tilted away from the soft wind, he can hear the early morning buzz of children greeting the day. Twenty busy figures gather themselves in straight desk rows, the warm glow of a burning fire hidden in the heavy metal of a tall potbel-lied stove. A short sprite of a man scurries into the room, the children rise, and the day begins.

High above, a sharp crack of thunder breaks the stillness. Lower now, their billows filled with rain, the dark clouds extend heavy about the old man, the cracked cement blocks and piles of cow manure. Stooping, he climbs over the rubble and steps out into the dimmed light. Spreading two strands of loose barbed wire, Johnson steps onto the cemetery grounds. Above the entrance, the letters *Oto* are welded. The graveyard is grown over with high grass and sprouts of scrub oak. Small, thick sage and spreading locust trees obscure many of the markers. Picking his way through the fallen stone and brush, he stands before one concrete-bordered plot. Sister Julie and her three babies. 1918. Flu sweeping through, the sounds of coughing and dying. Billy there, 1932, dead before we could get him to town. Clarence, barely sixteen, not even a headstone, crumpling metal marker, name barely recognizable, 1936. Wiping away the crusted dirt with his sleeve, he squats on thin legs, the taste of rain fresh, the wind moving to the north blowing cool through his flapping shirt. How many here? Thirty? Forty? All of us raised here, brought up together, grown, gone, or dead away. Damn. It ain't right. Stuck off alone out here. Pasture taking over. Maybe come out Sunday and get some of this cleared. Can't let it go like this.

Pulling his cap down against the wind, Johnson walks past the entrance to the highway, returns to the pickup, and drives back east to town. He keeps his eyes to the road, working his jaws, holding the steering wheel tightly. Spots of rain splash in the dust on the windshield, and rivulets of muddy water cloud the glass. He stares into the brown droplets and begins to hum lightly. Pulling the wiper knob on the dash, the old lips form words, and the frown slowly fades from his worn features. He thinks of the voices he will never hear again, and his eyes form pictures of the people he will never see again.

Passing through Clayton he forgets Bob Walker and the home, and the waves from the street go unacknowledged. On the Seneca road, he begins to sing. He cannot remember when last he has sung, and the rasp of his voice startles him, but he continues. There is a groping; then the tone raises and the crack in his throat retreats to the unexpectedly resonant sound of an old church song he recalls without knowing:

Comin' home, comin' home,
Never more to roam.
Open wide thine arms of love,
Lord, I'm comin' home.

The old dim eyes brighten, and his thoughts are of the supper that will be waiting and the old woman who will be watching for him. The singing stops. The rain heavily beats against the pickup, the sounds filling his head with their poundings.

The deepened ditch of gravel driveway welcomes the old man. He is home. Broken stalls peer vacantly from within the darkened doorway of the small, tin-roofed barn. Next to the barn stands a shed with torn shingles clinging in patches on the sloping roof. It has not been repaired in years, and the winds blow through the cracks. Manure-spattered boards protect the entrance to the inner room. Carl Johnson's milk shed. On the walls, hanging in cobwebbed neglect are rusted, broken hobbles and unused lanterns, useless in the skeletons without glass. The room is unlit and dark. A tractor seat is propped at an angle in the center of the room, tilted onto the floor, knocked over and left this morning.

A moss-grown stock tank stagnates beneath the creaking windmill. Encircled by the wooden corral, its heavy metal circled black with mud and age, the tank echoes with water that slowly spills from a long pipe that reaches from the well.

Clutching his collar, he hurries past the outbuildings into the rain toward the house. He falls back against the closed door and then stomps into the kitchen. With a towel she wipes away the dripping water and pulls a chair from the table. He smells the biscuits, can almost taste the thick gravy simmering on the stove.

She removes the wet cap, hangs it on the nail by the door.

"How as Bob doin', Carl?" she asks.

Wiping his face, he hesitates, then answers, "What the hell makes you think I been to see Bob Walker?"

"I dunno, just figured that's where you was. Usually go by 'bout this time every week."

"Well, I didn't today. Had other things on my mind. Damn but supper sure smells good."

"Be ready in a minute. Wash up."

Dipping his hands into the basin, he rubs the soap against his palms then cups the water and splashes it onto his face. Reaching for the towel she offers, he dries the moisture and says, "Ma, I been thinkin', maybe we oughta move to town this year. You know, be closer to your work and all. Course I ain't sayin' we just have to, but it's worth considerin'."

Roberta Courtney Meyers

Bone Dream

(for female voices)
From *The Chaco Canyon Dream,* a Modern Opera

VOICE 1   The skeleton
             touched my eye.
             I probed her gingerly.
ALL   She was beautiful
             white
             like the first snowfall of the world.

VOICE 1 & 2 Delicate one
             with bone turning
             to ivory ash
             from burning desert sun.
VOICE 3   Wise one
             holding
             secret centuries.
VOICE 2   Silent one
             speaking Anasazi tongue
             with an unhinged antelope jaw.

ALL   She sang puzzles
             voiced soundless songs
             of wind and sand.

VOICE 1   Gentle blue spirit of the long white mesa.

VOICE 2   She crooned the lasting universe.
VOICE 3   On bone she strummed old music.

ALL   She chanted the canyons
             against ancient story pictures.

VOICE 1   She wailed silently.

ALL (*whispered*)   Those with no ears heard the song.

Terry Song

In These Times

You who were
are no longer and what I was I'm not.
Am I to know myself?
— MARVIN BELL "You Would Know"

"Step on a crack, you will
break your mother's
back," children
chanted on the schoolyard
sidewalk. Was it too many
children in cracks that finally
wore your heart to the thinness of trying
to keep them in shoes
and oranges, much less
in tow Sunday mornings, having put
rolls on to rise, cut up a
hen to fry for the preacher over
after, while you
hurried the five girls, Grandpa
leaning on the Model T horn, shouting,
"Jewel, don't you have those kids ready
yet!" You handed the four boys
hankies, dimes for the collection plate,
and pinning hat to head and
humming, strode out to
meet impatient eyes.

This rare weekend of escape to the lake,
alone on the small dock and my children
clambering like crabs up the sandy
slope back to the cabin —
you were twenty years

older than I am now
that last day you watched us
scrabble up the same steep
slope, dangling
your legs from the dock's
edge, your hair
already escaping the white straw
hat. You laughed,
"I think I could live
forever."

        And oh! the next morning
when Aunt Betty shook Grandpa away, crying
"Papa! Papa! Mama's dead!"
I was a sorry river
shrivelled to salt,
a heart heaving and cracking
like boulders in the arroyo
when rain comes too fast.
Such loss was everything
when I was eleven. Why
did it have to be you? And still,
so many questions:

Who would you be now
in this age as mass
collapses to infinite density, time
accelerates, tracking the speed of
light across our backs?
I need to know.
Our families are small.
No one home to sow
seeds or gather eggs.
Who could even tell
a story? What steady
hands to guide small fingers
in the knotting of thread,
the stitching of hems?

I need you now as you were
then when the waters
flowed below your pasture and squirrels
chattered through your
tree. I need your creeks
that swell in the
spring, creeks with
trees that dangle grapevines and roped
sandbags to swing on.
      If I could see you
      in the thin morning light,
      coming from henhouse, apron
      full of brown eggs, a fat
      hen by the feet, wings
      splayed from your hands,
      then I might know.
            But your apricot jam is gone.
            Even the old ladies don't roll down their
            stockings anymore. And the boxes of
            dresses and hats you gave us,
            the handbags and high-heeled
            shoes have gone
            the way of all playthings.

How am I to know
what street to raise my
kids on? The stars can point a way,
but city lights confuse.
Prices are high, and the calendar
falls in on itself.
Please, come
sit awhile with me; we can blame
the thoughtless Oklahoma summer
days that unfolded so slowly
I could not get here in time
to ask you these things.

Terry Song

In Bread We Trust

We cannot live by bread alone,
especially from the makers of Rainbo
or Mead's fine inflated white
fluff that never knew a
crumb, much less
mold no matter how
stale or old.
Even as civilization rose
out of grains ground on stones
and baked between glowing
coals, so it shall
fall beneath the:
Give us this day our daily
       monocalcium phosphate,
       sodium stearoyl lactylate,
       ethoxylated mono- and
       diglycerides —
       calcium inappropionate.
Even in the back of Lucero's
on Espina Street
where they are making the *pan del
muerte* for All Souls' Day,
and in the concrete and cinderblock
enterprises
calling themselves bakeries,
it is all dead bread, pale as a
corpse's face, where we should
catch one morning, walking by,
the aroma of wheat fields soaked in
sun and waved around in cool
breezes, the dry chaff of

buckwheat, oats, corn, and
rye from the mills and metates of
earth, golden
loaves, body of
Christ, we are taking the name
of Bread in vain.
Accept no substitutes.
Do not be deceived by Mrs. Wright's
caramel-colored light wheat
or even Roman Meal.
Let the memory lingering on our
tongues be rain
and sun on fresh plowed
earth. When there is little
left to believe in, let us
waken the sleeping
yeast, nurture it in embryonic
warmth in the fires
of our own small kitchens. With our own
hands let us raise the house called
Bread, breathe its honest
fragrance and be
filled.

Karen Thibodeau

Pasha Rajah's Feather

Once there was a very beautiful, very long, very delicate peacock feather which came from the palace of Pasha Rajah. He ruled the Kingdom of Famaj, that is whenever he happened to think of it. Pasha Rajah spent most days choosing his turban fabric, or looking for his ring, or ordering his Noble Fly Whisker to remove the flies from his nose. Yes. Flies mysteriously settled on Pasha Rajah's nose as he spent hours seated on his throne choosing this, ordering that. The Noble Fly Whisker spent hours waving them away with the very beautiful, very long, very delicate peacock feather. One day the great feather disappeared. Flies settled on Pasha Rajah's nose.

"Oh where is my fly whisker?" he cried.

Pasha Rajah let it be known throughout the land that whoever could find the royal feather would be richly repaid. Heralds announced: "Hear ye, hear ye, the Royal Fly Whisker's whisker is missing. Anyone who finds this precious feather will be rewarded with a permanent seat beneath Pasha Rajah's throne."

Heralds searched the entire Kingdom.

They looked in the graineries,

        they looked in flower beds,

  they looked under beds,

they looked inside teacups

       (in case the feather had shrunk).

    They looked under haystacks,

        they looked in children's toy boxes,

  they looked in birthday present boxes,

      they looked in wooden boxes,

        they looked in golden boxes,

  they looked in cereal boxes

      (except there weren't any),

    they looked in boxcars

        (being little cars in boxes),

   they boxed each other's ears

  when they got tired and crabby,

they felt boxed in,
they looked in pillboxes
          (because the feather was being a real pill
                 by not showing up).
They gave up and went to sleep on the spot.

In the town lived a curious child named Rosalind. She never missed a thing. When her mother lost a sock in the laundry, she found it in an apron pocket. When her father lost a shoelace, she found it in her mother's noodles. When her dog lost his bone, she found it in her mother's soup pot. When her teacher lost his glasses, she found them on his head.

One day she went for a walk through the streets of Famaj. She walked down a street called Zeather. She walked by a shop called Meather's. She stopped by a carriage called Deather's. She talked to the driver named Beather. She met a horse named Weather. She saw that Weather was indeed wearing a very beautiful, very long, very delicate peacock feather. The Pasha Rajah's Noble Fly Whisker's whisker was found. A great celebration was made. The people of Famaj danced the courtage. Everyone sang until the bells rang. Tables filled with feasts lined the streets. People danced and sang and ate until their hearts giggled. Rosalind went to the palace of Pasha Rajah.

"A permanent seat beneath my throne, for you, oh clever Rosalind," beamed Pasha Rajah. But Rosalind had a mind of her own. She looked up. She looked down. She looked sideways. She saw nothing that she wanted. She announced her heart's desire.

"I wish to have a small palace of my own next to yours. That way I will indeed have a permanent seat beneath your throne, for my palace will always be beneath the shadows of your palace, and I will not have to look at your feet."

Pasha Rajah had to agree with Rosalind. He set at once to building. It was an unusual experience for him. He had never done anything for anyone else. He had chosen the color of polish for his toenails. He had decided on the direction of the royal bed. He had chosen the flavor for the royal lollipops. But he had never thought about what someone else would like.

At first all these decisions stretched his brain. He tried to think what Rosalind would want. He complained of headaches. However, as the days went by and he chose the gold tiles for the entryway, aqua tiles for the bath, pink flower vases for the sun porch, singing finches for the bedroom, a tinkling fountain for the portico, pink frosting for the outside walls, and slates of cinnamon for the roofs, rivulets of sparkling cider to run around the tiger lily beds, licorice sticks to fence the sweet peas, and chocolate bricks to mark the garden paths, he began to enjoy himself. It was an unusual feeling. He began to please himself by pleasing Rosalind. When she smiled at the chocolate bricks, he smiled too. When she laughed at the licorice sticks, he laughed too. When she sighed over the pink frosting, he sighed too.

Creating a palace for Rosalind gave him so much pleasure that soon he began to think of doing things for other people in the Kingdom of Famaj. In fact, Pasha Rajah became known throughout the land for his exceptional kindness, his witty gifts, and his generous heart. Furthermore, because he was so busy, flies had not time to settle on his nose.

Utah

My brother, Tom Austin, and I coauthored a collection of essays on the landscapes of Kansas and Utah. It won a prize in the Utah Arts Contest, and that's how we became part of the TumbleWords project. Reading and giving workshops with my brother has been a "real" experience, mainly because he's the eccentric one of the family, his eccentricity coming in part from having served as a police chief for over ten years. Our most interesting experience so far has been reading in a nursing home. Somehow I had believed that we were to read for "alert" senior citizens, so we were unprepared for the audience that greeted us. One lady was completely doubled over in her wheelchair, one man soon nodded off, and audible moans and groans punctuated my reading. I ended quickly, leaving the floor for my "show-stopping" brother.

Tom's usual opening routine is designed as a transition between my work and his. He accomplishes that by giving me a hard time, declaring, with just the right flip of the hand, that I'm the boring one of the team, the artsy one. "I'm the storyteller," he asserts, "so now you'll have something really interesting to listen to." He always carries on for about five minutes, expanding on the theme by stressing how slowly I write compared to him (which is all too sadly true), much to my discomfort. This time, however, two of the ladies (who were surprisingly alert and displayed astute judgment) bristled up, coming to my defense. "We didn't think she was boring at all," one lady stated loudly. "Not at all," the second one agreed loudly enough to make the dozing man sit up and look about in bewilderment.

After Tom finally settled their feathers, he launched into his reading. Not only did one of the men constantly lament, "I want to go back to my room"; a three-year-old, who had somehow wandered in, burst into tears, sobbing for his mother. I thought it was one of our best efforts ever, and only what Tom deserved.

Seriously, though, we enjoyed the experience of reading to an older audience. I felt our lives had been enriched, and Tom, after all, is only nine years away from getting a senior citizen discount on his meals. I am his younger, normal sister.

MERRY ADAMS

Merry Adams

Winter Camp

The eyes are not here
There are no eyes here
In this valley of dying stars
    — T. S. ELIOT

When a person has been overwhelmed by the virulent forces of evil — disorder, contamination, ghosts, bewitchment, death, or dreaming of stars — the Navajo conduct a ceremony called *haneelneehee bihochooji* (the Evilway.) During part of this long, complex ritual, the patient is blackened with charcoal, and spruce bundles are fastened to the soles of his feet, his knees, stomach, chest, shoulders, hands, forehead, and crown. These bundles, made of spruce and turkey feathers and tied with yucca strings, symbolize the effects of ghost sickness, which include mental distress, insomnia, bad dreams, anorexia, and emaciation. In the winter of 1989–90, I came down with all of the symptoms of *bi-hochooji* (ghost-side) illness.

The winter had been devastating for our community, a small, isolated town in southeastern Utah that borders both the White Mesa Ute and the Navajo Reservations. The tiny college where I was teaching, where 65 percent of the students were Native Americans, had been called a cancerous growth, and its much needed expansion was being fought by neighbors. Along with the controversy about the college, the community was riven on all sides by petty discord, but there were even more serious traumas. One of my friends, blind and stroke-prone from advanced diabetes, became totally bedridden. A fire demolished another's home. One of my students had been raped, and her children threatened if she went to the authorities. Another told me he could hear tormented voices from hell. A third left my office hurriedly to vomit in the restroom after telling me of being attacked by her favorite uncle.

The stories of conflict, abuse, and tragedy continued day after day. Even more traumatic were the deaths occurring in the families of people I cared about. Within a period of five months, three died from cancer, one from respiratory problems, one from cardiac arrest, one from suicide.

The shadow of suffering spread to the seemingly inanimate elements. The land itself lay in anguish from a prolonged drought that was sucking dry the entire Southwest. Even the hardy cedar trees, long acclimated to surviving on little moisture, were beginning to die.

Carolyn Forché has said that whatever is spoken upon the earth remains, even after the speaker is gone, waiting to rise up in a swirl around those who listen. So after the devastating fall quarter, the voices of the sufferers, both people and nature, began blowing around me with increasing velocity as story after story was added, weaving themselves into a stinging wind devil of anguish:

> Since he's a doctor, he knows what lies ahead. We're afraid his bones will start breaking or that the cancer will travel up his spine into his brain.
>
> All of Autumn's dolls were burned.
>
> He took me up on the mountain road. He said he'd hurt my kids.
>
> My husband is dying, but I'm not going through with him what I did with my baby, laying her in the grave and all.
>
> Dad won't take his oxygen, and he won't go to the doctor. I think he wants to die.
>
> I'm tired of lying in bed all day and all night, of looking out and seeing nothing.
>
> Yes, they tied my father up, but I don't want you to write about it.
>
> My father hit me so hard I went crashing out an upstairs window. I hated him.
>
> I guess I went kind of crazy when my baby died in the fire.
>
> I can hear things in hell — people crying. Now I can't 'member things so good.
>
> We know there isn't much hope.

The accumulation of deaths and traumas and unresolved conflicts, most of which reverberated on a subterranean level rather than on the surface, finally cracked me like the earth itself. After the haunting suicide of a friend's fourteen-year-old son, which culminated all of the tragedies, I found myself unable to eat, unable to sleep, unable to teach, and one day, unable to stop sobbing.

Because of the deaths and my inability to work, I didn't think I could ever return to the classroom. Never before had I been so faced with my own vulnerability, with my inability to cope, with the weaknesses that flawed the fragile glass of my psychological makeup. I weighed less than a hundred pounds. And I had nothing left to give to anyone.

That night, after hours of uncontrollable sobbing, my wrestling became in-

tense. I knew I might never return from the dust-deep, lunarlike internal landscape where I was heading, and, just as certainly, I knew I couldn't go there
because I still had a child to raise into manhood.

So the dead of winter, both internally and externally, gripped my world as my
brother and I drove south from Blanding. We were headed for a winter camp in
the desert, a place of purification and visions, but I did not think of that. I moved
as an automaton, doing what I was told, doing what everyone else had determined best, resolute in one thing only — to regain a semblance of my normal
world, if it were possible, for my son's sake.

"I'll force-feed her every two hours," Tom solemnly promised our mother as
he loaded the back of his truck with enough food to last us two months instead
of the two days we proposed to stay. Huddled against me, nearly crowding me off
the seat, his springer spaniel, Ellie, shared her warmth. A skiff of snow lay over
the land, maddening in its scantiness. I felt the earth cracking, suffering, dying.

An hour and a half later when we pulled off the highway onto the single-
tracked, deeply rutted road that only a vehicle like Tom's big four-wheel-drive
Jeep pickup could traverse, I was struck, even through the stupor of emotional
exhaustion, by the fact that the sand was not the normal beige color, but rather
shades of orange: the color of dancing flames, of crepe flowers, of the sky at dawn,
of various round, succulent fruits such as oranges, tangerines, apricots, and
peaches, and in places, a deeply singed shade that had no equivalent. As I took
in the variation of hues, something deep within stirred back to life, as if I had
been given a nutrient. I had been color deprived, color starved by the darkness
of death and pain.

Symbolic immersion into utter darkness during the Evilway ceremony is necessary before the power of malignity can be replaced by good, before Monster
Slayer and his twin brother Born-for-Water can cut the yucca strings and unravel
the bundles from the crown, shoulders, hands, stomach, and feet.

In Blanding I had walked among the stone gods of pain and malevolence,
having nightmares about a land where stars had no light. But in the desert, with
the burnished orange of the wind-swept sand, the silver hair of the sand sage, the
red of the mesas, and the cream of the Navajo sandstone, the bundles of pain I
carried began to unravel.

As first one bundle, then another, was cut, the haunting voices began to fade.
This was a different world. It was a desert, yes, a land by definition barren, aus-
tere, even brutal, but the dust that in Blanding lay strewn so thickly over new

graves here had life and light and color of its own. The voices here were different as well. They did not press around me. I had to listen carefully to hear them at all.

We continued along the truck-wracking track until late in the afternoon when we arrived at a windmill, a dome of Navajo sandstone, and a hoary old cedar tree. "Let's stop here, Sis," Tom said. "We can get some shelter under that cedar." Incapacitated not only by anemia and severe weight loss but also by innumerable layers of clothing, I waited in the truck while my brother set up camp: building a fire, making a windscreen, beginning supper. Despite his promises, we hadn't eaten since morning, so my salivary glands started working overtime as the aroma of the anticipated feast drifted toward me: Rice-a-roni in a particularly appealing shade of gut-green cooked in a rusty Dutch oven over a cedar fire. I ate with keen relish for the first time in weeks.

The moon rose, huge, full, orange-tinged, over the hush of the cold desert night. Ellie still huddled close against me even though Tom called her a black-and-white-spotted turncoat. I had needed a friend, and by some miracle, I had two of the best with me.

The cedar fire, its fragrant incense wafting toward us, died back to small yellow-orange flames that occasionally popped and crackled. Both Tom and I could "feel" the sheltering presence of the cedar tree, probably hundreds of years old, under which we unrolled our sleeping bags. Edward Abbey had tried to pierce his cedar with a finite human mind, finally giving up the enigma as part of the mysterious "other" that lies outside the comfortable periphery of our human-made existence. Neither philosopher nor out-and-out rebel, I merely sank into my nest of blankets and bedroll, comforted by the presence of the dog on my feet, the indomitable tree above my head, and my big brother nearby.

I awoke early with the moon going down in the west while the sun rose in the east, dismayed to find that during the night my faithful foot warmer had landed on my thick-lensed glasses, brittle in the below-freezing temperatures, breaking the frames beyond repair. I could not function without my glasses. Period. With what I could tell from my nearsighted, astigmatic glance, Tom still snored peacefully away. He would be of no help. After I scrutinized the glasses again, I determined that, despite the fact that both sides were cleanly snapped just above the nosepiece, I could fit the lenses back into their respective places. With the greatest of care, I manuevered the frames onto my nose. After doing so, the desert curved and wavered around me in strange ways until the slightest misbobble sent the lenses, first one and then the other, popping out to land with soft thuds on my bedroll. Still, if I was careful, if I had the most precise of postures, if I balanced the glasses perfectly, I could see. I did not realize then that the shattering of my old way of perceiving had been essential for new vision to begin.

Necessity calling, I set out to find privacy and then to explore the desert quiet. Foot warmer crowded close behind.

I clambered around the dome of sandstone, holding my glasses in place with one hand while I looked at the stone sparkling in the morning light. The light seemed to come both from without the stone and within it, as if it had been trapped there eons ago when the stars yet sparkled upon the ground — before coyote had tossed them up into the sky. I could see this was a land of living light, not a wasteland where the stars lay dying.

Despite the beautiful sight, I still felt very tired. Exhaustion seemed a lifelong condition for me. I had been weary since childhood. But, for the moment at least, I had no students knocking at my door, no failures to regret, no tragedies to face.

I rounded the top of the rock and stumbled across the remnants of an old cowboy camp with stumps still in place and ancient tin cans the same rusty orange as the sand they were sunk in. Time stops in the desert. The camp had probably been inhabited in the fifties before the environmental movement made everyone aware of recycling, yet little had changed. When archaeologists a thousand years hence dig in the soft apricot sand, they will be amazed at the petrified perfection of the remains. Even bones, as Abbey noted, become exquisite in the desert, scoured white by the wind and sand.

Every now and then, as I bent my head to look, one or the other of my lenses would fly out. The first time one hit a rock, I panicked; then I became frustrated and angry. I didn't want to return to Blanding yet. Except for my son, I didn't want to go back ever.

However, my fantasy of remaining until I too had been scoured exquisite by the wind was soon dismissed. When I circled back to camp, the mound beneath the heap of blankets was stirring. We ate Rice-a-roni for breakfast. "This'll put a little iron in your blood, a little steel in your spine, a little grit in your teeth," Tom assured me when I commented on the rust scraped from the bottom and the sand folded in from the top. And, indeed, I could already feel the magic of the nourishment working.

After eating, we decided to explore the surrounding area before heading back to town and harsh reality. Several factors went into our decision to break camp early. Before we had stopped for the night, Tom's pickup had been shifting with difficulty, and he suspected that he might have lost fourth gear. With fourth gear balky, he feared the entire transmission might go out, and to reach civilization would require a strenuous walk. The second factor, of course, was my glasses.

Still, we had the long, bright morning in a world where time had stopped.

Walking with Tom became an exercise in minute observation. He called my attention to details I normally would have overlooked: a circle enscribed on the bank of the dry wash, the tracks of tiny desert birds, the dung left by a ringtail cat, the tail trails of desert mice and kangaroo rats, the wide-spaced prints of a bounding coyote. Because we were constantly looking down, my lenses would periodically fall out, first one, then the other. Later, as I scrambled up a steep embankment, they both popped out at once, scudding in different directions. For the first time in weeks, as Tom retrieved them and tried to help me fit them back into the broken frames, I laughed.

Moments later, skirting along the top of the ravine, we found thousands of desert crystals, huge chunks of quartz, lying randomly like ungathered treasures along the surface. Suddenly, I wanted the crystals — I wanted to take them back with me to the other world, the world with no living stars, so I gathered up one here and one there, scarcely knowing what to take and what to leave, so many were so beautiful. The desert, despite its apparent sparseness, is generous with its wonders. It yielded three crystals in exchange for the promise to return to that spot someday, come back a different person, one who had incorporated wonder and beauty into my being, a seer of good as well as evil.

As I look through the crystal, the desert world around me mysteriously transforms. We descend into a deep dry wash. The tangerine-colored sand, almost elastic in its resiliency beneath our feet, is rippled by an ancient wind that spoke once long ago and left its sound imprinted forever afterward upon the earth. Its primeval song rises now as we walk down the narrow ravine. The earth has her own voice. Here on her soft skin, we hear the slow, steady beat of her life, a strong counterpoint to the ancient wind.

We have descended into a wrinkle. We can see only what is before us and below us, and, if we look up, what is above in a sky so pure it is a blue blade in my eyes. I cannot look upward long. Yet each thing I see with my tunnel vision speaks with a quiet voice of beauty and balance: the frost-touched purple arnica, the sparse grasses that shine with fragile fire, the sturdy clumps of squawbrush, the mysterious desert circles. The sandpainting is the beginning itself: the beginning and the ending swirled by the hands of the first ones, the sky people. From the summit of Spruce Mountain, Talking god, with thy white face, with thy white cane upon me, come thou to my home. In the first, second, third, and fourth shelves of the skies, remove the spell, remove all evil.

I walk among the gods, touched by their hands, the orange sand becoming my skin; the crystals, my eyes; the wind, the whorls of my fingertips; the silver sage, my hair. Suddenly my sight is swept outward as the entire world falls away. In the distance, mesas float in purples, blues, lavenders, scarlets, creams — the air itself is the purest of golds, and the silence of sacred time distills upon us all.

As we limped along at thirty-five miles an hour northward back toward Blanding, fourth gear definitely gone, Tom looked at me with a grin. "Someday, Sis, we're gonna laugh at this."

With that future firmly in mind, still holding my broken glasses in place, I nodded. "Yeah, I know," I said as I turned my sight toward home.

Tom Austin

Day of Days

It started early, that day of days. I was sound asleep in my upstairs room when I was awakened by the sound of the elm tree outside my window whispering that a storm was coming. I hated that tree. It stood right outside my west window and touched the screen. When the wind blew, the tree limb would move back and forth across the wire screen sounding like someone scraping his fingernails. (I didn't stop to reason that such a person would either have to be standing on a ladder or else be twenty feet tall.) The tree looked like a black skeleton against a bright white winter moon, and in the growing season I was sure that the thick foliage hid most of the loathsome creatures of the world. I hated that tree.

The wind was blowing gently through the west window, and the tree limb was scratching across the screen. I could hear distant thunder, and the breeze smelled of rain. I wasn't disturbed. It was a Kansas August. We needed the rain. I shut the window and lay back down. I closed my eyes and slid slowly back into sleep.

A daylight bright flash of lightning and a tremendous blast of thunder made me sit straight up in bed. That one had been close! I looked out the north window into the backyard. The storm was just breaking. It was raining hard, and another flash of lightning showed the orchard in bright relief. I closed the north window and started back toward my bed.

The boat! I hadn't tied the boat up high. There were two rules that Granddad had imposed with regard to my using the boat. I had to tie it to a tree high on the bank in case the river came up unexpectedly, and I had to bring the oars up to the machine shed. The boat, this night, was tied to my pier/stump at the edge of the water, and the oars were in the locks. It hadn't looked like rain when I'd left it in the early evening, and it had seemed like too much trouble to subscribe to the rules. Just this once I hadn't obeyed. Now the storm had struck.

I jumped out of bed, jammed my feet into my tenny runners, and slipped down the stairs. I didn't bother to put any clothes on. (One of the advantages of living on a farm is no one cares if you run around in your undershorts.) The rain was coming down in sheets, pounding at the face of the earth, so anything I wore was going to be instantly soaked anyhow. Better to wear just my shorts than to try and explain wet clothes to Granny in the morning. I stopped momentarily at the back door and looked out. I was scared. The thunder and lightning were almost constant, the wind had reached nearly hurricane levels, and the rain made a dull roar on the tin roof of the machine shed. It was incredibly wild, but I knew I had to go down to the river. I had violated the rules, and the boat was important to me. I couldn't risk losing it to the river, or losing the privilege of using it. I took a tentative step onto the back porch. The violence of the storm and the coldness of the rain that pounded on me snatched away my breath. Suddenly, I heard the tornado warning whistle screaming in town. The wind was apparently blowing just right to carry the sound out to the farm. If I wasn't struck by lightning, or sucked up by a twister, I would probably still drown in the rain. I was resolute. It was my fault that the boat and oars were at risk. I had to continue.

I ran to the trees that bordered the river and stopped a moment. Jeez it was dark! Even the lightning flashes didn't penetrate the blackness under the trees. My feet knew the path to the boat by heart, so I plunged into the forbidding darkness. My head was down to keep some of the rain from my eyes, but it didn't help. I literally could not see my hand in front of my face. I ran headfirst into a tree. It hurt, but really I was more surprised than anything. I knew the path perfectly, yet a tree had seemingly grown up in the trail during the few hours since I had last travelled it. My arms flapped and my feet scrambled as I fought to keep my balance after I'd rammed the tree. The path was based on good ole blue-gray clay, and it was slicker than about anything I can think of (snot on a doorknob comes to mind). My feet started skipping, spinning, and churning the clay. I was out of control, I was off the path, and I was moving downhill gaining speed as my size twelves acted as skis. I started screaming — not the nice genteel shrieks my sister gave as I pounded on her, these were deep-down, gut-wrenching howls of terror. My feet got ahead of my body, and I smashed down onto my scantily covered butt with a sloshing slam dunk that drowned out the roar of the thunder. I was still gaining speed, and my hair was drawn straight back behind my head by the draft I created as I sliced through the night. I went over the first bank gaining a little altitude as I hit the rise, and then slamming back into the clay as I descended the second bank toward the water. I was going well over a hundred miles per hour, and I was still accelerating. I shot out from under the trees, and the scene before me was irradiated by the almost constant lightning. I could see it coming. My legs were slightly splayed apart, and heading right for my vulnerable crotch was a cottonwood sapling about an inch in diameter. My screams became hysteric as I realized what was about to happen.

It hit me. (I should probably say I hit it, since I was in motion, but I still think I saw the damn thing move so as to catch me square in the tenders.) I grabbed at the area of my anatomy that was wounded by the malevolent tree, and realized I was slowing down. The tree had caught my shorts, which were being pulled ever tighter against certain delicate areas of my body. Quicker than a goose fart, my gonads were clenched tighter than if they were caught in a vice. I screeched with agony; then my shorts tore away, staying on the tree as it flipped upright. They flapped in the wind like a flag of victory.

As my shorts ripped off, I spun backward, and once again I started to gain speed. I knew I was about to die. I got back up to a hundred quickly, since the second bank of the river is steeper than the first. I shot into the air again (there was a lip right at the water's edge that acted as a ramp) and splashed into the river about halfway across. The waves I created nearly drowned me. My mouth was still obscenely open, uttering the screams that my balls were transmitting to my mind. The river water was blessedly warm after the chill of the rain, and I began to calm down. I stood up (the water came just under my knees), and I splashed over to the boat. It was tied high, and the oars were gone. Granddad had apparently checked to see if I was abiding by the rules and had secured the boat and oars before he'd come in for supper. My trip had been for nothing.

The chaos of the storm had somewhat stilled, but the rain still fell in constant sheets. I crawled out of the water like some creature from the age of dinosaurs just trying out newly formed legs. I was coated with blue-gray clay that no amount of rain would wash off. I tried to ascend the bank. It took me over an hour, slipping backward one step for every two I took forward. I finally had to dig holes for my feet, and even then I slid back to the river twice more. There was almost no hide left on my behind by the time I made the top. The rain had slowed to a drizzle, and I could hear the rumble of thunder as the storm moved east. I went to the basement door and eased it open. The last thing I needed at this point was to wake up the grandparents. I knew I'd need a shower before I could return to my bed. The shower was in the basement. I eased the door down over my head (it was one of those that was horizontal and heavy) and stood for a moment in the quiet darkness. I was finally home. I took a step down. I knew exactly where the light switch was. I took another step down, reached for the light switch, lost my balance, and thumped the rest of the way down the concrete steps. I lay there on the cement floor, among the dead bugs and other nasty things, and felt like crying. The fall had disoriented me, and as I stood, I fumbled around in the intense dark for the light switch. I found it. I put my right hand on the switch and my left hand on something solid to steady myself. I flipped the switch. Instead of the bright light that I'd expected, I heard an electric motor start, and suddenly my left hand was being chewed by some unseen monster. (The cream separator is to the left side of the door in the basement. I'd put my left hand on the belt drive, and when I flipped on the switch the motor had started, taking my hand around the pulley under the belt. The only thing I can be thankful for is that I was not facing the separator when I turned it on. Remember, I was stark-raving buck-ass naked. It could have been serious. My little sister might have, in that moment, gained the big sister she'd always wanted.) The pain was incredible, but I kept my mouth shut, enduring.

The incident with the cream separator oriented me, and I finally reached the lights. I stumbled to the shower trying to hold both my injured hand and my wounded gonies with my good hand. I turned on the shower and spent an hour trying to scrub off the river clay. (I had so much clay jammed into the crack of my butt that I finally had to use a toilet bowl brush to get it out. I was already rare from the multiple slides down the bank. Oh, the pain!)

I carefully crawled (naked) up the inside stairs to the dining room. I eased open the door and entered the house. I didn't dare turn on a light and risk waking the grandparents. I made my way carefully through the dark room. Just as I was reaching for the door to the stairway that led to my room, the dining room light came on with a glare that nearly blinded me.

"You okay, boy?" Granddad asked.

I looked at him, and he had a big grin on his face.

He knew.

I never violated his rules again. Ever. (Well, almost never.)

(This was just the beginning of a day that turned into an epic adventure.)

I slunk back to bed (thoroughly humiliated) after having watched Granddad experience a good laugh at my expense. I lay gingerly on my bed for several minutes and finally went back to sleep.

"Tom! Tom! Get out of bed!" she yelled up the stairs. Granny was never a particularly loud woman except when it came to getting me out of bed. I still firmly believe that she sat at the kitchen table and watched the clock until it read 6:30. Then she'd jump to her feet, run to the stairway, and scream up the stairs like some leather-lunged carnival barker.

The 6:30 wake-up call came, and I rolled from my bed. I could barely walk since various (tender) portions of my body were raw, and others (even more tender) had dark bruises, not to mention a rather large bump on my forehead and my left hand swollen to twice its normal size. I dressed carefully and went down the stairs to breakfast. Granddad had already gone to the tractor and the north forty, but he'd told Granny about my ordeal of the night before. She had an amused look on her face as I sat carefully in the kitchen chair.

"Nice storm we had," she commented.

"Yeah," I replied.

"Got about an inch of rain," she said.

"Yeah," I said.

"You got a close-up look at it, or so Dad said."

"Yeah," I replied.

"Must've really poured," she said as she turned toward the sink.

"Yeah," I agreed.

It was quiet for a moment, and then she turned back toward me. "I can't fix your shorts," she said. "Dad brought them up from the river, and I looked 'em over. They're pretty well destroyed. I guess we can buy you a new pair at Penney's when we go to town."

"Yeah."

"I went down over the bank with Dad, 'cause he said you'd left some fascinating tracks in the mud. You know, they kinda looked like two scoop shovels slidin' side by side. Must've been quite a ride."

"Yeah."

"Dad hung your shorts back in the tree where he found them. He said that a ride like that deserved some kind of monument." I thought I detected a trace of a chuckle in her voice.

"I'm gonna go chop weeds," I said intelligently as I pushed back from the table.

"Okay. It was nice talkin' to you this morning," she said.

"Yeah."

"Tom," she said to my retreating back, "Doug is coming down in about an hour to help me with some flowers. [My divorced mother and siblings (two) lived on the next farm just west.] Would you bring up the wheelbarrow when he gets here?"

"Sure," I replied and made my escape out the back door.

Well, the day was looking better. Tormenting my little brother was nearly as much fun as beating up my little sister. I rubbed Rusty's head (my Airedale dog), and we walked together toward the fencerow and the weeds. I took a good grip on the swinging scythe and swung it viciously both forward and back. The weeds sheared off near the ground. I imagined that I could hear them screaming as they fell, and that made my mood come up a little. I loosened up as I worked, and even my bruised tenders began to feel better. I worked for a while, then I looked down the drive. Here he came. The little innocent red-headed boy on his bike.

"Hi ya, Doug," I yelled as he leaned his bike against the fence.

"Hi," he responded with a mixture of caution and suspicion in his voice. "Where's Gran?"

"She's in the house," I replied.

He went in the back door, and I snuck in the front. I knew Granny wasn't in the house 'cause I could see her in the flower garden out back.

"Hey ya, Dougie-Wougie," I said as I caught him in the front room, knowing how being called Dougie-Wougie pissed him off.

"Shut up, and don't call me that or I'm gonna tell," he whined.

That was always his major threat to me. He was gonna tell.

I grabbed him around the neck and gave him a good knuckle rub on the top of his red burr-cut head.

"Don't Tom. I'm gonna tell."

I wanted to get him really mad. That was an integral part of my plan. I had to get him so mad that he would chase me. I drug him back out to the kitchen and threw him on the floor. I grabbed him by the back of the pants and literally mopped the floor with his chubby body.

"I'm gonna tell." He was almost crying.

"Mamma's boy," I said with my voice dripping sarcasm. (I can use clichés if they were actually said!)

His arms and legs started thrashing. "I'm gonna kill you, you bastard," he screamed.

He was mad now! I figured the time was ripe. I let him go and took off running through the house with Doug close behind. I ran through the front room, up the stairs, down the stairs, around the living room, and out the front door. I'd put a little distance between us by this time, and as I exited the screen door I took the time to push in the lock button. It would automatically lock when it closed.

Doug hit the screen door in full running stride. I'd stopped in the front yard to see what would happen, and I was amazed. I'm still amazed when I think back to it. I expected the screen door to bulge a little and throw him back into the front room when he hit it. Instead he diced himself completely through the wire mesh, and the door literally exploded. I still get cold chills thinking about the total destruction that I accomplished by simply baiting Doug and latching the door.

He started caterwauling so loud that I bet they could hear him across the river. Granny could sure hear him, and she came around the corner on a dead run. He wasn't gonna have to tell. The evidence was pretty plain.

Well, I won't go into all of the things that were said, or how Doug stood behind Granny with a smirk on his face while she dressed me down. I won't relate how I made a silent sacred vow to rip his little red head from his shoulders when I next caught him alone. I won't tell about how Gran preached to me about becoming a responsible human being, or about not picking on people smaller than me, or about "love thy brother."

I listened humbly to Granny for fifteen interminable minutes, knowing that Granddad would simply have nothing to say to me (absolutely nothing, that was always his punishment, not to speak to me), and that I would have to pay for the ruined door. At twenty-five cents an hour (what I was being paid for chopping weeds), it was going to take me a while to pay for my mistake.

Gran finished ripping on me and turned back toward her flowers. I watched her and Doug leave, and then he turned back and stuck his tongue out at me. I took a step toward him and stopped as he clutched Granny's skirt.

I grabbed the scythe, and the dog and I went back to making the weeds scream.

Noontime came, and with it the inevitable silence from Granddad after he heard the story. I went outside as quickly as I decently could. Doug had made faces at me while I sat impotently across the table with rage building in my gut. I ferociously attacked the weeds and kept at it for a solid hour until I heard Granddad's pickup head back for the field. I wiped the sweat from my face and made my way toward the house for a drink. I slipped into the kitchen and took the water jug from the refrigerator. I guzzled the cold water, put the jug back, and walked into the yard. I went out through the gate and was on the outside of the fence when I heard Doug call my name. I turned and there he stood, inside the nearly brand-new aluminum kitchen storm door, (this door was located on the east side of the house, opposite the one I'd destroyed that morning,) giving me the finger. He wasn't just flipping me the old original birdie. No sir, he'd added an up and down pumping motion to the action and had his hand well above his head. I grabbed up a rock that was about double the size of my fist, and I hummed it in his general direction.

Now, I was a pitcher of some reputation with the American Legion ball team.

I had excellent control and great velocity with my pitches. I still cannot explain why the rock hit the door. Perhaps the anger made my arm stronger, or maybe it was just fate. Anyhow, this rock (it seemed to have eyes and homed in exactly on the spot where it would do the most damage) hit the door right in the center of the aluminum panel just below the glass. The partition burst backward, and the glass fell out on the concrete. The door collapsed with a terrible amount of noise. (Have I mentioned that the storm door was less than a week old?) I saw the look of fear, amazement, and shock on Doug's face (the only redeeming thing about the whole episode was that I scared the shit out of him), and I took off running for the river with Rusty close behind. I knew that I could never, never return home. I'd become a fugitive.

I went over the first bank and took refuge in the cave that cousin Kenny and I had dug under the big walnut tree. I was determined to stay there until I died of hunger.

I stayed in the cave about an hour and then decided to take a walk up the river. (It got pretty boring in the cave with no one to talk to but a dog.) I felt about as low as a human can feel (whale poop on the ocean floor comes to mind), and I was sincerely trying to figure out how I could ever possibly redeem myself. I had managed, in the course of one short day, to destroy both entry doors on my grandparents' home (have I mentioned that the storm door was nearly new?), as well as the relationship with them that I had spent years building.

The dog and I walked for some distance and arrived at the fence-line between our farm and the Neely place.

(At this point it becomes incumbent upon me to explain to the reader about electric fences. Electric fences are a popular method by which a farmer may keep his livestock from straying into his neighbor's fields. This is accomplished by stringing a single bare twelve-gauge wire around the field where you would like to secure the livestock. The wire is then attached to a charger that is plugged into an electric outlet. Most of them use household current and work on a one-second-on and one-second-off pulse. The household current runs through the bare wire that surrounds the field, and when the animals touch it they get a mild shock. It causes enough discomfort that the animals become conditioned to stay away from the electric wire. There are some drawbacks that are consistent with the chargers that run on household current. One is that weeds eventually grow up onto the wire, effectively grounding it and putting it out of service. Another is that if a bull is big enough, mean enough, or just dumb enough, the household current has little effect on him. To overcome these shortcomings, some genius invented a wire charger that operated from 220 volts. They called it the Weed Burner because it would fry weeds off instantly when they touched it, or ignite the hair on a bull's ass if he backed into it. A. B. Neely was too old to keep the weeds cut, and he had an old Angus bull that was dumber than a stump, meaner than a two-headed snake, with a hide thicker than plate steel. A. B. bought and installed a Weed Burner fence charger on the line between our place and his to contain said bull. Therein lies the story.)

At the fence-line between the Neely place and ours, I stood for a moment and looked north toward where the river disappeared on the horizon. Maybe I'd just follow it toward its end and die a noble death during the search. As I stood looking I was seized by the desire to relieve the call of nature. Luckily, being a male of the species, I am able to relieve that particular call while standing on my feet. I unzipped and looked for an appropriate place to make the deposit. (It is very important to pee in the right place. It makes the effort much more satisfactory.) I noticed that several of the weeds in front of me were misshapen and curled curiously over as if they were sick. I decided that a good shot of nitrogen would help them (urine has a surprising amount of nitrogen in it, a fact I learned in vocational agriculture), and let loose the golden flow in their direction. As luck would have it, Rusty decided to take advantage of the weeds and the break from walking to likewise take a pee. He watched me a short moment and decided that my judgment concerning the placement was correct. He lifted his leg and looked off toward the west while he did his duty. Suddenly, his eyes bugged out, he was seized by a case of the shaking shivers, and he let out a horrible screech and fell over on his side.

"Holy shit," I remarked cleverly, wondering what had happened to my dog. His actions added velocity and distance to what I was doing, and I arched the stream over the weeds. Instantly I was grabbed by the "Jigger" (I bet you didn't know that boys have cute little names for their things), my eyes bugged out, I shook like a cat crapping a peach pit crossways, and I screeched at the top of my lungs. Something had hold of my most precious possession, yet I couldn't see a thing. Suddenly, I was released and fell on my side next to the dog. I couldn't move for many long seconds. Finally, some feeling was restored to my muscles, and after five minutes I was able to stand. Rusty stood up, looked at me as if I had personally attacked him, and headed for home at a dead run. I checked ole Jigger carefully to see if there was any permanent damage but found nothing except a certain insensitivity that worried me for a couple of days. I did learn a valuable lesson from that particular episode and wrote a letter to the inventor of the Weed

Burner fence charger requesting that he put a warning label on the device that stated: "Warning: It is hazardous to your 'Jigger' to pee on the Weed Burner fence wire when the charger is activated. Such action can cause personal injury to both you and your dog and can make it extremely hard for the dog to trust your judgment in other instances."

I don't know if he took any notice of my request, but I did begin to look carefully before I peed thereafter, and I finally did restore the dog's faith in my judgment some years later.

After my "accident" with the electric fence I decided to return to the scene of my former crimes (that is, the destroyed doors) and started slowly for home.

I met Granddad as he was coming out to look for me. (It seems that the dog came home without me and hid in his house. Granddad got concerned about my well-being since nothing had ever scared that particular dog before.) I inwardly cringed as we walked toward each other. I'd never had this most important man mad at me before, and he certainly had every reason to be now. I stopped in front of him with my head down and tears sliding down my face.

"You got to learn that you can't always run from your troubles, boy," he said in his quiet voice. "There comes a time when you can't run no more, and you have to face up to what life brings you." He wrapped his arm around my shoulders (making me cry all the harder) and walked me back toward the house. It was the first time he'd shown me any affection, or even understanding. His words still echo in my mind and have been a standard in my life.

We were almost to the house when he cleared his throat and spoke again.

"You owe me $56.50," he said.

It took me all summer to pay him off.

Kate Boyes

"I Hold with Those Who Favor Fire"

Some say the world will end in fire,
Some say in ice.
From what I've tasted of desire
I hold with those who favor fire.
— ROBERT FROST, "Fire and Ice"

1960

I cut my one political tooth on what my father still calls *the* Kennedy campaign. I was eight, and my father had just started showing up again at his parents' house where he'd left us two years before. He appeared on the front porch one Saturday, took us kids to a movie, and bought us all the soda pop we wanted. We wanted a lot. A few weeks later, the sound of angry voices woke me in the night. I heard my father's voice, and I wanted to go downstairs to see him, but the heat of the argument filled me with fear. I watched for my father through the bedroom window and waved when he left, but he was looking down at his scuffed boots and didn't see me.

Then he started coming regularly. He was waiting for us at my grandparents' house when we came home from school, and he left before my mother came home from work. He had a job now, he said. He was working on John F. Kennedy's presidential campaign, helping elect the man who was for the little people, the people like us who could be somebody if they got a chance. Of course, the job didn't pay anything—not yet, anyway. But if Kennedy won the election, everyone who worked hard on his campaign would go with him to Washington. And when my father got to D.C., he'd pass the good luck along, maybe finagle jobs for his friends, maybe give us kids an allowance.

When I heard this news, I danced around the kitchen. My father made his living trapping beaver and collecting pop bottles for refunds. Although he tried to parlay his third-grade education into a regular blue-collar job, he hadn't had any luck so far. I knew money was a problem between my parents; if he had a real job, that problem would be solved. My parents might get back together, I thought, maybe as soon as January when Kennedy and my father went to Washington.

So I helped him campaign, which meant plastering our county with Kennedy's face. We began with my father's car. He was fond of what my brothers called tubmobiles, bloated luxury cars he'd seen on a new car lot ten years before and could finally afford. Any big car skidding that quickly into his price range was a lemon, but he never quite caught on to that. His cars seemed grotesque to me, their headlights and grills glaring, their fins like those of the sharks we watched on *Sea Hunt*.

But when he covered his car with Kennedy stickers, it became festive. He started conservatively, one sticker on the back bumper. Then two. Then he covered the back bumper and the front. The stickers crept backward and forward around the rocker panels until the car was ringed with red, white, and blue. He used four bumper stickers to attach a Kennedy poster to his door, then more to stick posters on the other doors. He wired a poster to the front, like a clown's nose, and it gave the headlights a happy gleam and the grill a grin. Finally, he stuck a poster on his roof so the Russians could see it with their spy satellites. I felt like I was riding in a parade float whenever we drove off.

Campaigning was quite a bit like being in a parade because we smiled and waved and shouted, "Vote for Kennedy," as we drove along. So my father said I had to look good, which meant wearing a dress. I hated dresses. They were something women wore, and I was never going to be a woman. Women made men miserable. And Jackie Kennedy was the worst! One day my father shoved a clipping from the food section of our newspaper into my hand. The article claimed JFK's favorite soup was bouillabaisse. "That's a lie," my father said, so angry he could barely drive straight. JFK didn't like that stuff. He liked the kind of clam chowder we ate, with milk and potatoes — not the red kind. My father said Jackie made her husband eat bouillabaisse to get ahead in society. I imagined Jackie, with her little smile and her pink pillbox hat, forcing Kennedy to eat strange soup. "Just like a woman," my father said.

I didn't like wearing dresses, but my father said sacrifices make good things happen. I knew all about that. I'd decided a year ago I wouldn't eat dessert until my mother had another baby. After three weeks, our cat had kittens; I figured that was close enough. And every day I tried to be good so the dark shadows that frightened me at night would stay in the far corner of my room. My father had already made a sacrifice. He'd gone down to the Salvation Army thrift shop and bought a pair of dress slacks that only had to be rolled up a few times to fit him and a white shirt with cuffs that weren't badly frayed.

We campaigned first in remote sections of our rural county because my father said that's where the little people lived. I held posters on my lap, handed them out the window of the car to my father, and then watched him nail them to telephone and utility poles. It was illegal to nail posters to the poles, but that was only because Republicans owned the phone and power companies. My father hammered posters up fast, so fast the county sheriff couldn't catch him in the act. All the sheriffs were Republicans. He kept the car running, just in case we had to make a quick getaway.

My father left the radio on, too, and I listened to interviews with the candidates while he nailed up the posters. That's when I started campaigning for more than the chance to help my father land a job. Nixon couldn't be trusted — you could hear that in his voice. He was like Ed Sullivan, only not funny. But Kennedy was a Democrat, an Irish Catholic, one of us. He sounded like he really could make our lives better, like he could prove that all politicians weren't bad. I would have done anything for him.

After the poles were covered with posters, we went on to store windows and front yards in our county's one large town. I didn't like campaigning in town so much. I had to wait for my father in the car while he went inside stores and houses to talk to people. He was often gone for a long time, especially at bars. My father said the owners liked Kennedy one day, but then they'd listen to Republicans on the radio and change their minds. He had to set them straight, so we went back to bars again and again. And the woman in one house must have needed plenty of convincing, too, because we stopped there often and stayed for a long time. Sometimes my father would rip down a Nixon poster on the way over to that woman's house and let me use his carpenter's pencil to draw on the back while I waited in the car outside.

And then one day my father said I had to do some campaigning all by myself. He wanted a store owner to put a poster up in his window, and for some reason my father refused to go into that store. He stopped his car half a block away from the place, handed me a poster, and leaned over to open the car door for me. Then he stayed crouched down as he made a U-turn and drove off. My father didn't know that my mother shopped at this store. I knew the owner and he knew me. Before I could ask about putting a poster in his window, he said to tell my father to stay away from his store, his house, and his wife, and then asked if I'd heard him.

I couldn't answer because I had been chewing nervously on a corner of the poster, and bits of cardboard were stuck in my throat. I hurried outside, but my father was nowhere in sight. Then I felt something dribble from my mouth, and

I looked down and saw a red stain on the white collar of my dress and on the poster I was holding. The cardboard's sharp edge had rubbed the skin off a late-erupting six-year molar. So I waited for my father and watched a trickle of blood and saliva drip down the poster, drip down JFK's face from his forehead to his chin.

1961

I had been out of school for two days with an ear infection when news of the Bay of Pigs invaded our home. My mother was working late, so my father took the opportunity to eat a good meal at my grandparents' house. At the supper table that night, he spoke of nothing but revolt and counter-revolt, espionage and sabotage.

I was well enough to sit up on the couch but too sick to eat with the family, so the affair seemed distant to me, unreal. The news flowed in from the kitchen, the meaning obscured by a fever fog. I held a bowl of potato soup on my lap and tried to listen. But my head drooped until the nape of my neck rested against the prickly back of the horsehair couch, rested there while I drifted in and out of half-dreams of dancing St. Joseph aspirin, rectal thermometers, and Cuban cigars. The couch needled me like a newly trimmed beard, causing just enough discomfort to keep me from drifting off completely.

The conversation seemed to fit the category of "Important But Not Really." The invasion was like a drought or the price of coal. Would it make any difference in how often my brother punched me in the arm while we waited for the school bus? Would it make my teacher stop ridiculing my handwriting in front of the class? No, no, so I put my soup bowl on the floor and lay down. I covered myself with a wool blanket and would have slept if someone hadn't mentioned The Bomb.

I don't remember when I first heard that term, but now it penetrated through my fever like the flames of a brush fire. I knew suddenly that The Bomb was what I had been dreading each night for years. Until the Bay of Pigs, The Bomb was a nameless creature hiding in the shadowed corner of my room after dark, too impossible to believe in, too dangerous to scoff at. Now the creature had a name. Now even the adults believed.

My father brought good cigars with him that night, and he and my grandfather had each smoked one before supper. Cigar smoke still swirled in currents near the ceiling. Blue haze came with my father, his visits obscuring the house with smoke that rose and hung in the air, lowering above our heads. The men sat at the supper table long after the food was gone, each having another cigar, and the haze dropped until curtains of blue clouded the air above my face, making me cough.

Life with my father had always been like this, but I had been too young before to understand that. Objects and events were obscured; the truth was never clear. Dark thoughts came with waves of fever, and I remembered all the times my father had let me down. Once, when he still lived with us, he said he would see us at supper, but he didn't come home for weeks. Another time we tracked him through five states and asked him to come home, and he told us he would. He said he would meet us the next day at a little motel we knew. We waited at that motel for days, my mother, brothers, sister, and I sleeping crosswise on the one bed in our room until we had only enough money to buy gas for the trip home.

And all those promises during the Kennedy campaign. I worked with him right up to the election, and then Kennedy was president and my father was gone. He was in Washington, I was sure, and would call from there any day. Or I would find a letter in the mailbox with a D.C. postmark, and there would be a picture of him by the Lincoln Memorial or the White House and maybe a few dollars for us kids. We didn't hear from him in January, but I figured he was busy with the inauguration. When he finally came to borrow money from my grandparents, I found he had been living the whole time with another woman in a town twenty miles away. He was one of the little people, but his actions made me feel even smaller.

My father said Kennedy wouldn't try a stunt like the Bay of Pigs invasion, but Kennedy himself said he was responsible. I didn't know who to believe. Sacrifices were being made — by my father, by Kennedy — but it felt like they were sacrificing the rest of us, and nothing good was happening. My feverish thoughts circled around and around the darkness of deception.

Then I realized it made no difference in whom or what I believed. The Bomb was on the loose; nothing else mattered. I would continue to curl like a fetus against the innermost brick wall of our school when we practiced for a nuclear attack, but I would secretly believe that surviving an attack was the worst fate, that quick death was a friend. In time, living with imminent death around me would make annihilation my familiar. And I remember thinking that night that no sacrifice I made would ever turn down the flame of danger that burned so brightly now before my eyes.

1968

Washington explodes. The event is billed as another Poor People's March, a non-violent plea for help like Martin Luther King, Jr.'s march a few years before. But more is at stake now, and this march will not be the same. Hot winds from Southeast Asia scorch our lives, and the little people — the tinder — have caught fire.

Busloads of us drive to Washington to tell the government we are mad. I am at the end of the line, and there is no room for me on the last bus. No room, either, for the two Vietnam vets who have been drinking in an alley nearby. They wander over, hear the local organizer give his spiel, stand looking at the concrete, at each other, at the half-empty bottle one holds in his one remaining hand. Information seeps slowly through the alcohol, and they stand there while the bus pulls out. Then they want to go, must go. One cries and wipes his face with the bottle's brown paper sack. The organizer is driving a car to Washington; the vets sob and plead their way into the car, and I go with them.

We travel through the dark to D.C. The vets sleep, one in front, one beside me in the back. The organizer owns this car, has visited Africa, and wears a head-band with no sweat stains, so I am suspicious and say little. I notice, though, that he has a long gash across his temple. He says a cop clobbered him during a demonstration. The new purple wound is crudely stitched, the skin pulled so tight it shines in the dashboard's light.

The vets wake about an hour outside the city, and they sing along with the radio. They are singing "MacArthur Park" when news comes that the march has turned violent. The vets keep singing, even when Richard Harris is abruptly silenced for the announcement. They keep singing, and the organizer and I strain to hear which sections of the city are under fire, what curfew has been set, when the National Guard will arrive.

The organizer decides to skip the action tonight and join the demonstrators tomorrow. He has a friend we can stay with, and he asks the vets to quiet down so he can hear if the section of D.C. his friend lives in is still open. He's clearly annoyed by their singing. The vet in front sits quietly for a minute then sobs loudly. The one by me pulls a knife out of his boot, leans forward, holds the knife by the driver's cheek with his one hand, and says he and his friend sing whenever they want.

We are near the city, and we are sad. We travel toward D.C. in the night, toward the center of our sadness, into the heart of our fear. We have been travelling here all our lives. "Surfin' U.S.A." comes on the radio, and no one moves, no one speaks. The knife catches the headlights of a car behind us, flashes, then loses its gleam when the car passes.

The organizer starts singing. There is a sack of sandwiches, beer, and apples by my feet. The food is there, and I haven't touched it, even though I haven't eaten for two days. Now I pass out sandwiches. I ask the man beside me to cut an apple in two so we can share it. He cuts apples for all of us. Then he uses the knife to open a bottle of beer for his friend, one for himself, another for the driver. They drink. We all sing. He puts the knife back in his boot.

Before we finish our meal, we reach the edge of the city. Tear gas stings our eyes and throats. Even with windows up and vents closed, tear gas enters the car like an evil thought. Streets are littered with papers, clothes, blankets, but no people, like the streets I've seen night after night in my dreams of nuclear war. The gas films our eyes, hazes the air; street signs slip out of focus just when we think we've found our way.

A service station owner is boarding up his windows, but he lets us buy gas and use his phone. The curfew has begun, and the National Guard is on the way. Hurry, we say to the organizer, who calls his friend. Hurry, we say to the vet with two hands, who pumps our gas. I wash the car windows because there is nothing else I can do.

There is a bridge over a river. On one side is the world where power rules. And on the other side, which is our side tonight and has always been our side, the little people pump gas, use the phone, wash windows. We hurry, but we are not fast enough. There is a bridge over a river, and from that other side comes a truck like a cattle truck but full of power. Men are standing in the back of that truck. They hold their weapons straight up like candles, and the bayonets on those weapons are cold, silver flames.

The National Guard surround us in a moment. The organizer hides behind the gas station, but they drag him back. The sobbing vet drops the gas hose and runs for the river. When he is tackled and hits the ground, a sigh as large as his longing for life before the war escapes and blows cinders into the air. The other vet crouches in the car and tries to cover himself with a blanket, but his good hand is gone, and his clumsy fumbling attracts their attention. They pull him out by his empty sleeve. Gas is still flowing from the nozzle the vet dropped. While three Guards surround me, I watch a dark rainbow flow from the hose, pool on the concrete by their boots, and swirl around the car's tires.

They search the men. They thrust their hands roughly into the vets' crotches. They knock the organizer's head hard several times against the car, and blood oozes through the stitches of his recent wound. The Guards around me hesitate, but they are ordered to make a search. I am fifteen, these men are young, and we are all at our first dance with life. We are so clumsy, touching and being touched. In the truck, men hoot and make suggestions to those who will search me. I hear this, and I hear the officer in command make his own sexual suggestions. But what I hear most clearly is one Guard asking the other two to screen me from the gaping men on the truck. And what I remember most clearly is how that Guard acted efficiently, quickly, finished the search fast.

Then we wait, each of us with our three Guards, while the one in command decides our fate. The other groups exchange unpleasantries, shout and are shouted at, argue politics. My Guards put the gas hose back on the pump and then talk quietly to each other, to me. We watch vibrant color bands of petroleum reflect in their newly shined boots. We hope no one lights a cigarette. We are, all four of us, afraid to be here tonight, to be around the people we've come with, to be the people we have become.

The officer decides we can go as long as we leave town. We are in the car, and we are going, gladly. We are going, the key is in the ignition, and the commanding officer taps the tip of his bayonet on our window. The vet with one hand rolls down the window while we think about gasoline near our exhaust pipe, about speeding down the road, about being someplace else in some other time. But we wait while the officer leans in until his face is close to the vet's. The bayonet hangs between their eyes, gleaming red in the light of the gas station's neon sign. The officer says he should arrest us, would like nothing more than to arrest us, but he's been ordered to "save the jail cells for the niggers."

I want to tell him that isn't fair. I want to say we are all black tonight. The vet beside me senses that I want to speak, that our lives, a moment before heading out of town and into the anonymity of the highway, are now turning back toward danger. He feels the spark of injustice that rushes through me threaten to immolate us all, and he moves his body so that I would have to crawl around him to be seen or heard by the officer. I am fifteen, and I have not seen what a bayonet thrust can do. I am fifteen, and I have not seen a body charred. We drive away.

We drive away from Washington in the night, holding fear close to our hearts, travelling into a world of sadness. In ten days, the vet who cries will be drunk and will say something foolish on a street corner; four riot police will beat him with clubs. I will watch the beginning of the beating, but they will see me watching and drag the vet into a stairwell to finish. Then he will be flushed into prison.

The organizer will take me to Abbey Hoffman's apartment, blindfolding me with his clean headband and making me swear I will never tell anyone else the way. He will sit in a book-filled room and plan events that set Chicago on fire during the Democratic convention later in the summer. He will be on trial for years.

The vet with one arm will leave town after his friend is arrested. He will leave thinking he has survived war in the jungles and war on the streets of this country. But he won't know that the hell of both will hound him for the rest of his life.

I will live on the streets of a city. I will hold the muddled heads of drug users on my lap and tell them what I think is real and what I hope is not. I will huddle in the darkest corner of a room while police fire live ammunition into the crowd outside, and later I will see bullet holes in the building, deep pock marks in the red bricks at head level. One day a man will shove me into his car, and it will take a few minutes for me to realize that the man is my father and that I am going home, going home to wait for the world to end.

Ken Brewer

The Importance of Missing the Mark

Commitment

Deciding to become a writer is dangerous. It guarantees nothing but the realization of how little one truly knows and how much patience, commitment, and acceptance of cosmic irony one needs. I made that decision in 1965 when I was a graduate student in English at New Mexico State University.

My mentor there was the poet Keith Wilson. His advice was to expect at least a ten-year apprenticeship period: ten years of learning, of commitment, of patience before any major publications, before I could say with any confidence that I had become a writer, or even worse, a poet. Ten years, at least, of cosmic irony. It has been twenty-five years. I do occasionally admit to being a poet.

I am also a teacher, like most poets in the USA. Our system of higher education supports most poets and many fiction writers and playwrights. I know very few writers who actually live on the earnings of their writing, and those who do probably spent a long time in the teaching mills before they could. For most of us, writing is a second occupation, a "shadow occupation," as Sam Hamill calls it in an essay in the *American Poetry Review*. That, I guess, is part of the irony: what we commit ourselves to seldom becomes more than a shadow seeping below the country's footsteps.

I teach writing: poetry, nonfiction, and, occasionally, fiction. I teach introductory, advanced, and graduate levels. I hesitate to ask my students to make the sort of commitment I believe is necessary to "become a writer." Of the twenty-five hundred or so creative writing students I have taught, perhaps five have made that commitment. Two have begun to make a mark for themselves — after at least ten years.

My point here is that beginning writers — young or old — seldom understand what writing demands of its victims. I often receive phone calls, especially during periods of economic woe, from beginners who want me to "look at" their writing. Usually I think, they want me to tell them how wonderful it is and how much money they will make — they need the money soon. Ten years is not soon enough.

The pattern of development that has emerged in the USA is this: you begin by taking creative writing courses (high school and college), then publishing in the school magazines. If you are "committed," you begin to submit to local and regional journals, then national ones. The idea is to build a vita of publications leading to a first book publication, usually a chapbook issued by a small press. Eventually, you either win a major literary competition or have a book accepted for publication by one of the larger publishing houses — or a well-known university press. This pattern is most common for poets. Of course, if you persist, if you live long enough, you will win the Pulitzer, the Nobel, and the Ronald Reagan Award — the USA's version of knighthood. If you're doing all of this for money, your odds are probably better trying to win a Publisher's Clearing House contest.

Not everyone chooses this path, of course. Some refuse to load their poems into the shotgun of mailings and blast them at journals they've never even looked inside, or to dog it out on the reading circuit — a reading here, a reading there, plus a summer workshop gig for one week with a dozen beginning writers who want to hear how good their work is and how much money they will make.

Some countries have pubs, some have salons. We have the creative writing workshop.

Though I make my living teaching such workshops, I am not convinced that they represent the only way to learn to write in the USA, or even the best way. I work hard to keep attentive to what writing is all about. Workshop discussions can deteriorate into "technical writing" briefs — cold, precise word processing — or dogfights with everyone barking at each other where a line should break. Of course, we need to learn our craft, but, above all, we need to remember why we're learning it. More often than not, we miss the mark. Learning to hit it takes patience, takes years of trying.

When I shoot a mature rooster pheasant, surely one of the most beautiful of birds, I cannot find the words to express that feeling. I can describe how my golden retriever worked the scent, doubling back, circling, nose in the snow and tail thwacking the bitterbrush and thistle. I can describe the burst of feathers and whirring as the pheasant finally flew, but I would have to say it was like a jack-in-the-box popping out through dry leaves and a chandelier made of bamboo shoots and whistles. But even this is "missing the mark," because I have to describe what it is by saying what it is not, as if all things are somehow the same. And, finally, the clean shot, the gun tight to my shoulder, the report, the way the bird seemed to freeze in midair then fall, a graceful, bloody death, every bit as beautiful, as ugly, as a graceful, bloody birth. Still, I miss the mark. Words are not as accurate as steel shot.

Writing and Waltzing

How, when, where, and why did I become a writer? I don't know exactly, but I think it had something to do with waltzing. I never learned to waltz, yet many people think I'm a good dancer. Fast dancing, that's what I'm good at — isolated, alienated, standoffish, fast dancing. I move well — for such a big man — when I can set my own rules, dance my own steps, find my own rhythm in the music. But I can't waltz.

I remember taking waltzing lessons, as well as foxtrot, rumba, and tango, when I was in elementary school — the P.S. 62 Ballroom Dance Class that ended the school year with a formal ballroom dance. I hated the entire experience. Not only am I a "big man"; I was also a "big boy." Actually, I was a fat boy, which meant I could never dance with the cute girls — the ones whose initials I wrote secretly in my notebook. I was stuck with the tall, skinny, gawky girl whose bony sternum met my eye level in waltz grip; or the three-foot dwarf whose hair stood straight in the air like an electrified pompon. Of course, as I look back on this (as I write it), I realize what those two girls, who are probably charming, attractive, middle-aged women now, must have felt having to dance with the fattest kid in school who always sweated a lot.

So I didn't pay attention, got terribly ill the day of the formal ballroom dance, and stayed home, leaving, I guess, giant and dwarf to dance with each other. My failure to learn to waltz was the first sign of a lifetime of disasters.

Ironically, I love to play waltzes on my guitar; of course, I never learned to read music, so I play my own versions. I also write open form poetry rather than traditional, formal poetry. Politically, I'm independent. Religiously, I'm nothing. My taste in music ranges from Rimsky-Korsakov to Paul Simon to Lightnin' Hopkins to Emmylou Harris; some would say I have no taste at all. My favorite novels are The Tin Drum and The World According to Garp. I wear a three-piece suit to school one day then a sweater and Levis the next. I like a meal of bologna-cheese-and-onion sandwiches with Grand Marnier mousse for dessert; some would say I have no taste at all. I like strong, independent women who let me win all the arguments.

But I can't seem to stay married to such women. I don't communicate well about important problems. Isn't that ironic: a writer who can't communicate. Oh, I'm good at talking, as long as it's about writing or literature or current events. But when it's how to pay the bills without going bankrupt, or how to deal with troubled children, or how to tell a wife that I'm depressed because I can't seem to write anything worth a damn lately—these are the times I become a human conch shell sitting in a chair and hoping, I guess, for someone to put her ear to my mouth, or my heart, and listen without my actually having to speak. So I listen to my own voice inside that hollow, empty shell, and I listen to music—alone, of course, the same way I dance.

I'm at the trumpet's end of my second marriage, it sounds like, and I'm beginning to realize, as I write this, how I have designed my life. I could have saved this marriage several years ago when my wife and I joined a dance club. At one particular dance club evening, my wife chided me for never having learned to waltz. Adult that I am, I immediately pouted, sat out the next four dances, drank three scotches, and flirted with half a dozen other women (though I doubt they realized I was flirting). Eventually, I danced with my wife again, but only when the band hit "Proud Mary" and I could do my extravagant, self-indulgent, get-down, boogie, swing-spin-hop fast dance. If only there were such concatenators as gods! Such a moment would bring forth an epiphany. A bolt of lightning would strike the lead guitar, screech the voice of the God of Sudden Insight throughout the Country Club ballroom: "IF YOU DON'T LEARN TO WALTZ, YOU'LL SCREW UP THIS MARRIAGE, YOU IDIOT!" But there is no such god, so it took me ten years to realize the "sudden insight" in this act of writing: if I had learned to waltz, I wouldn't be alone right now.

Waltzing is a graceful, elegant motion. To waltz is to give, to feel, to join, to love. Two people hold one another, swirl through a bounded space, know exactly how, when, where, and why they do what they do.

I can't waltz. I'm a writer.

Maps

My family has strong women, their strength coming from years of quiet suffering, from years of forced independence, from years of unresolved anger. The men in my family die young, from the miner's black lung, the alcoholic's cancer, the down-and-out white folk blues. I'm the first man in my family to graduate from college; indeed, I'm one of the few to ever finish high school. I suffer like my mother and sing the blues like all the men — but quietly and to myself.

The zygote didn't split, I guess. Too much booze gives me a headache, and I don't feel much anger. The easy answer is that my early childhood "determined" this duality. I was born nine days before Japan bombed Pearl Harbor. My father was already in the army and didn't return from the Philippines until late 1945. My mother raised me, protected me, nurtured my loneliness with her constant womanly presence.

When my father finally had to become a father, I'm quite certain he was frightened. Tearing down and cleaning a rifle is one thing; a child is something else. Tossing a hand grenade into the air does not easily change into tossing a breathless son who howls at the very sight of this stranger. My father was always a soldier to me, as if I could never quite see him behind all that jungle camouflage.

Alfred Korzybski writes, "The map is not the territory." I believe that is true of how we perceive and understand other people, including our parents. My experience of my parents is *not* them. It can only be *my* experience of them. Nor is what I now recollect necessarily accurate. It can only be my imagined recollection. Not photographs, not journal entries, not my grandmother's account, nor any other sort of record can give me my parents — only their maps.

My father lived through malarial dreams and alcoholic weekends while I lived through P.S. 62 and Thomas Carr Howe High School. My mother suffered quietly through everything. Yet I only saw her in tears twice; I never heard her shout.

When I was in sixth grade, I played hooky a good deal. The sixth-grade teacher, Mrs. McDaniel, had embarrassed me in front of the entire class the first day of school. When I went to the blackboard to work a math problem, she said I made my eights as fat as I made my body. So I spent most of that year angry at her and spiteful. One afternoon I had two of my Catholic school buddies at the house — they sometimes had holidays we public schoolers did not observe. We got into a raucous rubber-band-shooting battle throughout the house. I should explain here that my parents were seldom home during the day since both worked every day but Sunday, so I was left to myself most of the time. My mother collected salt and pepper shakers — must have had five hundred pairs on display in various places throughout our very small house. She had converted a dining room into a bedroom by hanging curtains across the entrance and stationing two bookshelves to serve as room dividers, loaded, of course, with salt and pepper shakers from all over the country and several parts of the world.

Since there is no suspense as to what happened, I'll make the point quickly.

While running from a flying rubber band, shot from the end of a ruler, I toppled one of the bookshelves, smashing dozens of salt and pepper shakers. That night, my mother sat in the middle of the living-room floor where I had left my shattered souvenirs — and she cried. I felt like one of the rubber bands I had stretched too tightly — one that snapped and bit my heart before I could let go. My father's belt thrashing the back of my legs would have been easier to withstand.

The only other time I saw her cry was on their twentieth wedding anniversary. My father disappeared from Friday afternoon to Sunday night on one of his drunken weekends. I was in high school then, playing football and thinking about girls. When Dad finally showed up, he presented Mom with a set of Blue Willow dishes. He was still drunk and barely managed to get the two large boxes into the house before he passed out at the kitchen table. My mother and I dragged him to the bedroom; then she sat on the floor next to the bed and cried. I carted those Blue Willow dishes through several states and two marriages of my own. I sold them eventually for $10 at a garage sale. That's more than I make on most poems I sell.

I am mostly a stranger to my parents as they are to me. I cannot say that I know either of them very well. Since I left home for college, I have spent fewer than a dozen months with them, broken visits of a few days, a couple weeks at most. I have my mother's eyes and hands, her way of suffering, never shouting. I have my father's failures, my father's nightmares, and his Kentucky blues.

Beyond them both, I have words. This is why I write and, I guess, what this essay is, after all, trying to tell me. I write to save myself. I know these words are maps; they are not the territory. Without them, though, I would be truly lost.

Marilyn Brown

On the Way Home with America

Tag Haggarty ate at the same time I ate in the lunch house. At eleven forty-five he passed the door of my classroom so fast I saw streaks of overalls and sometimes heard a crash close to the office. He was always close to first in line. By the time I got to the old house in the schoolyard, he was waiting at the window they had punched out between the living room of the lunch house and the kitchen where a couple of ladies leaned far out with ice-cream scoops full of potatoes or yams or spaghetti and slopped them on the tin plates. I was late. I stood at the door sometimes in and sometimes out, where another lady took our dimes. Sometimes the dime lady was the taxi driver America Laughingheart. Sometimes she stood back in the kitchen with a towel on her hair pulling utensils off the racks and pushing pans into ovens. Every time I went by I looked for her. She smiled at me.

When Tag dropped his chili on the floor, she came out and bent over it. She got down on the floor, and there wasn't room to pass. She wiped up the floor and wrung out the rag in a bucket. Tag started to cry.

"Hey! Are those tears?" she said to him.

Tag started to shake.

"Don't let it get you! There's more," she said.

He put his fists in his eyes.

"Come here." She was kneeling down in front of the window. A bunch of us, hungry as maggots, stood beating our tin plates against our legs, and she pulled Tag into her big arms and put his head on her shoulder. He all but disappeared inside of her big arms.

"There there. Let's get you another plate." When she stood up, all the tables on the lunchroom floor rocked under her weight. The people in back of me started to shout. America didn't even look at them.

"Come over here," she said. "Here's another plate and another spoon."

Tag sat in front of his chili with his face in it. He didn't move for a few minutes. America sat with him and kept her big white arm on his back. It swallowed him up.

I would have been embarrassed if I were Tag. But I couldn't stop looking at

America Laughingheart with the red hair tied in a loose bun on the top of her head, the huge peonies on her dress.

My class came through the lunch house before Jessica's. I sat by Suzanne or Katie and ate as fast as I could so Jessica's class could come in. We ate without talking. Henry put his face inside the bowl, and when he came out of it there was nothing there. Chili day was all right. Only a few people snubbed it and grabbed handfuls of crackers or carrots as they left out the west door.

Suzanne was talking. But I watched America Laughingheart if I could. When she disappeared into the kitchen I still watched for her. I saw her walk back and forth in front of the window carrying big pots or pans of rolls.

I threw up one day, and the children sitting beside me left the lunch house without finishing their food. America came out to the table and scooped my vomit into a pudding-mix box with the same spoon she was done dishing up the macaroni and cheese with.

"I'm going that way," she said. "I'll take you home, honey. Something disagreed with you. You got folks at home?"

I didn't know. Grandpa Callister was minding the store. I stood around and waited while America Laughingheart pulled the big canvas apron off her head. Her hair slipped out of the bandanna on her head and fell around her shoulders. There was something in the pit of my stomach that tasted like apple seeds.

"Well, let's go. I got the horse on the west road."

I found Jessica and told her I was going home. She was rubbing crackers between her hands and letting them fall out on her macaroni and cheese like salt out of a salt shaker.

"Who you going with?" she said crushing crackers.

"The taxi lady."

"Mother won't like it going with strangers."

"She's not strangers. We know her. She serves lunch every day. She lives in Covered Bridge."

"She smokes," Jessica said.

"She does not," I said.

"She does too. I'll tell."

"Go ahead," I said.

When the door opened, the sunlight reflected off the wet floor and hit my eyes. The cooler air rushed in. Three more people left without finishing their food. I had a headache.

"Come on," America said. She waited for me outside the door wrapped in her big shawl. She turned and I followed her. Suzanne, or someone behind me, shut the door with a bang. I thought that was rude. But I didn't stop to think about it. I walked into the hot sun without seeing America. I knew she was there. The sun was sharp in my eyes.

"I have just one stop to make," she said.

Standing on the road looking bored was the horse in front of the big cart. He wore patches over his eyes.

"General Sampson!" she called.

The horse jerked the harness and stamped. She ambled up beside him, and he nuzzled her hair. He lifted his big nose and pulled it back from his teeth black around the edges. He had a few teeth left. They looked like stakes hammered into old gums.

"Are you all right, honey?" America said.

I was shaking.

"That sweater can't keep you warm." She gave me a blanket. It was blue with white fuzz balls on it. Used to be yarn. I sat on the cart bench and pulled the blanket up around my shoulders.

"You still sick, honey? I got some peppermint tea would give you a new look. Your eyes is pale. There's a few things growing right around these parts that kick you into synch. I've had that pallor before, and it goes away with some singing too."

So she began to sing. I pulled the blanket up around my shoulders. It smelled like horsehair.

"Robbers are hurting, the barons are closer, begum," she sang. "Pearly hearts cross on the trees in the tiddely tum."

"Is that a song I ever heard before?" I asked her.

"What kind of songs you heard before?" she asked me.

"I never heard that one."

"Singing is good for what ails you," she said. She took up the song again. "Favors are cheating, and summers are fleeting begum."

"What does *begum* mean?" I said.

"It's the magic in it. When you say *begum* you're calling up the ground," America Laughingheart said.

"The ground?"

"The ground is your friend. You ever thought of that?"

No, I never did.

"It's what you come from. It's what you go to. It holds you up. It keeps you walking."

She hauled the horse around in the middle of the road. Clop clop clop. It pulled us past the house built by the architect Lloyd Wright.

"Some people is rich, some people is happy," America Laughingheart sang. "I bet all my money on herbs and honey, begum."

When we came to a light, she pulled the horse to a stop by lifting the reins above her head. "Whoa, General Sampson," she sang. The horse shook his head up and down, snapping the leather in her hands.

"You ever thought about being rich?" America asked me.

"I wished we had a car," I said. "My mother has to walk to the Startup Candy Company."

"Why that's no good. I thought Mr. Potter lent you that car."

"We went up to Covered Bridge to get it." Grandpa Callister said Mrs. Potter opened the windows to let in the breeze on the hot night. A man in the yard watched her take off her clothes. That was the last time anybody saw her alive, and after that nobody ever saw that man again, either.

"There ain't nothing wrong with wishing for a car."

"Why didn't you wish for one?"

"General Sampson and I are old friends."

I waited for a minute in silence.

"How do you think General Sampson would feel to be traded in for a car?"

"Not very good," I said, looking ahead on the road.

"It's a matter of what's real and what isn't," America said to me. "General Sampson is real. A car isn't."

"A car's real," I dared to say.

"You think a car's real," America laughed out loud. "Look at over there in the cemetery." We were drawing close to it now. The horse was tugging the cart through the light. "If there's something alive somewhere in that van, you'll never see it. That vehicle looks like an overfat hog. But there's nothing in there at all. Life is the only substance, honey. And don't you forget it. Look around you. Do you see anything that wasn't touched at one time by life. Wood in the houses, rocks made out of grass a million years old. The dirt comes through the peppermint leaves, and you make tea out of it."

"The tin was rocks once."

"Well, say, I guess you're right about that. Where did you get your smarts?" America said.

"My father draws guns for the war."

"That ought to make anyone quite smart," she said.

I pulled the blanket down from my ears and looked out at the men in the graveyard in white pants and shoes. They were throwing shovels up and down with dirt in them.

"Somebody's either coming or going," America said.

"They're throwing dirt on somebody," I said. "That's their van, and they just put somebody in, and they are throwing dirt over them."

America slowed General Sampson to a slow crawl. She sat up tall and stretched her neck up. Usually folded up into rolls, she was long and white when her head went up.

"Are you sure about that, Lindy?" she said. "I don't see it that way."

I stood up in the cart. The blanket fell down.

"I see them taking dirt out of that ground. Isn't that what they are doing? They're digging a hole to put somebody in that ground."

"How can you tell?"

"Maybe there isn't a way to tell unless we ask them."

"Are you going to ask them?"

"Do you want to ask them?"

"Does it matter what is really going on?" I said.

"You can't always see what's real," America Laughingheart said. "What is real? Is somebody going in or coming out? Do we need to know?"

"I saw you at Mrs. Potter's funeral."

"Were you sure it was me?" Then she laughed.

"It's easy enough to tell it's you."

"Not always. Sometimes I'm different. When I'm with General Sampson I'm one person. When I'm at home alone I write songs. I think about my boy and wonder if he's grown up like you."

"How old would he be?"

"Older than you. Maybe twice as old as you. Are you ten?"

"What happened to him?"

"I was building a fire down on the corner of the west forty, waiting for Caleb to fetch some more firewood. We was going to try to save the sheep," America said.

"Did they die?" I said.

"Not a one of them," America said. "We rounded up every one of them that was frozen inside a wall of ice. The fire in the middle of it kept them warm. But Caleb was carrying Bowie on his back, and the Indians came and took him. Wounded Caleb. And eventually I lost them both."

"How old was Bowie?"

"Near four months old."

"Why?"

The cart came up to the Sinclair. It looked dead. Mr. Potter was at Covered Bridge, and the Stuart boy who ran the station had put a sign on the door in pencil that said Back at 2:00.

"That's half an hour from now," America Laughingheart said, glancing through the window at the Coca Cola clock. "I wonder if Potter knows those Stuart boys aren't worth drinking from the crack in the teacup."

"Why did the Indians take the baby? I thought you was an Indian."

"I never knew my father," America said. "My mother was whiter than you, and she give me this red hair."

America got down out of the cart when we pulled into the Sinclair. General Sampson snorted. She stood and tied General Sampson's reins into a knot on his leathers. She was still glancing over to the cemetery looking philosophical while it looked to me like the men were throwing dirt onto the grave. She went up to the green door and looked in at the window. "Look. If your folks is home anyway, I'll wager they haven't got peppermint tea. I'll stir some up on Hammersley's hot plate."

"There's something in the air about this quiet," America said.

"What do you think they are doing?" I said.

"I don't know, but I intend to find out. As soon as I fix you up I'm going to go over there and ask them."

She pulled the blanket around me and tucked it into itself. She reached to the top of the door frame and pulled down an old key. "Hammersley knows I'll never tell anybody who'd do him any harm. You're not a robber, Lindy. I can see it in your eyes. You live long enough, you see signs written all over people that tells you what they're going to do next."

"How do you know?"

"You just know. You see lines around somebody's nose, pimples on somebody else's ears. It just happens certain ways like the laws of dirt and leaves."

The station was almost dark at quarter to two. The slanted sun came in the garage part only and fell on the cement and oil. In the back of the garage stood a long dirty countertop covered with green oilcloth and loaded with what America said were car weapons. "Screwdrivers, pumps, wires, and screws. Without these screws what would we do?"

She plugged in the hot plate and rummaged around in the cupboards for the tea. There were two or three sewed-up bags made out of old flour sacks and dumped in an old spark-plug box. "Get me some water, Lindy," she said.

If the water was as dirty as the skinny tin faucet over the iron tub, I wasn't going to drink it, I thought. When I pulled the handle forward, the water jerked out red.

"Let it run," America said. "We'll boil it. You're not afraid of boiled water, are you?"

I didn't want to say.

"It's all right, a little iron in your blood," America said. "'I drink the earth. I eat the earth,' the old Indian prophet said. Time is we are all one inside of each other."

When the water cleared up, I ran a teakettle full.

"Sometimes these Church folks around here get to thinkin' they're the only ones know anything. You're one, aren't you? Oh, don't get me wrong, I like them all right. But there's others know a few things themselves. The old Indian prophet, for instance: 'Let the wind say what it wants to say. Let the rain say what it wants to say. Let the ground come up through the wind and the rain. We are all one.'"

I would have asked her what she was really talking about, but I thought it wouldn't have done me much good to ask. When I looked up to the back window, I saw a couple of heads go by. The faucet on the outside of the station whirred on.

America Laughingheart ran to the window. "I'll be bamboozled if it isn't the Stuart boys after some water too," she said. She put her nose up to the glass and peered out on them for a long time. "They are gone over to the cemetery," she said. "Look at that. I'm too late. The white van is pulling away."

I could hear the water heating up. It sizzled along the burner.

"If you don't mind it, I'm going to sing a long song," America said. It didn't matter what I would say. She was about to sing something I had never heard before.

"The wind in the treehouse will sing you to sleep. The moon in the clouds will rock you free. Your head in the leaves is the fruit on the bough, and I'm rocking you now."

She twisted the tea leaves into a piece of the flour sack, put it in the cup, and poured the hot water into the cup. "I'm rocking you now," she repeated. "The wind in the trees is rocking you now. Oh, I'm rocking you now."

Katharine Coles

Death Valley

After a painting by Maureen O'Hara Ure

More delicate than the historian's are the mapmaker's colors."
    — ELIZABETH BISHOP

At the Homeless Shelter School

Leon's lucky pebble
is an entire desert
shaded in all the colors —
red, ochre, violet —
brown ever dreamed of flaming
under the sun's mirages:

that desert once held
the sea in its lap
and now holds a mere
hallucination of water,
bedazzled aridity,
and a floor stark with salt's
impossible formations.

Anyone Leon shows
has to guess where it's from.
Now the pebble sinks
into Leon's deep pocket.
Leon paints a red car,
sets it ablaze, sends it
over the cliff. At its window,
the requisite self-portrait.

the mouth's 0 of alarm.
"Where I'm going," he's written,
obediently, underneath.
He turns away from the camera,
will not say what he
and his father are hiding from.
The pebble has no weakness,
none it hasn't folded
tight in a gritty heart

beating so slowly
no one, in a lifetime,
detects that core of motion,
incomprehensible,
empty of any wind,
any stirring of sand or thirst,
any love or other violence
to send a flicker through it.

Family Vacation 1: Dante's View

The Ford's blue wind
wavers on the air,
then falters, then winds down,
its engine puffing steam.
Dust settles around us,

but heat still blurs our vision,
the desert clarity.
here the terrors are only
in fire, geology
the surface below expresses
in folds and rutting slabs.

We don't know how to read
the earth's explosive map.

Mother points and names
conglomerates and limestones,
igneous diorite
pressured over eons

then thrust up through the crust
to rest against the turtlebacks —
how the very ground,
tentative, could open
any moment to take our bones
into the fossil layers,
the history of oceans,

of uplift and erosion.
We are children, tired,
restless under the heat
pressing us into the car seat,
but safe, somewhere to go

if we ever get out of here.
Below us, fields of salt
stretch under the sky
like glaciers, cool to the eye.
Father hasn't moved
his hands from the steering wheel.
Mother opens the car door
to a blast of arid wind.

Family Vacation 2: Last Chance Range

All the clichés: a grave,
railways drifted over —
not with snow, with sand.
Something built, abandoned
to what we can't imagine:

a desert valley so vast
we could cross for days

and not seem any closer
to the mountains on the horizon.
We look out of the windows.
Inches from our tires,
the road meets the view,
opens behind held breaths,
as if gates in our hearts,
creaking, have swung wide.
The wagon bucks and heaves
over the thrust fault's ancient rock.
Why would they bring us here,

into such precarious balance?
As if the rock will hold.
My father's face is set,
but behind his closed mouth
something flickers, like joy.
In the front seat, Mother's bandanna
glows red, combustible.

Artist's Palette

The painting is not the landscape,
though we enter it, stroll in
under cliffs so bright we almost
fail, now, to believe —
because what we remember,
the stark mineral brilliance,
couldn't, at last, be real.

The poem is not the painting.
The mind works the space
between page and memory,

a place recalled, acrylic
gold and red, the complete
frigidity of salt.

Now we sit in a studio
high above our valley.
The windows open to storm.
Clouds muscle over
the snowed-in peaks of mountains
fifty-odd miles away —

a view domesticated
by habit, double-glazed glass.
We never tire of working
intimations of ice and sky
we delineate, try to enter.
We fail to enter our pasts,
much less other lives

less open to comfort than ours.
The poor will always be
with us, or without.
What we see is vast,
cool, immutable
rock and ages — not
the particular lives of the city,
its houses reduced beneath us
too small for habitation,

for their iced-over kitchen windows,
knives laid on the tables,
for the hands descending hard
or reaching up, open,
to melt a space on the glass.

Winter Solstice

What we desire is more
distant, elemental.
From whatever threatens to move us,

we want to make some beauty
to cauterize the wound—
how Leon wound himself
around my legs, and held
so tight he bruised my thighs,

and then, as I was leaving,
told me to close my eyes
and dropped his charm in my palm—
it still held his body's heat—
the pebble, to carry me home.
We return from the desert,
or from this afternoon's luncheon,
coffee, our voices and hands
fleshing out shapes on the air,
and let our houselights blaze

profligate on the twilight.
Again the dark descends
too early over the houses,
the freeway overpasses,
the abandoned parking lots,

where shelters made of cardboard
and scraps of carpeting
bend under the blizzard.
Our windows give us back

only our own reflections.
We couldn't see out if we tried,

not if we extinguished our lights,
cupped our hands to the glass —
unless we walked into the storm,

let its weight accumulate
and press our limbs to ice.
We wash the dust from our hair
and lie down on fresh sheets,
and dream we drive to the edge,

then over, into free fall,
family faces pressed
against the sandy windshield,
descending into the valley,
into prehistory,
as if this past, recharted,
could burn us clean of our lives.

David Lee

The Landrum Geese

What time is it? Is it time yet for supper?
Go up to the house and tell LaVerne
to get some supper ready I'm hungry
no don't, goddam get back here right now
don't go messing with her about no supper
she's in her wrong moon turn this week
don't say nothing at all right now
she'll do it her way or not
you go and piss her off
it could mess up the rest of your life
and ruirn the whole evening
yours and my goose both would be cook

I known a man name Goose once
I grown up with Goose Landrum
that's what we called him
his daddy and granddaddy too
I never known that one
it wasn't their real names
they had Christian ones
his daddy was Harold
and I don't know his granddaddy's
but it was something
Leon or Albert like that I imagine
his was George
we never called that to him
where'd I put them long-handle pliers?

it started with his granddaddy
which had his wife and this new baby
which later would of been his daddy

out to take a ride in the wagon
with this new team of horses
he was breaking in on a Sunday
so them horses spooked up a rabbit
scairt themselves to death and took off
like a slobbering whirlwind
he thrown her the reins
grapt that baby up and jumped off
tried to holler her to keep them
headed on the road best she could
till they given out
it was too late
sed her dress blown up in her face
she couldn't of heard him if she tried
screeching too loud by then
them horses sounded like a thunderbolt farting
she'd have to figure it out
without his help
she's a schoolteacher so he wasn't worried
it's her job to get paid to think of something
he had to carry that baby
all the way home walking
we didn't have no hitchhiking back then
most people had other things to do on Sundays

she got back that afternoon by about 4 o'clock
he was setting on the furniture rocking
when she come in the door
sed by god I'm hungry what we having for supper?
she sez whar's the baby?
he sed it's asleep in its bed
you sure are nasty you better take you
a bath after we eat something today
she never sed nothing
walked in that room to look at the baby he thought
started humming hisself a tune
got lost studying how it went

till he heard the cock
looked up and she had the rifle
pointed right at him out of the closet
he jumped and she shot
the middle rafter right out of that rocking chair
he run to the winder
tried to pull it up to jump out
it was froze he heard that gun go cock
ducked down on the floor
she shot the winder right on the crossbar
all four pieces of glass fell out
one of them didn't even break
anothern only busted in half
he crawled to the door till he heard it again
come up running hit that door
turned down the porch and saved his life
she shot that door through the heart and lungs
right where he would of been
if he'd of stood on the other side or went straight
he run as far as he could back behind the barn
where he could look through the board gaps
to see if she was coming after him
but she never
I think it's the bushing in the solenoid not rubbing
get me a screwdriver down here

he waited the rest of the day out there
by hisself to see if she'd leave
or burn the house down
nothing else happened
sed his dog wouldn't even come out
for company it was so ascaired too
stayed under the porch the whole time

he waited until after dark for something to happen
finally when it didn't
he snuck back up to see if she'd hung herself

or was hiding with that gun
got to the winder she was setting
in his chair staring at the bedroom door rocking
never even looked round sed
your supper's on the table if you want it
got up and went in and shut the door
he'd never made a sound so he never known
how she supposed he was there
that one friend of yours sez
all womern can see in the dark
I spoze they can hear through it too
it was catfish and mashed potatoes and fish gravy
with the head on looking at him
on that plate all in a bunch cold in grease
but he ate ever bit of it
he didn't think it was a good idea not to

she never offered to talk about it
and he had a story made up to splain
how she got free wagon-driving lessons
that could of costed upwards of 4 dollars
never got to use it
that baby was the only one
they ever had

from then on after that
you could walk up behind him
goose him or clap your hands
he'd turn inside out with a spasm
oncet these boys blown up
this blasting cap outside Josey's grocery store
he fainted right by the meat counter
talking to Jim Kennedy about bologna and viennies
if he seen a gun he'd go white as a Yorkshire hog
you couldn't of offered to paid him enough
to come to town on the 4th of July

they'd of had to given him a transfusion
everbody called him Goosey
from then on

that baby grown up the same way
he was Little Goose in town
him and this womern had this baby
they name George which was my friend
before she run off to Oklahoma with a Indian well digger
his daddy was a Campbellite
didn't believe in no divorce or piano music
he waited for her to come back someday
but it was too late and she didn't
what they called him then was Poor Goose
he's ruint all over town
they'd all pray for him with the sick and afflicted
even the Lord known who Poor Goose was
but she was gone for good

before that
before they dug all them dry holes on their place
before Goosey the granddaddy hung and killed hisself
after his wife took off when Poor Goose grown up
even before he got behind on the taxes
and lost part of their farm and Kay Stokes picked it up
somebody give the grandboy they called Baby George
these 2 gooses for a birthday present
to be funny about it all
but he raised them for pets around the house
so one day eating supper they seen
them 2 going off down the road through the gate

Poor Goose sed there they go
you better get them back inside the fence
and close that gate if you want to keep them
that boy run out to do it

in a minute they looked out the winder
he had one goose under both his arms jumping up and down
they could hear him hollering through the wall
Leggo goose, leggo me goose
went out on the porch sed what's going on?
boy turnt round still jumping
both them long-necked gooses had leant over
and bit him on the pecker
he squoze so hard one passed out
they thought it was dead
its head down flopping like a well bucket
and they'd have to eat it but it wasn't
othern hung on until his daddy
jerked it loose but it was a tragedy
that goose flopped its wings and give him
a bloody nose
and it broke that boy's pecker
must of busted something in there
turnt off to the east
almost like a L ruirnt
took him both hands to pee from then on
he was so embarrassed of it
he never did get married by choice
sed he never had no inclinations or otherwise
it was too much pain for being married to be worth it

so after that
after all the womern left and Goosey hung hisself
and Poor Goose and Goose Neck
which is what they called him at first cause it looked like one
was living alone out there together
for the rest of their lives
about to lose the rest of the farm during the drought
with no money coming in to nobody
before they noticed it them two geese
turned in to over a hundred
you couldn't come up to their gate even

here all them gooses would run up
with their wings and tongues out
hissing and squawking like a oil well fire
even the Jehovah Witnesses couldn't get up to their porch
they'd of busted your knees flopping their arms
then you'd slip on goose shit and fall down
they'd bit off all your private parts and ears
before you could crawl off and get away
and that saved the farm
is it a rag up there
I can wipe off this oil with?
no dammit not a clean one
one I can use on oil
you wearing a T-shirt?
take it off and give it here

M. L. Basinger come in
with the drilling and well supply
had his machinery and parts spread out
acrost his property
people started sneaking in and stealing it at night
dogs didn't help
they'd bring dead meat and feed them
walk around and take whatall they wanted
he's about to lose everything
when he heard about the Landrum geese
went out and offered them 5 dollars apiece
for as many as they'd sell him
made enough to pay the taxes
and keep the rest of the land
it stopped the stealing right now
bunch of field hands cut across Basinger's
one evening after work singing out loud
just got the gate close
there was all them geese
if they'd of kept singing it might of been all right
but they turnt round and went quiet

like something was the matter
that was what them gooses was looking for
it was like a bale of cotton busted in a hurricane
scairt them so bad they couldn't get that gate back open
tried to run but they couldn't get away
one fell down and about drowned hisself
on dry land holding his face in the dirt
so them geese wouldn't get his eyeballs and nose

tried to climb that fence with the barbwire on top
cut their hands up like it got caught in a gin grinder
tore their britches almost off going over
one got tangled up and his foot stuck
hung him head down on the fence
but them geese couldn't get to him on the other side
his face a inch away
this one goose trying to get its head through the fence
hissed till he had goose spit down the side his mouth
screamed so loud they thought it was a fire truck
all in the Spanish they couldn't understand a word of it
but them geese seemed to know what he wanted
made them so excited
you could hear it four miles away
had to cut him down with some pliers
they thought his ankle was busted
never found out
he hit on his head come up running
none of them field hands said they didn't never
see him again he was gone
them geese chased him down the fence
trying to get to him heading straight south
they had them some plans worked out for him
M. L. Basinger after that put up a sign
sed Keep Out This Property Is Protected
by Landrum Attack Geese
You Come Through This Gate You Will Probley Die

it was such a good idear
everbody wanted to buy some of them geese
even Charley Baker for his junkyard
and tied that sonofabitch dog up with a chain
but somebody told them idiot kids of his
they could populate with a goose
so he had to let them go
but it was worth a try he said
that dog was too mean even for him
but it never bit them idiots even oncet

that's how the Landrums got by and
held on to their land selling geese
for all them years till they give it up
but now you know something most people don't
who lived here all their lives
they think them people was call Goose
because of what they raise
that's how come nobody can pass a history test no more
they don't know before from after
and most don't give a dam either way
just what's on television and have supper ready on time
which if you push too hard on when she aint in the mood
can get you in a lot of trouble
set the whole thing going all over again
like the way it works when you don't pay attention
sometimes your goose don't get cook
you have to live with it
and that can last a real long time
get in and turn the crunk over
let's see if this sonofabitch'll start yet
we'll drive to town and buy something to eat
if you need supper that bad before it's ready

David Lee

Willie and the Water Pipe

Then you have done a braver thing
Than all the Worthies did
    — JOHN DONNE

Willie Dalton would of laughed
if he'd been there
for his own funeral
8 men carrying his box
anyone could of
carried him off like a flour sack
he never stood 5 foot tall
in cowboy boots or weight
a hundred pounds a day in his life
his own family sed they thought
that Dr must of throwed out
the baby and got the other part
to breathe he's so runty

he's a horse jockey
didn't have much choice of it
broke 3-year-olds ever spring
at all the ranches around
one time a man sed
in front of him it wasn't ever
no horse alive Willie Dalton
couldn't ride and he sed
that's a pile of crap
any horse could of throwed him off
on a day but he'd try
and get back on
it was some thrown him

right back off again on his ast
but he made good money at it
busted almost ever bone
in his body and his privates
one time or the other

it was a 4th of July picnic
we had for the whole town
back then ever year
had running and jumping
rassling in it
so Leon Bilberry this one year
whupped everbody that tried him
he sed it aint no man
in this town I cain't kick his ast
them words never even hit ground
before Willie Dalton was at him
jumped right on his head
wrapped him up with his arms
one leg around his neck and the othern
under his armpit and elbow
hollering like a strangled bobcat
he'd pry something loose Willie
would grap him another way
couldn't shake him off
Leon sed it was like a octopus
had his testicles wrapped
round his head
finally he fell down
whichever way he rolt
Willie went the othern riding him
like he's breaking a mule
kicked his sides so hard he thought
9 ribs was busted
it was only 2
till he gave up Willie sed
say calf rope he did

say I give he did
say I won't never rassle Willie Dalton
never again he did
on his mother's white butt her watching
anything to get him off of him
he wouldn't rassle nobody after that

but what Willie done
that nobody else in our town
ever done before or since
was clean out the water pipe

town water come from
the mountain 7 miles
for ditch water and 4 drinking
so 1 spring both pipes clogt up
they fixed the drinking by geography
went halfway down and cut
it wasn't no water
so half of that back up
till they found the plug 3rd cut
and got it out
but the ditch water was different
not plugged off just partly
couldn't get no full stream of pressure
they didn't know what to do
so at the town board meeting
Willie Dalton sed for 2 bottles of whiskey
I'll clean that pipe out
they shut off the water
from the dam and he clumb in
the next day crawled that pipe
7 miles down mountain
through a 16-inch hole by hisself
with a flashlight
breaking up the bumps
to the bottom with his body

all day
when they opened that headgate
it was 9 dump-truck loads of gravel
and rock come out that pipe
he'd loosened up going through

he crawled that pipe
30 years ever spring
by hisself for 2 bottles of whiskey
even after he had a cancer
like half a cantaloupe
hanging off his neck
his whole skin yellow as squash
almost ready to die
that last time he didn't come out
till after dark
only 4 people left waiting to see
some of the rest sed
he's dead we'll warsh him out
in the morning sometime
give him his 2 bottles of whiskey
Roy Talbert sed you gone open them
we'll have a drink?
Willie sed bullshit
that's all

they was sitting on his mantle
the day he died a month later
not even opened
with a letter they read
sed if I'm dead you can open these
and all have a drink now on me
wasn't one man in town
even Curley Robinson who would
touch one of them bottles
I expect they still setting there
and the water pipe sealt itself up

2 years later with mud and rock
they never could clean out
all the farmers had to go to wells
because Willie wasn't there no more
they had to find another way
to get by without him

Patricia McConnel

Edna

Six foot two, blue eyes, and the heavyset sensuality of Percheron mares — Edna
is big assed, big busted, just big. And blond. A Viking goddess drunk and careening down Gaffey Street at 2:15 in the morning in a white convertible with the top
down and four or five men, drunk too, all of them just as big and brawny and
rowdy as Edna. Dock workers, merchant seamen, waterfront thugs.

I know where she's going: to her house on Point Fermin, where she will take
them all on. Everyone in town knows Edna and what she does.

They've tried to close down her beer bar on Gaffey Street. The town is out to
get her. But she is careful: checks IDs on everyone who looks under thirty, won't
allow dope in her place, throws out brawlers, bodily, into the night, and if they
try to come back in, she personally knocks them out. But they can't close her
down for that — it's her right as the owner to keep the peace. Hookers don't even
try to work out of her place. Every female in our little seaport town is terrified of
Edna, and no woman has been seen going in that joint in anybody's memory.

The story I heard is that although they want to close Edna down, they can't
catch her at any violations. But what everyone secretly suspects is that the cops
are scared as hell of Edna and her boys and won't go near the place. When the
fights happen, they are earthshaking. Bodies fly and blood flows. The regulars at
Edna's tend to hang out there all the time, so it may be a kind of self-regulating
closed loop. If they're at her place, they aren't at some tamer bar with lesser
mortals they could probably snap like matchsticks. At Edna's they're all more or
less equally matched, equally belligerent, equally rowdy, and never call the cops
no matter how bad anyone is hurt. They go home and pour whiskey on the
wounds and go back the next night.

It all works out.

The reason I see Edna and her gang roaring down Gaffey at 2:15 A.M. is that
I am on my way home at the same time. I have a job as a cocktail waitress at The
Bridgehouse, a suffocatingly dull neighborhood bar operated as a money-
washing front by a collector for the Mafia — Freddy the Legbreaker, he is known
as locally. But I don't know that yet. I just know it's the only job available for a
twenty-one-year-old girl with no skills. They hired me, with no experience,

because they want a B-girl and I am sexy, in a short-legged sort of way. But I don't know that yet either. Why they hired me, I mean. I know well enough that I'm sexy. Just not how to handle it.

I'm fascinated and a little titillated by Edna and always hope I'll see her again on my way home. But I have no desire to go near her. She scares me just like she scares everyone else. And most of the time I don't think about her. I'm too busy trying to learn to be a halfway competent cocktail waitress, and doing badly at it. For one thing, I'm afraid the guys that hang out at The Bridgehouse assume that because I work there I must be easy — I got propositioned my first night on the job. That they should assume such a thing insults me, and I am defensively prim.

Scotty the bartender keeps calling me down to the end of the bar to command me, in an irritated whisper, to talk to the guys at the bar and get them to buy me drinks, and although miserable, I try to obey, saying things like, "How are you tonight?" and "Wasn't it a beautiful day today?" Scotty gets furious if a guy offers to buy me a drink, and I say, "No, thanks," so I take to drinking crème de menthe and soda because it doesn't really taste like liquor.

I can't remember orders for more than two drinks at a time, and I get completely confused when I lean over a table to serve a drink and some guy stares at my boobs — which are very nice, I must say, but I don't want anyone to notice. I try to discourage smart remarks by looking stern. I only manage to look grim, and people who are there to have a good time don't leave me very good tips.

I have been at The Bridgehouse less than a month when the unthinkable happens: Edna and her crew come in. They are already drunk. Edna knows everyone in the place and greets them all boisterously. Have all these quiet nondescript guys, who come here to drink after work, had their day — or night — with Edna? I stand paralyzed as she makes her way along the bar, slapping backs and planting noisy kisses. I am hoping desperately she and her gang will sit at the bar, but no, they choose a big booth at the back.

There are five men with Edna — six drinks to remember — so I grab a pen and a cocktail napkin to write them down on. I don't doubt that something terrible will happen to me if I don't remember the drinks right. When I reach the table there is some hilarious comradely rousting going on, something about someone getting caught with a chicken leg in his pocket, and I stand, more or less at attention, waiting for them to notice me. I have my stern look as my only defense. Edna is wearing a Hawaiian shirt, men's trousers, a mariner's cap, and longshoreman's boots — and is disconcertingly sexy, making me feel idiotic in my pale blue nylon blouse with white fuzzy polka dots. At last Edna's voice rises above the others: "Hey, boys, order up. The lady is waiting." Obediently they quiet down and give me their orders: all straight shots of whiskey or vodka, a couple of boiler-makers. I escape without having to say a word, and as soon as I walk away the hilarity resumes. I am sure they are laughing at me.

When I return to the table with the drinks they all quiet down without an order from Edna. I must reach across the table to serve the men on the inside. I tremble, keep my eyes lowered. They are all watching me. Edna says, her voice suddenly lowered a few decibels, "You're new here, aren't you, honey?"

I nod yes.

"Well, listen. Don't let old Scotty give you a bad time. He's really okay, you know?" Then she raises her voice so it booms the length of the bar: "And don't let any of these motherfuckers give you any shit because I'll clip the balls of anyone who does!" Everyone laughs. I feel sure I am going to faint.

Then I realize one of the men is speaking to me. "Aren't you Patty?" I'm so surprised I look up. The man who has spoken is a huge dark-skinned man with the body of a wrestler, oriental features, and a Charlie Chan mustache. He looks dimly familiar. He grins a giant's grin, warmly. "I'm Felix. Remember? The beach. I'm a friend of Leonard's."

Jeesuz. I remember him alright. He asked me out once, at least five years ago, on the beach, in a gentle voice, no drunk, not so huge then, and I wanted to go out with him. But my mother wouldn't let me go because he was Samoan, and I was embarrassed when I told him I couldn't go, bitter at my mother for her prejudice, unable, of course, to tell him the real reason. Now I barely manage to answer him with an "Oh yeah," and put down the last drink.

I hear Edna ask me how much they owe, and I manage to answer as her table resumes its high-decibel cacophony. Edna pays. I take the money and flee, and I'm abjectly grateful when they leave without buying another drink. When I clear the table, I find that Edna has left me a ten-dollar tip.

I'm so amazed I tell Scotty about it. He grins, says, "Ol' Edna, she's a great gal." When I tell him I knew Felix as a teenager, Scotty frowns. "Stay away from Felix, kid. He gets crazy when he drinks, been in a lotta trouble. He's done time for attempted rape and assault. He's bad news, that guy." Now I wonder if my mother, for all the wrong reasons, saved me from a drunken beating or even rape. Jeesuz.

A couple of weeks later Edna and Felix come in together. This time they are very drunk, and quarreling. I'm relieved when they sit down at the bar. It is Satur-day night and the booths are almost full, so I'm busy. I don't know what starts the fight. When I hear the bar stools crashing to the floor and turn around, Felix is pulling some guy up off the floor by his shirt and pounding him in the face with one hand, holding him up with his other hand. Edna is yelling at Felix to stop, pulling on him, but she's so drunk she can hardly stand up, much less muster the force needed to pull him away. Everyone in the bar is motionless, shocked, transfixed. Next thing I know the guy Felix is beating is on the floor, and Felix is stomping on his stomach. Edna is screaming now, but Felix is crazy and fixated. He stomps and stomps until the guy vomits so hard that a stream of liquid shoots up like a geyser and actually hits the ceiling. At this point I run into the head and hide in a booth. I'm shaking and crying, and I don't come out till Scotty opens the door and tells me we are closing up. He tells me that Edna finally pulled herself together enough to land one hell of a blow on the side of Felix's head, which seemed to snap him out of it. Then she led him out of the place like a puppy.

For a while Scotty and I point out the stain on the ceiling and tell people how it got there, until we realize that nobody believes us. But I don't work there long after the fight. It is the first of a series of events that get the message through to me, dumb as I am, that The Bridgehouse is not a place for the fainthearted, or for people who aren't into dedicated self-destruction.

But all this is almost forty years ago, and Edna's Place has long since been torn down, The Bridgehouse is a TV repair shop, and I have put on a lot of miles and forgotten all about Edna and Felix.

Until recently. I run into Scotty, tending bar in a Las Vegas club. He doesn't remember me at first, and I have to feed him reminders. "I'm the one who couldn't remember more than two drink orders."

He says he's had a lot of waitresses like that.

I say, "I'm the one that hid in the ladies' room when Felix stomped that guy's stomach."

Then he remembers. He remembers the crème de menthe and soda, too. He teases me about how naive I was.

I say, "Scotty, I was the world's most unlikely B-girl. Why did you hire me in the first place?"

"You looked pitiful," he says.

Scotty tells me that the last he heard of Felix he was doing a long stretch for manslaughter — a second conviction. He doesn't know what happened to Edna. She just disappeared.

"Y'know, Scotty, at the time I thought I was scared of her. But now I think I envied her. She did what she liked and didn't give a damn what anybody thought.

She was a lot of things I wasn't. I was so scared of sex, scared of all those guys in the bar. So the idea of her making it with all those men at once just fascinated me. You know, like we're mesmerized by horror movies. We don't really want them to happen to us, but we're spellbound all the same."

"You were scared of sex? Huh. I always thought you were bursting at the seams. But what's this about Edna making it with all those men at once? Where did you get that idea?"

"Why, Scotty, you can't tell me you didn't know. The whole town knew!"

"The whole town knew what it wanted to think. Edna was just a roughneck. She liked to drink and fight and carouse, and she liked to play poker."

"What about all those guys she took home when the bars closed?"

"Poker. I went there lotsa times. I know. Nothing but poker. Edna wasn't interested in balling any of those guys. Even Felix was just a buddy. She was probably a dyke."

I remember her gentleness toward me, the warning to the whole place to leave me alone, the ten-dollar tip. But even so, I'm not sure Scotty's right. Edna was a brawling, wild, strong woman, and the only people she was comfortable with were the waterfront outcasts. She didn't have any choices back then, in the fifties.

But with one brick removed, the whole construction crumbles: me, bursting at the seams? With *lust*, is that what he means? Suddenly it all is shining clear. All that defensive primness: it was *me* who was obsessed with sex. I made Edna the nympho I didn't have the guts to be. Poor Edna — because she was a maverick, she was a natural to bear the projections of a whole town's secret guilty selves.

But what if Scotty is right? Did she *want* me, for chrissake? Is that why she responded to me so gently, so protectively? If Edna did lust for me, and if I had had the sense to know it, would I have had the courage to let her into my life? Into my bed?

Probably not. Those were the fifties; women didn't even dare to not wear makeup in those days. Even a rumor of lesbianism was enough to cost a woman her job and, most of the time, her family as well. Anyway, I was such a dope. She probably just felt sorry for me.

But now, with a couple of drinks in me, I want to find her, throw my arms around her, tell her I got smarter and tougher and braver later on, tell her that . . . well, maybe I could have loved her.

I don't say any of this to Scotty, of course. But he and I agree that she isn't alive now. Nobody lives past fifty at the pace she was going.

She probably knew that.

Wyoming

In Pine Bluffs, a ranching community in the southeast corner of Wyoming, my visit was distinguished by an untimely blizzard — the season's first — which swept in the night before, when I was already ensconced in the local motel. I woke up ready and raring for a day of workshops in the schools only to find that the schools were closed! But thanks to a counterblizzard of phone calls from the teacher-organizer, over two thirds of the students enrolled in the workshops came to school anyway. This may have had something to do with the persuasive powers of their teacher, but I chose to think of it as testimony to the hunger for poetry in their young lives. We had the whole school to ourselves, could've paraded up and down the halls bellowing out our words if we chose. The snow never did stop falling that day; the evening reading was postponed until I could reschedule a return trip in the spring.

In Lovell, a community in the far north of Wyoming, my morning workshop was held in the detention room of the high school, a setting that inspired the celebratory poem that I've enclosed.

WORKING IT OUT
            (for the students in the Lovell High School poetry workshop, 1/20/94)

In the detention room
where, after school,
troublemakers squirm
before the unbelievably slow motion
of the clock,

we made poetry, eighteen of us.
Our words, free as they were,

could not make the angles
of the four walls any less severe;
they could not cleanse the yellow grime
of ten thousand wasted hours
from the neon lights, the stains
of all those petty crimes paid for here —
ill-timed cuss words,
sleeps that were too deep . . .

But for an hour at least
the white noise of the radiator
was drowned out, the air was filled
with words worth breathing.
I have to believe that we left something here,
that this afternoon's contingent of offenders
suffered less because of us.

— RICK KEMPA

Laurie Ann Ihm

Tishnish — Spring Song

Tishnish was fishing quietly and smoking his pipe when the daylong drizzle turned into a steady mist. It looked somewhat like ice melting on his small round cheeks. His oiled buckskins did not alter in the moisture, nor did his long and curly brownish hair, which flattened under the long stocking cap. And even his pipe, which burned red with aspen chips and wild tobacco, was not changed by the heavy mist that tinged at the edge of a winter's frost. The only change around him was the white grass that slowly accumulated into a sloppy white blanket. It was like sitting in a field of cottonwood seeds.

Finally Tishnish rose and took his trout to a nearby cliff where hot coals burned slowly, hidden near some willows. He prepared the fish and fried them over the fire. And oh, did the fairies come to see where the wonderful smell came from? Kimmy offered to trade a pretty shell for a share of his fish. Tishnish just ignored him. The mist and snow continued to fall around him, and another little fairy came to him and offered to trade a mug of his honey wine, cool from the river bottom, fresh from last fall's harvest, for a bite of that fish. But Tishnish continued to keep to his thoughts and take his time cooking. He was singing a song to himself while the snow piled higher and higher around him.

At last the fish were well prepared, and he sat down in a small cave that lay hidden in the cliff wall. The fairies sat in an aspen outside and felt distressed that they could not enter and join him.

Suddenly Tishnish heard music outside, and this was the first time he paid any attention to the fairies. The music was the calling of spring. A female called in a high, long melody that sent all living creatures to stand still and listen. It was a voice that cried for the departure of death, rejoiced for the rejuvenation of new life, and danced with all youth. It called for the gathering of the aged ones. Tishnish listened and found that he no longer desired to eat but to feel each emotion the song provoked. When the song ended, the snow stopped falling at once, and the evening stars slowly undressed across the sky.

Then the fairies moved toward the doorway of the small cave and watched Tishnish listen. He asked them to find the song maker and invite her to share his trout with him. They returned immediately with a shy young girl. Tishnish knew at once who she was. She was the one who has always sung to the flowing rivers, to the falling leaves, to the dancing flames, and to the racing winds. And Tishnish had never recognized her songs until now when she sang to the spring snows. Her voice was thin as a leaf. Her face was childlike, even though she was as old as life itself. She was beautiful, and her name was Randy.

Randy sat and ate with Tishnish as her companions watched. And it wasn't until she finished, which was only a few bites later, that he offered to share with the other two. They immediately entered, laid their gifts near him, and served themselves. Soon the fairies were talking and laughing — except for Randy who was still so very shy. Then she asked to be excused and soon left.

Tishnish was now lost in his thoughts again; only this time Randy had filled him with wonder. He knew that she must be the spirit who calls to the changing seasons. She would soon return after the leaves reached their maturity, and after the rivers flowed strong. He would then wait to hear her song, again, as she would call to all the living creatures. She would invite the chill to ring through the air, crisp as an iceberg ready to shatter. Tishnish would wait for her song and invite her into his home once more.

Rick Kempa

The Wind

We live on a hill that rises from the middle of a sprawling little city in Wyoming, in a land of much sky. Ours is one of a row of town houses, by no means a romantic dwelling, but it's modern, efficient, comfortable, and built with at least some attention to the weather. The view is what recommends it most: the swirl of town lights beneath us; the interstate — dividing line of the world — in the middle ground; the angular horizon of buttes and crags, and on the best days, in one particular notch in the bluffs, north-northeast, the far-off glint of the Wind River Mountains.

Being a confirmed view man, one for whom the top of a tree or mountain or double-decker bus has always been alluring, I am willing to put up with a lot of abuse for the sake of my horizon — the higher rent, for instance, that is affixed to a housing complex called "Hilltop Manor." But hand in hand with the view comes the other legacy of living closer to the sky, the most obvious fact of life on the hilltop, the wind.

All of nature has ceded this territory to it. Nothing grows taller than knee-high up here, even in the best of times. The seedling of any sort that manages to sprout here is destined to be a dwarf. The antelope in their restless grazing periodically scour this place, the birds alight on eaves and wires in a calm hour, but except for a few rodents that hide beneath rocks and a few humans behind walls, no creatures live here.

Even we humans have granted wind its dominance, limiting our spring-planting projects to ground huggers like grass or shrubs. This is not to say that our sights were always so contained. I'd like to see the architect's vision for this place, concocted in some controlled-air dream factory in Denver. The six cherry trees, one in front of each town house, are evidence of our initial false assumption as to who or what would rule here. As spindly and squat as the day they were transplanted, they are growing downward, if at all.

No matter where one goes, folks are always bragging about their weather, and we're no different. Ours is not your ordinary wind, we say. We've seen it blow holes in billboards or flip over trucks on the highway like they were empty cardboard boxes. It's been known to take a freight train and put it in a ditch. Last summer in one of those mean dust raisers that pass for thunderstorms around here, the wind pummelled a two-story house being built a little ways down the hill, until it collapsed into a pile of twisted wood.

When we meet in the grocery store by chance, even before we ask about the kids, we talk about wind: "Ain't it something out there?" "What do you think is behind it?" Memory can be as compelling as the thing itself. Whatever else the weather might be doing — bitter cold or dusty drought — we remind ourselves, "It could be worse." Or if it's been nice too long, the cashier is sure to say, as if it's the Official Company Line, "Enjoy it while you can. You know it won't be long until . . ."

Or we joke about it, make it the butt of our bareboned humor. "It's snowing sideways again," someone will say, frowning out the window. We tell the thin-skinned newcomer that if it ever stopped blowing, "everything would fall over." We talk about the flakes that leave the clouds just this side of Utah and touch ground four hundred miles east, in Nebraska.

But at times wind is the fact of weather that one must take dead seriously. "It's a wonder the wind / don't tear off your skin," Utah Phillips sings, and that's no lie. Arctic air set into motion can literally burn or bite. Layers of skin can lose their life in a quarter hour's time. Protrusions like noses or tips of chins can be in mortal danger, anesthetized first, and then, in a stroke as clean as any surgeon's blade, excised.

Skin grows back or scars over, but once the wind's been under it, it stays there. Once you've been out driving on that open road fifty miles from anywhere and had to fight the wind with all your might to see who turns the wheel, or once you've been caught short-sleeved several hours up-trail on one of those days that started out so perfect, so blue, that you forgot the wind was out there (it *was* out there, prowling around the blue, quiet only because there was nothing for it to rub its back on), once *you've* been out there, you come to know that the wind is an animal.

When my wife Fern and I moved to the hilltop, we included the front and back yards in our homemaking plans, thinking, like the Denver draftsmen, that the outside world was ours to shape. Shrugging off the absence of trees, we bought patio furniture so that we might better enjoy the view. But the chaise longue shuffled around the deck without asking leave, the chairs flip-flopped daily through the dog's minefield, and the table with its umbrella threatened to take to the sky, passengers and all. We learned to fold and store the chairs each night, and we bolted the table down, but the wind whirling through the umbrella made an eerie high-pitched sound, causing the dog to bark and the neighbors to mutter. When I complained to a friend about these matters, she looked at me with eyebrows raised and exclaimed, "But the wind hasn't even started blowing yet!" Taking her comment as a warning, we changed homemaking tactics, sold off the lawn furniture (Barely Used! Lowest Price!) and, like the cherry trees, surrendered the outside space. We instead invited the best of it indoors by hanging prisms, sun catchers, and plants, and by frequently scrubbing our windows.

When the wind finally came that made the first ones seem like wisps, our task became one of trying to keep it out. It took us by surprise at first, in schizophrenic October, the month of sunbaked afternoons and frost-tinged nights. One morning I found the kitchen window open and papers strewn across the floor into the living room. My first thought at seeing the disarray was of burglars, for I distinctly remembered reaching over the sink the night before to turn the crank that drew the window closed. But the screen, still in place, belied that notion. A few minutes of on-site chin rubbing gave me a likelier answer: apparently I had left the window slightly ajar, and the wind, as insinuating as a screwdriver in a gloved hand, had approached at a certain precise angle and pried it open.

On another night, in November, when the wind shifted out of the north, icy pillars of air filled the house and sent me running downstairs to find the front door flung wide. Again, the fear of man beset me, more urgent this time. With my dog at my side and my clenched flashlight doubling as a nightstick, I searched every cranny of the house before I was satisfied that, again, the culprit was the wind. This time its assault had been premeditated: first it had threaded through the mechanism of the lock to see that it was not turned, then probed the latch to find it hadn't clicked, and finally had backed off, summoned its strength, and thrown its shoulder against the heavy wood.

This skirmish signalled the start of our winter's war. Armed with heavyweight plastic and duct tape, I sealed all the windows on the inside (which meant, of course, saying good-bye to the clear, clean light). When the wind mounted its offensives, the plastic bulged and strained like full-blown sails, and the tape that held the edges down began to come unglued. It was frightening to see how the air between the glass and the plastic was not static, not "the extra layer of insulation" I had been told it would be, but rather a restless, alien body striving to get in, vanguard of the invading force.

Every day I patrolled the borders, tape and scissors in hand, sealing off the icy little arrows that had pried up the tape or pricked the plastic. I nailed strips of wool along the edges of the door, so that it took a major exertion simply to open it. By Christmas, closets became refrigerator-freezers, and we joked about hanging our coats on the outside to avoid entering them. Then the joke became reality, as we surrendered those dark spaces and instead lay our coats along the bottom edges to trap the air inside.

One January night I sat on the sofa with a blanket draped around me and simply paid attention to the movement of air, the violence of it outside, beating the walls like drums, rattling the metal vent caps on the roof like cymbals. Inside, too, in spite of all I'd done, the cold air freely moved. I got down on my hands and knees to feel for its source, and the futility of my season-long defense became clear. In the cracks between the baseboard and the wall, long, thin planes of icy air seeped in. A jet of it surged in through each electrical outlet. The wind even infiltrated the molecules of the wall itself: the plaster was frigid to the touch.

At that moment, my season-long efforts seemed more the work of a madman than of a devoted homeowner. I felt a sudden, weird kinship with Bobby, the introverted boy-next-door of my youth, he of the famous obsession. All summer long, he prowled his back porch with a fly swatter, squashing every beady-eyed bug that landed on his wall. So diligent and so accurate was he that I kept expecting his work to be done, the world to be flyless. But no; every morning brought a new hatching, more toil for the slaughter boy. Similarly, no matter which way I turned in my poor wind-shriven home, the influx of cold awaited my petty efforts. "Shoddy construction," Fern complained, but I took the higher perspective, as I continued (how could I not?) to insulate. Ours were the labors of Sisyphus. We were part of a long tradition, Bobbie and I, which bestowed dignity if not meaning on our work. There was something ennobling about carrying on while faced with the truth of the old Chinese proverb: "There is no wall through which wind cannot pass."

The storm arrives one April night, a dark tide moving against all that is anchored, making the whole world scream, seeping into our porous dreams and playing havoc with them. In between my deep dives, as I approach the surface where trees are hissing and rainwater is smacking the window in waves, I think, "Hmmm. The street cleaner is out—how strange" (especially because I have never seen a street cleaner in this town). Fern, meanwhile, is imagining that she is lying in a small boat in a big surf, close to shore but getting no closer, being pushed toward it and pulled away from it at the same time. She sees the butt ends of the oars sticking out of the oarlocks above her, she wants to row, but she can't sit up; it's like her back is glued to the boat's bottom. And all around her and under her, separated only by some thin planking, is the crushing, thumping, seething force.

Claire, our three-year-old, trots into the room, yelling, "Mama, Papa, there's animals outside!" We assure her there's not, that it's "just the wind," that she should go back to bed. But as I draw her close for a hug, I realize she's trembling, and I see the glint of alarm in her eyes. What is the wind to a little girl but an unseen animal flinging its body against the house? I haul her aboard, settle her in between us.

She promptly sleeps, but not Fern nor I. Of our three dreams, Fern's is the one that compels our wakefulness. Even in the house, in bed, being in the windstorm is much like being in the surf. The panic, the threat of imminent drowning, is absent, but there's the same sensation of helplessness, smallness, engulfment in something with no beginning or end, with only variations in intensity. Relax for a second, and the next invisible thrust will convulse you, unbalance you. The whole damn house might get torn from its moorings, like Dorothy's.

"To him that hath no home, no wind is friendly," Montaigne wrote, and the wind moves Fern to commiserate. She imagines other people out in it—the hitchhiker cowering under a bridge, the motorist stranded on the interstate. She projects ourselves out there: "What if we were living in a tent?" she suddenly blurts. And what a thought that is, to have nothing but a thin sheet of nylon between us and it, the fabric flapping, bulging, the air streaming in through the seams, the terrifying tautness of certain lines of pressure. With a shiver, she moves toward my side of the bed. Her feet are so frigid they could keep an ice pack cold. She rummages for the heavy blanket at our feet, pulls it over us, gets my half as well because that's too much weight for me. Claire, half-smothered between us, lets out a yelp.

Once I spent a night and a day on a Carolina beach during a nor'easter, a windstorm fierce enough to test the limits of any tent, except I didn't have a tent. I was sandblasted down to my eyeballs and scoured on the inside too. A nor'easter is a gale wind that blows in from the North Atlantic in the fall, a dry run for the wetter, fiercer storms that'll come from those parts in winter. It's a wild, ceaseless thing that whips the waves to frenzy and idles the fishermen, easily deserves the name of "storm."

Time and again in the course of that eerie, moony night, I moved from behind one clump of dune grass to another, in a futile search for a niche of calmness. It didn't exist, of course, outside of the rented walls. No matter where I threw down my sleeping bag and crawled into it, the incessant hiss of sand in motion — louder always when you get down to its level — filled my ears. "Today's sand flat is tomorrow's dune," an old-timer at the chowder hall in Okracoke had said to me with a wink, when he heard I was heading down to the water. Out in the storm, where all I had to do to make a pillow was tilt my head and let the sand flow in under it, there was no reason to think he was speaking metaphorically. How many of these particles would it take to bury me, backpack and all, I wondered — five hundred million? A billion? Whatever the number, it seemed within an easy night's work of that wind. I ended up wandering, like the ghost of a drowned buccaneer, up and down the beach and through the empty streets of the old seaport, waiting for the first pot of coffee to call me in.

"The wind in one's face makes one wise," wrote the English poet George Herbert. This wisdom has nothing to do with words: yell into the wind and hear what happens. Nor for that matter does it have to do with thoughts. Wind can get your thoughts aswirling just like everything else, but it's one thing to be moved, and quite another to be organized.

But the wind will do what no other creature is allowed to — it will touch your eyes. The prophet touched the eyes of the blind man and he saw; he was forever changed. A hitchhiker I plucked from an Idaho highway one November day was so wind-battered that he couldn't answer the commonest traveller's questions — clutching for my atlas when I asked where he was going, staring and staring at it until it became clear that he didn't know *where* he was going, other than east, the way of the wind. His eyes, which had been facing into the big blow, were neither red nor swollen, but wide open — the pupils huge, unfocusing. They were *touched*, no longer organs for seeing but for feeling. He was obviously out of his element in the controlled air of the car, and when, soon after, I pulled over where our roads diverged, he plunged headfirst out the door like a grateful skydiver.

The wooden gate outside our bedroom is being flung over and over against the side of the house. Our neighbor's second-floor storm window breaks loose and plunges into our driveway, where it explodes. Impossible to lie still! Wrestling free of the sheets, I prowl the dark house, window to window, peering out — at what? The body of the wind is not the wind; the animal is invisible. I place my palm on a pane, hold it there, then watch the imprint generated by its heat disperse.

The presence of the past, with me in ways more real, more permanent than memory, the way one's lovers are: a night on a beach, the wildest night of the most potent, most unfettered season of my life. I'd travelled twenty-five hundred miles by foot and by thumb from the Arizona desert to be there at the dividing line of earth and water, simply to be there. That the line was a frothing, pounding pit of violence made it all the better; the last thing I wanted or expected was tranquillity.

I mounted the last dune to its crest, where the wind that knew no land came across to touch me, took off my clothes there, and faced into it. Under that big moon, the blue-black water shifted and pulsed and broke into flashing, flecking silver. The sand held an unearthly luminescence, moonlight conjuring moonscape. I was the first man, the only man, and even the existence of my own body seemed uncertain, for the wind did not blow against it so much as through it, flushing out my cells, imparting a vibration to all my molecules. Arms outstretched, head raised, I gave my voice — no melody, no message, just voice — to the wind.

For as long as we have lived here, our neighbors have had a string of clay bells hanging from the eave of their porch. Each bell (there are five of them) is of a particular weight and timbre, so that they ring, in endless succession, a line of music that has imbedded itself into my mind as the first bars of a nursery song: "Mary had a lit . . . , Mary had a lit. . . ." Only the fiercest wind waves, flinging them all together in confusion, disrupts the pattern, and even then not for long. I listen hard between each crest for the feisty little string of swimmers to grasp at, gasp for, achieve their melody.

In a solitary, receptive hour, this interplay becomes the pure strains of collaboration, wind and man working for once toward the same end. Musicians know that if the thing between them is going to have a life of its own, if it is going to *take off*, they must act not only on *it*, but on each other. So, too, in the ferment of the night. The hand that made the bells translates brute force into pattern. Consciousness, in whatever being it resides, always aims for this, to impose itself on the world. The wind, neither harnessed nor humanized, has an equal potency, improvising, insisting with its wild forays on its own preeminence, but above all — or rather below all — imbuing the inert matter with life, translating clay to chime.

But the wind is an animal, a body in motion. I awake suddenly and completely, without it (surprised as usual that sleep had claimed me). In its place are the far midnight sounds: the shudder of boxcars coupling in the train yard, trucks groaning on the highway as they downshift for the climb out of our valley. Most of all I hear, in the underlying, unsettling quiet, the passage of the present. The world grows larger and larger. Heat disperses, stars pile on stars, that intolerable infinity approaches. Suddenly I yearn for wind, as one does for a bedmate: part shield, part company. The wind is most felt in its absence.

Home Fires

Deer are swift and fleet. They appear out of nowhere. They disappear like an illusion, the flash of their tails a brief memory that hangs momentarily in thin air before fading into the pine trees. Their illusive quality teases, inviting one to follow, to chase.

According to Oglala beliefs, Mark and I are in the sixth cycle of life, when temptation comes in a form as seductive as the tawny deer. Usually by now a woman has already been tempted by the deer. At first, she is impressed by his prowess and the carriage of his impressive antlers. If she does, indeed, succumb to his charms, the moment he succeeds in leading her away from her family, he disappears.

For men, the temptress usually appears later in the sixth cycle. The Makaha believe that a man needs a woman's gentle guidance during this time, a gentle nudge back toward the direction of wisdom. She does this through ceremony and prayer. The occurrence of the deer does not come as a surprise. A wife expects her. She comes swiftly but is illusive, as difficult to stop as the passing of time, as impossible to hold onto as youth.

This is a time of restlessness, when true friends are needed, when sweet grass is burned, and sage is scattered in the winds.

Our anniversary is tomorrow—fourteen years of marriage, and Mark has spent the last twenty-eight hours fighting fire. No sleep, nothing to eat but Forest Service fire food, prepackaged snacks full of high energy, no-taste foods. I wonder what it would be like to be out there on the fire line with him. I envy the girls, the women, who stand next to him, shovels in hand, the comradery they no doubt share.

Hoping Mark would be home last night, I fixed porkchops—one of his favorites. When I headed out to do chores, a red-tailed hawk circled high above the barn. While I was outside, putting the sheep and mares in the corrals before turning the geldings out, the porkchops overcooked. The hawk flew off to the hay field in search of gophers. Mark didn't make it home for dinner so Matt, Sarah, and I ate the too dry chops without him. Around 9:30 P.M. his boss called. Mark would be out all night with the fire crew until replacements arrived. The storm yesterday afternoon, which had dropped little moisture but brought numerous lightning strikes, had left its calling card throughout the forest. Scattered "smokes" had been sighted all over.

The women's movement is a two-sided coin. What was once a man's occupation, fire fighting, is now a woman's domain as well. For those on the fire line, those who have passed their "step-test" and stayed in shape all winter by running or working out on the exercise equipment in the shop, a fire is an exciting thing. It is the climax to a drawn-out preparation. Green fire pants are donned, heavy boots laced, yellow lightweight jackets worn like secret handshakes at a fraternity gathering. And then there are the "hotshots" of this special club, the fire crews who spend their summers flying from one "smoke" to another, sporting shirts that say I Was at Yellowstone.

Even the local crews compete with one another, each fire attended becoming like a notch on a gun belt — signs of experience and a big paycheck. I suppose the rivalry is necessary, for they are expected to work nonstop, to be ambitious and tireless.

This morning the sun, even as early as 8:00, is hot. I am thankful that the night was cool, giving Mark some relief from the heat of the day. What must it be like standing at the edge of a fire line, feeling the rubber soles on your boots begin to melt while the white-hot sun beats down from above? What a reprieve it must be when the sun finally slips behind the tips of the orange-flamed pine trees.

Again, I wonder. Does he lean against a tall ponderosa, yards away from the burning trees, drinking water from the melted ice in his water jug? Does some seasonal firefighter, female, younger and fitter than I, watch with him as the sun disappears, while the children and I eat our overdone porkchops, adding calories to conjecture?

Trusting Mark has little to do with it. I trust him — trust his love for me and the kids, for our life together, for this ranch. But even after fourteen years of marriage, I still notice the way his Wranglers cover his muscular rear and thighs. I still appreciate how trim his waist is, how strong his arms are, still admire his dark, wavy hair and sexy mustache. Surely other women must too. If I sat next to him, quenching my thirst, with the roar of the blaze cresting above us, in the heat of the fire, so to speak, I would notice him. I would be tempted to make more of this bond of fire fighting than would be wise.

In bed alone, without Mark, it takes forever to get to sleep. Morning comes and he has not returned. I make coffee, filling the pot half full. Doing the morning chores on Sunday is a luxury. I bask in the relaxed pace, no need to hurry.

Able to do these things without him, I feel self-sufficient. I feel inefficient because the water level in the tank has gotten too low for the sheep to reach, and I did not notice last night.

"Damn," I say out loud. Why the heck didn't I pay attention when he told me how to turn on the timer to the well pump that runs water into the tank? I go and get the black tub from inside the barn, which we use to feed corn to the sheep. I get a bucket and carry them both out to the tank. Then, putting the tub on the ground next to the tank, I use the bucket to scoop water into it.

Mainly, though, I luxuriate in doing the morning chores. I walk the path Mark walks each morning. I am greeted by the low, throaty baa's that the sheep greet him with each day. I open the gate to the pen on the east side of the corrals and call to the geldings. "Here, boys. Heeeere booooys!" I try to keep my inflection like Mark's, the tone an octave lower than normal. The geldings surprise me by turning at the sound of my voice and slowly sauntering into the pen. They go directly to the small feed tub, and I remember that Mark grains them each morning. Latching the gate closed, I return to the barn to hang up the unneeded halters and get a bucket of grain.

Mark's presence is everywhere, his touch apparent. The floor of the barn is swept. The bridles and halters hang neatly on the wall. There is no more sweetmix for the horses, only oats. I wonder when he switched to oats, and why. Too much protein in the other, too high-powered a feed for hot, lazy summer days?

I think of the women he works with, especially the pretty blonde whom he hired on his range crew. She's a ranching girl, knows about feed and water tanks, no doubt. She doesn't know how Mark calls the geldings in, though. They wouldn't know her voice either, like they know mine.

The lunch hour comes and goes. I feed the kids and me tuna fish, same as yesterday. I mix up a batch of chocolate chip cookie dough called "sweet dreams." Too hot to bake, I decide to wait until tonight, when the temperature will cool. Baking is a wifely thing to do, and it gives me pleasure.

More than twenty-eight hours have passed now since Mark left. I picture him in my mind. He bends down to retrieve a tool, sweat dripping from his brow. He wipes his face, leaving a telltale streak of ash on his forehead. He is dead tired but works at the same steady pace as always. Others, less disciplined, lean too long on their shovels.

Hondo is sitting sentry in the front yard with Freckles next to him. He stands. Freckles watches him then gets up also. I look up the driveway and see the truck pull in. "Daddy's home!" Matt yells. Sarah runs downstairs to primp a little. I walk outside and take his thermos from him. All the water jugs are empty. His face is whiskered and sooty. A gray smudge of ash streaks his forehead. I think of other women but ask only, "Have you eaten?"

He smells of pungent, acrid smoke, and the mudroom fills with the strong odor as he takes off his fire clothes. I hug him, wishing for privacy, wishing I didn't have to wait my turn, wishing I had been with him up in the forest.

"Yeah," he says, "I ate in town. I just want to shower and get some sleep. They could call me back anytime."

I rinse out his water jugs and set them on the counter to drain. Then, changing my mind, I fill the sink with hot soapy water and cleanse the jugs thoroughly, scrubbing the black marks from the plastic.

"The water in the stock tank is too low for the sheep to reach. I couldn't remember how to turn the pump on."

He explains and I listen carefully this time. He heads down to the shower, and I fill the jugs with fresh water and put them in the freezer. Then I go into the bedroom and turn down the covers. The sheets are clean, tight, and crisp. Closing the blinds, I unplug the telephone and sit down on the bed. The room is cool and dark, and I wish, for the moment, that I could be just a wife and not a mother. I want to share his bed with him, enjoy the coolness of his skin next to mine while he drifts off to sleep.

He comes in the room and climbs in bed. "It's sure good to be home."

I know he isn't just referring to the comfortable bed. He means that it is *good* to be home, where his family is, where his wife waits. I wonder if he can sense my presence in the house as I sense his presence in the barn? Do the thoughts that kept me awake last night still linger beneath the sheets?

We kiss.

"I missed you."

"That's good," he answers.

And it is good. It's good to miss one another. For fourteen years it has been good. And for fourteen years he has been glad to come home, and I have been glad to have him home. We are lucky.

I close the door softly behind me. Outside, the sun glares in my unshaded eyes. I can hear the kee-r-r, kee-r-r of a hawk but do not see him. Down at the water tank, I climb the corral fence and reach for the pump's control box. I find the "on" lever and adjust the timer. Water gushes into the tank.

Next time I will remember. I put my hand into the shooting stream of water. It is cold and wet and forceful.

Vicki Lindner

Weather Report

When I moved from New York to Laramie, Wyoming, every afternoon about
three o'clock the sky would broil with coal-colored clouds, and it would rain,
even hail a bit; otherwise the weather was warm and sunny, crisply dry in the
cool summer night. But the Wyomingites I met ignored the pleasant climate
outside and warned me about winter. I rapidly learned that the high desert plains
of the Laramie basin boast the stiffest winds, most frigid temperatures, and deepest snow in the state. I could expect the town's streets to be buried beneath unre-
moved ice from September through April, and highways leading to the Denver
airport to be closed by blizzards for the Christmas holiday, certainly for spring
break. By the time a week of my first western summer had passed, I had heard
the old saying "Wyoming has two seasons — winter and July" more times than I
cared to count.

Everyone took cynical delight in recounting a "weather survival story" to the
urban creative writing professor. My department chairman, a gentle bearded expert on Christopher Smart, suffered his first great adventure when he was bliz-
zarded off a road coated with black ice and forced to hitch to a Rock River motel
shortly after his arrival from temperate Virginia. Wayne the Sheepherder told me
about his girlfriend, also new to the state, who bought seven horses and moved
seventeen miles southwest of town in an initial rush of enthusiasm for authentic
western life; his uncle dug her and her steeds out from under the thirty feet of
snow that buried them in September.

In the course of casual conversation at a picnic, new friends would recall fish-
tailing down Telephone Canyon in the path of jackknifing trucks, or driving
home on the wrong side of Highway 230 in a blizzard because the right side was
blocked by a solid drift. A young biblical scholar from Buffalo and his wife, who
deconstructs Emily Dickinson, described their futile attempt to reach Lake Ta-
hoe via Interstate 80 after a storm. When their Mazda van ran afoul of the notorious winds near Elk Mountain and skidded into a road sign, forcing them to turn
back, they realized for the first time that they were trapped in Laramie. Uneasily
I recalled a San Francisco poet's comment when I told him that I was about to
trade in my career as a freelance writer for some kind of teaching job at the

University of Wyoming — was it "tenure track" or "tenure tract"? He said, "It's *tenure track*, and it means you work like a dog, kiss ass for seven years, then get to spend the rest of your life in Laramie, Wyoming!" I soon found that my student writers' best plots also invoked bad weather: going into labor on the ice-covered "White Knuckle Highway" of the Red Canyon Pass, chainsawing wood in a blizzard, trusting a horse named "Nigger" to navigate home through a storm so dense it blotted out landmarks on a Powder River ranch.

Along with the stories I got plenty of advice. I was told to outfit myself with various combinations of windproof and waterproof down, Thermax, Gore-Tex, Thinsulate, and Polar Fleece from head to foot. A local artist loaned me an Alaskan oil rigger's heavyweight, grease-stained down jacket to wear instead of my Gianni Versace shawl-collared wool coat. The Suzuki Samurai with the ragtop I bought was greeted with dismay, although the minijeep sported the four-wheel drive I had been told was requisite. What I needed, Tim, my next-door neighbor, advised, was a three-quarter-ton pickup that could bulldoze its way through mountainous drifts. As the warm sun, minus East Coast sticky humidity, polished pollution-free skies, I was repeatedly informed how to weight my *vehicle* (the westerner's egalitarian term for four-wheeled private transport — be it pickup or Porsche) with seventy-pound sandbags and to outfit it with a survival kit — a coffee can fueled with candles that would heat like a stove, water, food, and a good-to-forty-below sleeping bag that would prevent me from freezing to death when my Samurai blew off the antarctic black ice like a typhoon-whipped firefly. And I would need an engine-block heater to keep the motor oil from chilling to a gluelike consistency, and should plan to carry my car battery inside at night.

Although winter had reportedly made its reluctant retreat only moments before my July arrival, I detected, beneath the grim stories and warnings, a tone of nostalgic yearning for it to hurry on back. Some commented (with ill-disguised optimism) that the fur on the marmots in the Medicine Bow Mountains indicated that the forthcoming cold season would be the roughest one yet. (I'd heard that one about the fur on the squirrels in Central Park.) Meanwhile, the Yellowstone fires of '88 began darkening the aluminum-bright sky with L.A.-colored smog; my skin burned in the thin, high altitude then developed brown flaky patches — precursors of skin cancer, according to the brochure in my number thirty-three sunblock.

Finding the upcoming winter hard to imagine, I took the ominous weather reports with a grain of salt. This proverbial Wyoming winter, I thought, must serve a psychological purpose in an economically depressed state. Like the murders, muggings, break-ins, cockroaches, and garbage strikes that provide the plots for a New Yorker's survival stories, surviving a hyperbolic winter gave the Wyomingite his claim to superior fortitude. Without a winter horror story, a Wyomingite could not declare himself a true descendant of the mountain man or prairie schooner.

Besides, the harbingers of western winter gloom didn't have the scoop on weather in New York. How could a Wyoming resident, living in air that is cleaner than that of most cities, even when blurred by a hundred-and-twenty-thousand-acre forest fire, appreciate the concept of a ninety-five-degree day when fuzzy air sops up the wet heat like a Turkish towel and coats the glittering towers of the World Trade Center in a glutinous carbon-monoxide aspic? Or imagine a dark December afternoon, when the sherbet wind off the fetid East River ices your instep, encased in the black strappy platforms you have no choice but to wear with a modish micro-miniskirt to the *Cosmopolitan* Christmas party at effete Mr. Chow's? Has any Wyomingite ever tripped over a large cardboard box heaving with the shivers of its human resident? Whereas the snowpack in the remote mountains that feeds the rivers that feed the prairie grasses that feed the cattle and antelope that attract the tourists is a necessary component of a fragile rural economy, weather in New York is a nuisance that has nothing to do with making megabucks in skyscrapers. The New York tax base would surely increase if Manhattan were roofed with a sky-colored Plexiglas dome!

It did snow shortly after Labor Day my first year in Wyoming—a solid, but ephemeral inch, which put out the forest fires—and I immediately purchased a pair of Pacs—heavy fleece-lined rubber galoshes that stick the wearer tenaciously to ice. "You *do* have to have them," the salesgirl at Dodd's Bootery and the customer standing next to the cash register assured me. I let these ugly, expensive polar bear paws offend fashion in the closet for a week, waited for the October blizzard that froze the Willie's Handcart party of emigrant Mormons in 1856, and when it didn't arrive, I took them back. That first spritz of snow was followed by a balmy Indian summer; sparse islands of cottonwood and aspen turned an acid saffron amidst the mauve and sage shadows of the prairie. I drove to the Cowboy Poetry Gathering in Riverton that November without witnessing a flake. The shearling-lined leather jacket I'd sprung for on a humid June day when the Orchard Street salesgirl promised, "If you are serious about this jacket and are prepared to pay cash, I'll make you an offer you cannot refuse," malingered in its garment bag. Westerners cast worried glances at the snowless skies and recited tales of other gruesome winters that started late. They reminded each other that the state gets most of its *moisture* (the egalitarian term for snow, rain, hail, and sleet) in March and April. Gradually I began to hear rumors of the truth: there hadn't been a classic freezing, snow-abundant winter in Wyoming for a number of years; agriculture and ranching, especially in the eastern and southern parts of the state, were threatened by the drought. Thanks to the global warming trend, which had not exempted Wyoming, the famous Wind River glaciers were melting. When it did snow, it didn't snow enough. Even in December, a balmy forty degrees, my students came to class in T-shirts and shorts.

Finally, a brief winter arrived. I saw flipped-over trucks on the icy road to the airport and comforted an ESL instructor who had smashed into a guardrail. I did experience one forty-eight-hour snowstorm and two weeks of below-zero cold. As the snow pelted and the thermometer dropped, I expected my friends and neighbors to be rubbing mittened hands and chuckling with delight as they awaited an opportunity to escape unscathed from another mythological highway accident. To my surprise, however, Wyomingites complained about the bitter cold — it had never lasted *this* long in recent memory — slipped and fell on the icy streets, shivered, kvetched that they couldn't start their cars, and told me I was deranged to walk four blocks one especially frigid night, though I had a scarf to wrap around my mouth so my throat wouldn't freeze, and I was thoroughly swathed in layers of Gore-Tex and Thermax. But as colleagues stopped by my office to commiserate about the blizzard that had trapped us in Laramie, and bundled-up strangers hunched over frozen engines in the street, I began to understand why reserved westerners like bad weather so much: it provides them with a valid excuse to encounter one another.

In my second year in the West I acquired my own winter weather story. As I learned, you only need one. I was driving home from Santa Fe in the March moisture season, when snow is barely stifled behind a muffler of grey clouds. Highway 287 from Fort Collins to Laramie was dry until I crossed the state line, whereupon a legendary ground blizzard materialized before me, a conjured witch's cauldron of newt's eyes and dry ice. The snow fumed and smoked and streamed across the highway, which I learned — too late to put my car in four-wheel drive and turn tail back to Fort Collins — was thickly coated with invisible black ice. The wind pierced my ear like fingernails scraped across a blackboard; my little jeep, minus sandbags, fishtailed and spun as I steered in the wrong direction and forgot not to brake, and in a nightmare's slow motion, observed rather than felt, it slid off the road and came to rest in a snowbank, facing the wrong direction, but—hard to believe—still right side up. Huge tractor trailers thundered down the lane my car had skidded onto before it went off the road. I squeezed out the small opening the snowbank left for the door, and stood in the middle of a primeval whirlwind on a glacier that could have been there before the origin of molecular life, wearing a Santa Fe costume—black leather jacket, tight jeans, Peter Fox ankle-length boots, and no gloves or hat. I watched a blurred herd of jacquard-print pronghorns threading through the white gusts in single file, as my mind leisurely reviewed the instructions for off-road survival. Unfortunately, I'd forgotten my water, food, and coffee-can stove, shovel and sandbags; I thought I should probably make the supreme effort it seemed it might take to get my hiking boots and Helly Tech water- and windproof suit out of my duffel bag, so I wouldn't freeze to death and then. . . . But I felt as if this adventure was not happening to the woman I thought of as myself—no doubt inventing the scene in the cozy office of her Manhattan apartment with comfortable steam hissing up its pipes—but to a character in a black-and-white silent movie. Perhaps standing in the vortex of a ground blizzard enjoying an archival film is what the next life for the marginally wicked is like.

I was soon rescued by a United Airlines pilot travelling home to his ranch in a three-quarter-ton pickup. The next day Highway 287 was closed, but they let Corky's tow truck through to remove my vehicle and all the others that had blown off the road. Corky said this was the first major bout of towing he'd done this year; if the weather didn't get worse soon, he would go belly-up. I dumped bucketfuls of hot water over the Samurai's engine to wash the snow out, bought a portable shovel at Kmart, and drove as little as possible for quite a while after that.

I write in the cabin I rent in a tiny community called Jelm, overlooking the Big Laramie River and the crumbling granite of low bald mountains, where it is easy to spot white-tailed deer and cruising eagles. A gale-force wind is slamming itself at the frail siding of my glorified shack like a big crazy man in a padded cell. Today it picked up the smokestack on the chimney as if it were a Frisbee and blew it out of sight; then it snatched aluminum flashing off the roof, twisting it into a strand of fusilli. I contemplate the knee-jerk metaphors writers use to describe wind—"howling" or "screaming" or "whistling" or "shrieking"—and am convinced these predictable personifications are false. The wind does make disturbing noises, but it is not its sounds that make you feel trapped in a private still center, but its physical force — buffeting, pushing, slamming, Bruce Lee punches and kicks. I wasn't able to get to the annual Fig Roast last night, because it was thirty below and my vehicle wouldn't start. I put my warmest wool dress on over my long underwear and under my shearling leather jacket and North Face down vest, and laced Thinsulate-lined hiking shoes over thermal socks, gathered the cake I had baked between triple-layer mittens, maneuvered my bulk into the plastic car seat, frozen to the consistency of a Popsicle, and pressed in the clutch. But the trusty Samurai couldn't so much as clear the pneumatic phlegm out of its throat. I went back inside and spent the evening in the rocker in front of the woodstove, ate most of the cake, and made another determined stab at becoming an alcoholic. I don't feel that sorry to be alone and trapped. For entertainment on nights like these I think, read, and play with Moonbeam the Cat. Television reception in these mountains requires a twenty-five-hundred-dollar satellite dish.

When my friends call from New York with exciting urban tales about museum exhibitions, gallery openings, movies, and plays they've seen, and the famous people they've met at the *Cosmopolitan* Christmas party, I offer them a Wyoming weather report. I tell them how it snowed sixteen soggy inches in the beginning of October, and Big Pete, who cuts my wood, said that same snow would be on the ground until May; we could look forward to the worst winter yet. In a deceptively matter-of-fact tone I describe weighting my Samurai with sandbags and equipping it with water, food, and a coffee-can stove. I recount driving home through ground blizzards that whirl up in front of my car like dervishes and obliterate all visibility, feeling my way back to the frozen river by the guide lights that mark the edge of the road. (I don't tell them that after one such adventure I slept in my office at night if I intuited so much as a single snowflake or puff of wind.) And if there's no current news, I revive the weather story that made me a legitimate mountain woman — how I blew off 287 last March. I don't mention that in three days the temperature is predicted to hit fifty, the glaciers are still melting, and the snowpack is below normal again this year.

John D. Nesbitt

Keep the Wind in Your Face

This is a story about a small-time big-game hunting guide whose name is Del. In this first part, he is out on the hunt, leading some horses after leaving off his hunters.

Del took the horses on about another half mile, coming to a stop in a grassy swale. He slipped bridles from Spud and Whisker, and he snapped on their lead ropes. Then he loosened their cinches and let them graze. Little Tulip, who took a hackamore rather than a mouth bit, grazed with the other two. Del wandered with the horses, keeping the lead ropes clear, listening to the dry munching sound as they put hooves and teeth to the brittle grass. The sun warmed him as he meandered backward, enjoying the idleness that the horses fell into so easily.

When he judged that half an hour had passed, Del snugged Little Tulip's cinch and mounted up. He tugged on the lead ropes to get his party in motion, and the group made its way to the road that, as the horses also knew, led to the bottom and then on out the other side and back to camp. It was not a well-worn road. Except in some places where the ruts were deep, it was smooth and mostly grassy. The group made its way quietly, dipping in and out of shadows. Little Tulip shied long enough to recognize a twisted stick for what it was, and then they all moved on.

Del enjoyed the cool shadowed smell of dust and grass and sagebrush, along with the saddle creak and the scuffle-clop of the horses' hooves. In the spare, quiet reaches of the autumn rangeland, life stretched out wide and open on all sides, hemmed in by nothing more than a grassed-over road and a dry creek bottom. A fellow could cut loose and drift out of himself, hover with the afternoon, and yet never leave himself or the watch he kept on the land. It pleased him to imagine his hunters, at a liberal distance from him and from one another, taking in the rippled, shadowy world in quiet solitude.

Del was rolling down his sleeves and buttoning his cuffs when Little Tulip stopped under him. Spud and Whisker had halted as well. Down the trail on the right, less than a hundred yards, a three-point buck stood autumn blue in the long shade of the rim. Del exhaled softly, his breath nearly whistling through his teeth and rounded lips. Little Tulip flickered her ears at the sound but held still. Del's gaze moved in a quick curlicue, taking in the antlers and the vital spot before resting on the eyes. The deer, standing broadside, had his head turned to stare directly at the man. Del relaxed in the saddle but kept his eyes matched with the deer's. Behind those eyes, behind the dark-haired skull plate, there worked a series of impressions. The deer would not know why two saddles were empty, why the man looked like a cowboy instead of a killer.

Spud breathed out heavily, Whisker swished his tail, and still the buck stood frozen. The guide relaxed his gaze, and then the buck turned to jog away. He moved into a bouncing trot, his antlers moving up and down and occasionally clearing the shadows and catching the afternoon sun.

You're on your own, Del thought. The deer had been moving north before it stopped, and now it kept that direction. Depending on how the hunters had moved, their paths might cross.

The guide got down from his horse and led the way down the trail. He paused where the buck had crossed, scanning the ground for a bare spot that would show a hoofprint. He found one. It was always interesting to see the track and know which animal it came from. The buck had been average-sized, bigger than a doe, but from looking at the track just by itself the guide would not have been able to say, with any certainty, whether a buck or doe had left it.

Del rose from his study and walked on, with Little Tulip on his right and the other two on his left. Every twenty or thirty yards he stopped to listen. When the shot came it was louder than he expected, first a crash and then an echo as it rippled across the cool air of early evening. The horses all flinched and then came to a standstill. Del waited with them, but no more shots followed, so after a long minute or two of silence he stepped into the saddle and moved them all north.

(Del gets the deer back to camp, which is an old ranch house. Ken, the man who does most of the talking in the next part, is a restaurant manager who has already gotten his deer and who is working on his eighth beer or so. Also present are Len and Chick Becker (brothers) and Ken's son Kenny.)

The Beckers were drinking whiskey and 7 Up as they scratched out a map of the country they had studied that day. Del washed dishes and listened with half an ear to Ken's monologues.

"Shit yes, it's been twenty-six years, and I can see those milk bottles just as clear as if one was sitting right here. They had *Moon Lake* written across the top of the wide part, the body, you know. *Moon Lake* in dark blue letters. And beneath that there was a picture of a pretty girl sitting with her butt to us, leaning on her right arm. She was sitting on the edge of a little lake or lagoon, looking across it at a crescent moon. *Moon Lake.* I can see it clear as day. I got up every morning at three o'clock and delivered those damn things all over town."

Len looked up from his map. "You delivered milk?"

"Yeah. My first year out of high school. I had my own route, my own customers, my own accounts. I delivered it in these glass bottles, with a label in dark blue letters painted right on the bottle. *Moon Lake.* Then after about a year they went from bottles to cartons, and they had stacks and stacks of those worthless bottles. I used to take them out to Walnut Creek, which was way the hell out in the boonies then, and shoot 'em up with a .22. I bet I shot a couple of thousand of 'em. And you know what?"

"What?" Len went along.

"I haven't seen one of the sons of bitches for over twenty years."

"Those old milk bottles are worth something now," Chick declared. "People use them for wine carafes. They're probably worth ten dollars each."

"At least," Len said. "That's what you get your ice water in when you go to one of those restaurants with a high h.p.q."

"What's that?" Kenny asked.

"Hanging plant quotient. You know, the kind of place with a lot of hanging plants and ceiling fans and brass fixtures." Len smiled. "You see a lot of those old milk bottles in those kind of places. Classy, you know, in a down-home way."

"Shit," Ken muttered. "I bet I busted enough of them to furnish all my steak houses with carafes, and then some. And every damn one of 'em is shot to smithereens. I bet I destroyed two thousand of 'em."

"Well, they're gone now," Len said, "but I'll keep an eye out for them, and if I see one, I'll let you know. I have your card. You say the brand is Blue Moon?"

"No, Moon Lake. There's a moon, and a lake, and a pretty girl with her cute little ass poked at you. And it's all in blue."

"I'll keep an eye out for that one."

"Do that, if you would. Moon Lake. But they're probably gone, every last one of 'em."

As Del settled into his sleeping bag later that night, he had a clear image of a girl sitting by a lake, looking at a crescent moon, shining her blue moon of a pretty butt at the customer. Del understood how Ken probably felt, to have been so casual with all those bottles, which seemed so common, and then to realize they were all gone for good. Even if Ken could never get one back, it must make a very good memory.

Joan Puma

Lost in Paradise

The hideout was situated a third of the way down the length of Tupelo Valley, a green, elongated, glaciated (and, therefore, U-shaped) glen about three miles long and, say, a quarter of a mile wide. The valley was nestled at seventy-five hundred feet or so — an altitude that agrees with me. A creek wiggled down the center. On one side a precipitous slope of pines rose abruptly some four hundred feet until it levelled out some and gave way to a flattish high meadow poised right on the edge, hanging over the valley. It looked so smooth and green from down below, locals called it the golf course.

The other side, the sun-skimped north face, much gentler in its inclination, got the brunt of the weather and consequently was done in shades of tan with sage and juniper and cactus clumps and limestone cliffs and caves spotting its six-hundred-foot-high rise. Boxing in the far end of it, where the creek dropped down into the valley from the backcountry and the big ones, were foothills of pine, spruce, and aspen. If you wanted to get up to those big ones, the ten-, eleven-, and twelve-thousand footers and their still receding glaciers, this was the fastest way.

Near the cabins were some boulders and outcroppings of granite small enough to scramble up, high enough to present a fine view of the valley and the winding, deep, trout-inhabited waters of Tupelo Creek, and wide enough to accommodate the several bighorn sheep who, in spite of our presence, visited the little promontory daily while it was still warm. It was pretty much paradise alright. And I got lost there.

I set off one day to see if I could actually go on a hike alone. Back in the city I adored doing cultural things by myself — especially movies, but theater, concerts, art exhibits were fun, too, and had added possibilities of meeting interesting people, which are usually diminished whenever you go anywhere in someone else's company. I didn't mind long-haul solo car trips or bike rides in the country, either, but I never had much interest in hiking by myself. Maybe I should've signed up for Outward Bound instead of all those years in Inward Bound — therapy, that is. Well, anyway, here was the perfect opportunity. The season was over, no tourists or strangers or ax murderers were lurking about, and the weather at the moment was a gift — we were still in the middle of a hot spell — no sudden storms were expected. Of course, sudden storms are never expected.

I set off at nine o'clock for Windy Mountain, at 12,600 feet, the highest peak in this particular part of the Rockies. It was supposed to be a four-hour affair, so I packed my water bottle, a peanut-butter sandwich, and an apple, and took off, not saying a word to anybody. I didn't want company, and I didn't want anyone saying, "Oh, you can't go today. You've got to go into town," so I just left. Okay, I sneaked out.

I figured it was early enough to have time to go up by way of the north side of the valley — the long way. I passed under alleged eagles' nests — dark holes, minicaves in the pockmarked limestone wall that had been pointed out to me as such; I had no personal eagle-spotting experience myself — and sashayed around cactus and sagebrush and junipers, stumbling on loose rock, up, up, up — stopping many times to get my wind — and over the top.

I followed along on the dry ridge for a quarter of a mile and then veered off onto what looked to be a trail that cut through an alpine meadow that sloped gently up and into another meadow and another, which eventually would run into some scattered diehard spruces before even they must surely surrender to tree line. From here I could look off to the east and see the town nine miles away, out to the badlands the big river cut through, and follow the red dirt road snaking off the highway almost to where we had bailed out in the pines. The last lupines and paintbrushes of summer were hanging on for dear life, fading fast, but there was something even more engaging lurking in the tufts of grass.

Fossils. The hill, made of genuine original 100 percent ocean floor back in the old days before it got uplifted to become a mountain ridge, abounded in sedimentary rocks, many of which had fossilized coral or bits of shell or shadows or impressions of little shell skeletons embedded in them. I picked my way across the field — literally — with a fervor that helped me understand the "rush" in Gold Rush.

Apparently this fervor doesn't strike everybody, but it runs strong in me. Gathering rocks feels to me like what compulsive gambling must feel like — I'm unable to stop myself if the conditions are right. If I'm walking or hiking while away on a trip someplace and if the surroundings or the company happen to be sufficiently moving and the rocks particularly interesting and indigenous or the shells abundant and intact, I tend to constant bending over to pick up specimens — forgetting momentarily the goal of the walk or the hike — filling my pants pockets, shirt pockets, jacket pockets, daypack, and fists. Sometimes my blue jeans become too full and tight for me to walk. I used to take photographs whenever I travelled someplace, but for the last several years, I've taken rocks. Of course, this doesn't work in the city — only in the country, the hills, the woods, the beach.

I know several women who collect rocks, which has sort of slowly astonished me over the years as I made the discovery. I mean, sure, *I* collect them, but I had no idea how rampant the practice was. And many of these women were not now nor have ever been tomboys. What is it with these rocks, rock totems?

Many rock women and rock men I know have little shrines in or on or around which their rocks and shells sit — in baskets, on top of chests, in particular arrangements, patterns, configurations, resting on special mats or weavings. I'm convinced the impulse to pick up rocks and take them home is transcendental in origin, for us a backhanded way, disguised in late twentieth-century denial, that allows us to recognize, on some unspoken, unacknowledged level, that rocks are spiritual, are life. We can't pick up chipmunks and take them home or place them on our dashboards, so we bring home rocks.

My own personal stash of clamshells, conch shells, nautilus shells, sand dollars, wampum, igneous rocks, sedimentary rocks, metamorphic rocks, rocks shaped like slabs, like a potato, like the Buddha, like a Thurber dog, rocks with quartz crystals, rocks streaked with iron, rocks pink and aqua and black, rocks from New York, from Virginia, Texas, California, Wyoming, Utah, Florida, Montana, Hawaii, Idaho, and points in between, arrowheads from the National Museum of Natural History, a ten-year-old-but-still-barely-fragrant juniper stub, and assorted pinecones is kept in a large shallow, round basket and in a couple of leather pouches hanging in a closet, since they won't all fit in the basket. Each time I've moved, I've arranged these rocks and shells and cones in the basket quickly and in a way that seemed significant somehow or ritualistic or "right" and that "came to me," "hit me," like automatic writing, choosing what direction to place one or another, which ones to lie next to which, which ones to balance on top of others.

Eventually, I came to my senses and realized I couldn't carry that many rocks the rest of the way up Windy Mountain, or, for that matter, down either. And besides, it would be wrong to remove that many artifacts from their site. Rock-naturalist wags I've met in the woods call such a find a Leverite: "Leverite there." I know rock men, though, who have taken six- to eight-inch rock slabs, even eighteen-inch miniboulders, away with them. Too big for their pockets, they carry them out in their two hands or design conveyances for their transport—but this is not rock collecting, this is plunder. So I took all the rocks out of my pockets and pack and shuffled through them carefully until I finally found my favorite three. I scattered the rest as I continued on, which wasn't exactly the right thing to do, either, as even just moving a rock from its true site could be a cosmic no-no.

I got the water bottle out of my pack and took a slug and wished I'd brought a bigger bottle. Oh, well, I thought, I'll be back by three.

After several months in the West it began to occur to me what I now wanted out of life: to live with the pines and to be able to get lost. You couldn't really get lost in the city if you knew it well. Oh, there was the rare occasion when, say, I'd cut through a blockwide building in midtown to get from one street to another without having to walk to the corner, and suddenly a total blank calm would come over me, and for about twenty seconds I wouldn't know where I was. At first I'd frantically try to find the threads of reason and memory, but then I'd just let go and enjoy it. It felt wonderful, actually, all responsibilities stripped away, just dangling, living in the moment, and because I felt lost, that moment consisted of simply breathing. That's what nirvana must feel like.

I had gotten off the trail I had been following when I started picking up rocks, so I walked back in the direction I thought the edge of the ridgeline—and therefore the trail—was, but I couldn't find either one. Unfortunately, I didn't know which direction was which because I hadn't taken note of that particular piece of information, and I didn't have a compass, and the sun was too high in the sky for me to figure it out. But it seemed to me there was only one way to go. Before the fossil field, I'd been heading toward some sparse high-altitude spruces that covered the slope ahead of me in the distance like a badly moth-eaten blanket. I stopped. I had been coming up over a dry limestone-scattered rise and through sagebrush and scrub; the slope in front of me, which had trees, told me I must be on the south side. Going north. Made sense. After all, this wasn't quantum physics. I could figure this out. I sat down on a rock.

For some reason, what came into my head next were the north-south-east-west demarcation systems found in certain Native American or ersatz Native American contexts—in Sioux ceremonial traditions and in the book *Seven Arrows*, which, by the way, I've always liked a lot but which I've never been sure wasn't really the Native American *Lost Horizon*. If I remembered correctly, north was white; south, green; east, yellow; and west, black. Or was it white, *red*, yellow, and black? In the *Seven Arrows* version, north connotes the mind—wisdom and power; south represents the heart—growth, innocence, trust, and touch, the physicality of life; east, illumination, rebirth, and being able to see the big picture; and west, change and introspection.

I had no idea I remembered this much of it, but then my head still carried around the numbers of friends whose phones had been disconnected in 1976. So, big deal, I remembered it. How would this information, of infinite value I had no doubt, help me at the moment? My memory plunged even deeper. The animal of the north was the buffalo; the south, the mouse; the east, the eagle; the west, the bear.

I closed my eyes and heaved a few slow in-and-outs as calmly as I could. When I opened them, I looked up and quietly jumped as a golden eagle swooped very close to me and then virtually disappeared. I was practically sitting on the ridgeline and didn't know it. My heart dropped into my stomach. My stomach got excited and rippled with waves of expectancy, although I don't know what else on earth I could possibly be expecting now. I'd been waiting for months to see an eagle. This was my first—and at such a cosmic interval of my life. I ran to where I had lost sight of the great bird, which was dark taupe brown—the color of a beaver—and so much larger than the redtails or kestrels I've seen from the highway. I looked over the edge as it slowly flapped its wings matter-of-factly, every little—little for the eagle, that is—flap exuding an enormous sense of power. It must have a nest down there. Just before it got very near to the rock wall, it stopped flapping and resumed a slow glide, gently down the limestone face, its wings held out as it parachuted down the column of air.

There's an old tale certain white tourists—or maybe just me—are told with the greatest of earnestness in Browning, Montana, about how eagle feathers are gathered. I was a tourist at Glacier-Waterton Park for two whole days a few summers ago, travelling with Mrs. Cheesborough—who had said she wanted to "see" Glacier yet made arrangements for only two days. It wasn't enough time. Anyway, on the way back to Great Falls, we stopped at the Museum of the Plains Indian, where I was told the following tale. The young woman who told it to me, a guide, and another older woman who worked the museum cash register were Blackfeet; they both evoked a sense of spirituality—or I had projected it on them—I'd never experienced in any one-on-one interpersonalizing before or since, and certainly not in the gift shop of the Metropolitan Museum.

Anyway, in the gathering of eagle feathers, the gatherer purportedly journeys from the high plains to where the mountain walls rise up—what is now Glacier

Park—toward the end of the summer. On the edge of a rocky ridge the eagle-feather gatherer lays out a fresh kill so tantalizing, so plentiful and abundant, that the eagle who decides to claim it will become so committed to eating it all and, as a result, so full, and, indeed, so heavy from overindulging, it will be unable to fly and will need to sit on this cliff in a sleepy stupor until the digested food works it way out of its body. All the gatherer, who has been hiding until now, has to do then is reach up and pull out as many tail feathers as he or she desires.

Whenever I've told this tale to people I know, they've given me funny looks. The first time I related it to someone, I was brimming with conviction—it had been told to me only a few days earlier and, yes, it had sounded reasonable to me. It was only after the cynical response I got—"You'll believe anything an Indian tells you"—that caused me to entertain the possibility that it might be just a story. By now, whenever I tell it, it is with a great deal of sheepishness, although I still hold out a hope that someone else will find it as plausible as I did that day back in Browning, Montana.

Well, since I had no better alternative, and since I did get to actually see an eagle, and since this eagle *could* be a sign that I was supposed to head east, I did. I veered to my right, searching for a trace of a trail, feeling extremely New Agey. All the while, I was unable to shake the sensation that my destination lay west, to my left, even if my destiny led to the right. But I had to, like, go with this.

Jane Elkington Wohl

The Heart of the Egg

In the penlight's direct beam we see,
through lines and shadows of shell,
the unformed heart beating.
Barbara holds the parrot's egg
so even the children can see the rapid pulse.

She replaces it in the warmer and turns
to the incubators holding new-hatched parrot chicks.
Naked bodies flop against each other.
Purple-veined lashless lids cover unseeing eyes.
Heavy heads wobble on scrawny necks.
Beaks open wide for food.

Next summer these African Grays
will live in cages among Wyoming cottonwoods near the creek.
All day they will scream like small children
But now, in Barbara's laundry room.
among mismatched socks and small-sized flowered undies,
we see their hearts beneath loose pink skin.

Later my son and I hike up Tongue River Canyon.
We see only one fisherman before we reach the bridge
where the trail begins long switchbacks up the south side.
At each turn he wants to stop and rest
while I want to climb farther, push on
to see where this trail leads.

We pause by a rock taller than my car.
Its surface is pitted with small holes,
washed out by water or pebbles dropped from old mud.

High on the canyon's wooded wall, we look down
at the narrow stream below us, speculate
about a prehistoric lake, scratch among the dirt for fossils.

"Is this a dinosaur's egg, Mom?" he asks. "Could it be one?
Were they this big?" He stretches his arms
but cannot even span one side of this rock.
I shake my head, no egg.
But I lean against the rough surface,
feel it scrape against my cheek,
and listen for an ancient heart.

I remember this in the airplane,
looking down at the country north of Cheyenne
where water courses lace
late summer evening hills.
I follow each stream for miles,
through irrigation ditches, up hills to the source.

I see faint tracks crossing land and remember
that the Oregon Trail is still visible from the air.
I know this country as we fly over Douglas, Gillette, Clearmont.
Route 16 joins Route 14 east of town.
Cat Creek winds red through fields
of big round hay bales
their shadows stretching out eastward,
long black ovals.

Across this bumpy surface, rough as eggshell,
streams, roads, trails vein and shadow in the light.
I press against the small, thick airplane window,
looking hard at the steady evening sun,
shining straight across the curving land.

Contributors

ARIZONA

JAMES CERVANTES's latest volume of poetry, *The Headlong Future*, was the winner of the 1987 Capricorn Poetry Prize and was published by New Rivers Press in 1990. After much wandering, he has settled in Mesa, Arizona, and teaches at Mesa Community College.

JEANNE E. CLARK was born and raised in northwest Ohio. She holds a B.A. in English and an M.F.A. in creative writing from Arizona State University. She is currently on the Artists-in-Education roster for the Arizona Commission on the Arts and teaches at Arizona State University.

WILLIAM CLIPMAN is a poet, percussionist, composer, maskmaker, story-teller, and educator from Tucson. He holds a B.A. from Syracuse University and an M.F.A. from the University of Arizona. He works as an artist-in-residence with the Arizona Commission on the Arts and as a performing artist with young audiences. His publications include a book of poems, *Dog Light*, from Wesleyan University Press, and three solo recordings on the Stillpoint Music label.

DENNIS HICKMAN was born in the Northwest and spent his childhood in Idaho and Washington State. He attended Washington State University, the University of Washington, and Arizona State University and has taught in India, Bahrain, Alaska, and on the Navajo reservation in Arizona. In 1984 he was a cowinner of the Arizona Commission on the Arts fiction fellowship. He lives with his wife and two children in Sierra Vista, Arizona.

CHRISTOPHER MCILROY was born in New York City but moved west when he was six, in 1957. In 1987 he helped found ArtsReach, a nonprofit corporation that conducts creative writing workshops for Native American students. He is also an adjunct faculty member at the University of Arizona and an instructor for the Tucson Writers' Project. "All My Relations" is the title story from his collection published in 1994 by the University of Georgia Press.

RITA MARIA MAGDALENO received her M.A. in English/Creative Writing from the University of Texas at El Paso. She works as a roster artist for the Arizona Commission on the Arts and teaches part-time at Pima Community College in Tucson, where she lives. Her work has appeared in numerous magazines and anthologies.

PAUL MORRIS is a writer and translator whose work has appeared in journals such as *The Black Warrior Review* and *Cumberland Poetry Review*. In 1991 he was awarded a poetry fellowship by the Arizona Commission on the Arts. He works as a marketing writer, has been active in the Arizona Sanctuary Movement, teaches in the creative writing program at Arizona State University, and lives in Tempe.

JONATHAN PENNER is the author of two novels, *Going Blind* and *Natural Order*; a story collection, *Private Parties*; and *The Intelligent Traveler's Guide to Chiribosco*, a guidebook to a nonexistent land. His stories have appeared in *Harper's*, *The Paris Review*, and many other magazines. The recipient of Guggenheim, Fulbright, and NEA fellowships, he teaches fiction writing at the University of Arizona.

JEAN RUKKILA has published essays, poems, short stories, drawings, and photographs in numerous magazines, received several regional writing fellowships, and works in the Arizona Commission on the Arts Artists-in-Education Program. She lives in Patagonia, Arizona.

DEAN STOVER was born in 1953, raised on a farm in Iowa, and moved to Mesa, Arizona, in 1966. He attended Arizona State University and completed his B.A. in English education in 1975, and his M.F.A. in poetry in 1986. In 1991 he received a creative writing fellowship from the Arizona Commission on the Arts. Currently he lives in Phoenix and teaches creative writing and composition at Arizona State University.

JOHN SULLIVAN, a poet and theater artist who lives in Tucson, is a roster artist with the Arizona Commission on the Arts. In 1989 he received a Commission fellowship in poetry, and in 1993 another for playwriting. He is currently associated with Tucson's Theater Degree Zero.

LYNNE WEINBERG-HILL grew up during the 1950s on the south side of Chicago, worked briefly as a junior-high-school English teacher, then as a recruiter for VISTA. She then earned a master's degree in social work from the University of Michigan and moved to Arizona in 1973. She currently leads workshops for the Tucson Writers' Project.

COLORADO

CHIP BISSELL and his wife Donna have presented writing workshops for Grassland Writers. He is a high-school English teacher at Woodland Park, and has published four poetry chapbooks to date.

RAMON DEL CASTILLO has had two books published and works as a columnist for the *Rocky Mountain News*. Recently he was chosen as one of forty authors whose work is featured in *Cool Salsa* (published by Henry Holt, Inc., and edited by Lori M. Carlson). He holds master's degrees in social science and public administration, is close to finishing his Ph.D. in the Graduate School of Public Affairs at the University of Colorado at Denver, and is an adjunct faculty member in the sociology department at Metropolitan State College of Denver.

LORNA DEE CERVANTES, who edits the literary journal *Red Dirt* in Boulder, has published two books of poetry and has received a Patterson Poetry Prize. She teaches at the University of Colorado at Boulder.

JACK COLLOM: "Born in Chicago, 1931, . . . moved to Colorado, graduated Fraser HS ('The Nation's Icebox') in a class of 4, studied Wildlife Management at Colo. S.U., served 4 years USAF. Wrote first poems in Tripoli, Libya. Worked 20 years in factories, then became freelance teacher. Teach at Naropa Institute, occasionally other colleges, specialty is Visiting Poet in Schools. Author of 2 books of/on poetry by children." He has also received NEA creative writing fellowships in 1980 and 1990.

ABELARDO DELGADO, a specialist for the Justice Information Center in Denver, was born in Mexico and brought to the United States in 1943 by his mother. He has a bachelor's degree in secondary education from the University of Texas at El Paso, has taught school from the elementary through college levels, and is an internationally recognized pioneer in Chicano literature. He has received numerous awards not only in the arts, but also for his work in human rights.

MARGIE DOMINGO is a Chicana poet and native of Denver. She has published her poems in three books, *Let My Existence Be Born, Let Me Walk Beside You,* and *Las Mujeres de Aztlan.* She teaches creative writing at Escuela Tlatelolco Centro del Norte in Denver and gives poetry workshops in elementary schools throughout the Denver area.

PATRICIA DUBRAVA has had two books of poems published, as well as essays and short fiction in numerous magazines and anthologies. She reviews for *The Bloomsbury Review* and *The Small Press Review,* and her translations of work by the Mexican poet Elsa Cross will appear in a forthcoming White Pine anthology of Latin American women poets, *These Are Not the Sweet Girls.*

ANTHONY J. GARCIA is the artistic director for El Centro Su Teatro, a Chicano/Latino cultural arts center in Denver. Primarily a playwright and stage director, he is a past Theater Communications Group/National Endowment for the Arts Director Fellow. His play *Sarafin: Cantos y Lagrimas* was the winner of the Best New Play award given by the Denver Drama Critics' Circle.

RACHEL E. HARDING, a native of Atlanta, now lives in Denver. She has an M.F.A. in creative writing from Brown University and has published poems and short fiction in several literary journals. In 1992 she was awarded a fellowship in poetry from the Colorado Council on the Arts, and is currently completing a Ph.D. in history from the University of Colorado at Boulder.

JUDITH JEROME was raised in Texas among a large family of storytellers, has been a piano tuner and technician, and has raised three daughters. In 1993 she was awarded a Colorado Council on the Arts CoVisions project grant, and has been commissioned to write and perform local stories for the cities of Arvada and Lakewood. She has a B.A. in storytelling and mythology from Loretto Heights College and is on the artist rosters for the arts councils of both Colorado and Wyoming.

RICARDO LA FORÉ was born in Trinidad, Colorado, in 1943 and has been active in the Chicano movement since 1969. He is the former executive director of the Colorado Migrant Council and is presently an aide to U.S. Senator Ben Nighthorse Campbell.

JEANNIE MADRID, a performance artist and poet, lives in Arvada and has performed with Poetic Justice and the Colorado Symphony Orchestra.

JACINTA TAITANO MARTENS is a newly published poet who lives in Denver with her husband and has two grown children who are often the subject of her work. She is a co-owner of a chocolate shop and is involved with numerous community boards.

WARDELL MONTGOMERY, JR., lives in Denver, where he works for HUD during the day and performs his role by night as that city's "Urban Folk Poet." He has hosted a television show, written verse plays, and presented workshops on conflict resolution through the performing arts.

JACQUELINE ST. JOAN is an associate with the Rocky Mountain Women's Institute and a graduate student in the Creative Writing Program at the University of Colorado in Boulder. She has presented her work at the Rocky Mountain Book Festival and the Denver Press Club and been published in the *Texas Journal of Women and the Law* and *The Denver Quarterly*. Her recent work focuses on the seven years she served as a county judge and issues of women, law, and literature.

IDAHO

RICK ARDINGER lives in Boise and is the editor of Limberlost Press, a publisher of fine letterpress editions of poetry. A chapbook of his poems, *One Place for Another*, was published by Confluence Press in 1983. His first book-length collection, *Goodbye, Magpie*, is forthcoming from Floating Ink Books.

KIM BARNES was born in Lewiston, Idaho, and grew up along the North Fork of the Clearwater River, where she now lives with her husband, poet Robert Wrigley. She received her B.A. in English from Lewis-Clark State College and an M.A. in English from Washington State University in 1985. She is the coeditor, with Mary Clearman Blew, of *Circle of Women*, an anthology of contemporary western women writers published by Viking Penguin. The memoir from which her piece for this anthology was excerpted is forthcoming from Doubleday.

WILLIAM JOHNSON grew up in the Northwest and currently teaches at Lewis-Clark State College in Lewiston. His poems and essays have appeared in numerous journals and magazines, and he is the author of *What Thoreau Said*, published by the University of Idaho Press. A fly fisherman and amateur naturalist, he "writes about the spirit of place as a means to bring us together."

LESLIE LEEK is an Idaho native who grew up in rural towns where her parents published weekly newspapers. She is a recipient of a literature fellowship from the Idaho Commission on the Arts, and her collection of short stories, *Heart of a Western Woman*, was recently reissued by Blue Scarab Press. Leslie lives in Pocatello, where she teaches in the department of communication and theater at Idaho State University.

RON MCFARLAND was born in southeast Ohio, received B.A. and M.A. degrees from Florida State University, and earned his doctorate from the University of Illinois, specializing in seventeenth-century literature. He was named Idaho's first state writer-in-residence in 1984. He lives in Moscow and is the director of creative writing at the University of Idaho, where he has taught since 1970.

STEVEN E. PUGLISI, who is originally from New Brunswick, New Jersey, has been living in Pocatello since 1976 and is currently a visiting instructor in the department of communication and theater at Idaho State University. His collection of poems, *First Lights*, was published by Blue Scarab Press in 1990.

BOB SCHILD was born in Rexburg, Idaho, attended both the University of Idaho and Colorado State University, and was a full-time rodeo professional for many years, collecting numerous titles. He opened his business, B-B Leather, in 1961, and has often been a featured poet at the Cowboy Poetry Gathering in Elko, Nevada.

WILLIAM STUDEBAKER was born and raised in Salmon, Idaho, and currently lives in Twin Falls. He is the director of the Honors Program at the College of Southern Idaho and has had work published in numerous magazines and journals. When he is not at school, he's wandering the Great Basin/High Desert.

ROBERT WRIGLEY has been poet-in-residence at Lewis-Clark State College in Lewiston since 1977, though he has also taught at the University of Idaho and the University of Oregon. He has twice held the Richard Hugo Chair in Poetry at the University of Montana — where he once studied with Hugo — and lives with his wife, the writer Kim Barnes, on the Clearwater River. His new book is *In the Bank of Beautiful Sins* (Viking Penguin, 1995).

MONTANA

B. J. BUCKLEY "is a Wyoming-born and raised writer who lives near Florence, Montana, with her sweetheart and two huge Newfoundland dogs in an 8 × 17-foot cabin with no electricity or running water (and prefers it that way)."

DAVID CATES's novel, *Hunger in America*, from which this excerpt is taken, was selected by the *New York Times* as one of the Notable Books of 1992. His short stories have appeared in a variety of literary magazines, winning honorable mention in the Pushcart Prizes, among other awards. He lives in Missoula and is a graduate of the University of Montana.

PHIL CONDON was born in Wyoming, raised in Nebraska, and lived in California, British Columbia, and the Missouri Ozarks before moving to Montana in 1987 to earn his M.F.A. in fiction. He received the A. B. Guthrie Award at *Cut-Bank*, was twice nominated for a Pushcart Prize, and was awarded a fiction fellowship from the National Endowment for the Arts in 1993. His first collection of stories, *River Street*, was published by Southern Methodist University Press in 1994.

PETER FONG is a former coeditor-in-chief of *CutBank* magazine, and current editor of the Systemic Initiative for Montana Mathematics and Science, an integrated mathematics reform project. He received an A.B. from Harvard in 1982 and an M.F.A. from the University of Montana in 1992. He lives in the Bitterroot Valley with his family, and this last year he received a fellowship in creative writing from the Montana Arts Council.

PETE FROMM is the author of two short story collections, *The Tall Uncut* and *King of the Mountain*, as well as the novel *Monkey Tag* and the nonfiction work, *Indian Creek Chronicles: A Winter in the Bitterroot Wilderness*. He is the winner of the Pacific Northwest Booksellers Association 1994 Book Award, the Robert Traver Fly Fishing Fiction Award, the 1992 Writer's Voice "New Voices of the West" Writer's Exchange, and *Sierra's* 1991 Nature-Writing Award.

LOWELL JAEGER is a 1981 graduate of the University of Iowa Writers' Workshop and a 1986 recipient of a creative writing fellowship from the National Endowment for the Arts. He is the author of three chapbooks, as well as two full-length collections, *War on War* (1988) and *Hope Against Hope* (1990) from the Utah State University Press. For the past ten years he has taught writing at Flathead Community College in Kalispell.

RUTH RUDNER has had several books appear with different publishers, including Sierra Club Books, Viking, and Dial Press. She has been a journalist, with articles in publications from the *Wall Street Journal* to *Field & Stream* to *Wilderness*, and a contributing editor at *Skiing* and *Self* magazines, among others. She grew up in Rochester, New York, but has lived in Montana for eleven years.

NEVADA

SHAUN T. GRIFFIN lives in Virginia City, directs Nevada's homeless youth education office, and runs a prison poetry workshop. He has edited *Torn by Light*, the selected poems of Joanne de Longchamps (1993), and *Desert Wood: An Anthology of Nevada Poets* (1991), both from the University of Nevada Press. His own collection, *Snowmelt*, was published by the Black Rock Press in 1994.

STEPHEN SHU-NING LIU graduated from Nanking University, came to America in 1952, and earned his M.A. from the University of Texas and his Ph.D. in English from the University of North Dakota. His poems have appeared in numerous magazines and anthologies, and in 1992 he received a poetry fellowship from the National Endowment for the Arts. Since 1973 he has taught at the Community College of Southern Nevada in North Las Vegas.

GAILMARIE PAHMEIER teaches creative writing and literature at the University of Nevada, Reno. She has twice received creative writing fellowships from the Nevada State Council on the Arts, and a collection of her work, *With Respect for Distance*, was published by the Black Rock Press in 1992.

KIRK ROBERTSON is a poet and visual artist who lives in Fallon and has published seventeen books and chapbooks. His revised collection of new and selected poems, *Again & Again*, will be published by the University of Nevada Press next year. He is editor of *neon*, the journal of the Nevada State Council on the Arts, and the weekly music and book reviewer for a local newspaper.

GARY SHORT lives in the office of an abandoned silver mine in American Flat, population nine. He has been a fellow at the Fine Arts Work Center in Provincetown and a 1993–95 Wallace Stegner Fellow at Stanford University. His collection of poems, *Theory of Twilight*, was published by Ahsahta Press in 1994.

NEW MEXICO

HEATHER AHTONE, a Choctaw originally from Oklahoma, graduated from the Institute of American Indian Arts in Santa Fe with a degree in creative writing. She is currently back in Oklahoma to study film.

LEON AUTREY was born into a ranching family in 1941 and owns and operates the Autrey UL Ranch at Chupadera with his wife. He is the author of one book, *I Dreamed Last Night I Seen Daddy*, and has been a featured performer at Cowboy Poetry Gatherings in Elko, Nevada, and Lubbock, Texas, among many others.

JEAN BLACKMON's story "Rescue" won first prize in the *Writer's Digest* Annual Writing Competition, and her work has appeared in many magazines. She writes a column for her hometown newspaper and teaches at the Taos School of Writing. She and her husband live in Corrales, where they own and operate a small grocery store.

ARSENIO CÓRDOVA earned a degree in liberal arts from the New Mexico Highlands University in 1967 and now teaches theater at the Northern New Mexico Community College. He is a poet, storyteller, composer, and choir director who has been featured in *Barrios and Borderlands: Cultures of Latinos and Latinas of the U.S.*, published by Ruttledge. He lives in El Prado.

LARRY GOODELL was born in Roswell, New Mexico, in 1935, received a B.A. from the University of Southern California, and studied with Robert Creeley at the University of New Mexico. He has been an active organizer of poetry reading series, a teacher, publisher, and editor. Among his books and cassette tapes is *Firecracker Soup (Poems 1980–1987)*, published by Cinco Puntas Press in 1990. He lives in Placitas.

KENDALL MCCOOK, the son of a farm and ranch family, was born in Clayton, New Mexico, in 1945 and now owns a farm in Springer. He earned a B.A. in English from the University of Texas in Austin, then an M.A. from the University of Wyoming. After teaching for many years at both secondary and college levels, he published his first collection of stories, *This Land*, in 1984, and then a second, *What Price Paradise*, in 1987. A play, *I Wish You Well*, was produced in 1989. He continues to publish and perform "on stage, in coffeehouses, art galleries, and cabarets."

ROBERTA COURTNEY MEYERS is a multimedia artist who lives and teaches in Taos. She has had five books of poetry published and eighteen of her dramas and musicals produced in several states. She is the editor of Moonfire Press.

TERRY SONG grew up on a small farm in West Texas in the 1950s and early 1960s then moved to southwestern New Mexico, where her family still farms. She earned undergraduate and graduate degrees from Eastern New Mexico University and New Mexico State University, respectively, and now lives in Las Cruces, where she teaches writing and children's literature at New Mexico State University.

KAREN THIBODEAU works in theater, puppetry, and storytelling. She writes and directs plays for the Taos Children's Theater and travels as a puppeteer in the schools for the New Mexico Arts Division.

UTAH

MERRY ADAMS is originally from Kansas but now lives in Blanding and teaches at the College of Eastern Utah, San Juan Campus, "a tiny, unique institution, serving a 65 percent Native American student body." She has published in several regional journals and magazines, and "Winter Camp" has been accepted for publication by the Utah Centennial Project, edited by Terry Tempest Williams and Tom Lyons.

TOM AUSTIN writes novels, magazine articles, and essays and has won several awards from the Utah Arts Council. He is currently serving as both police chief and city manager for Santaquin City. He is the "eccentric" older brother of the "artsy" Merry Adams.

KATE BOYES serves as the assistant editor of *Western American Literature* in Logan, Utah. Her writing has been published in regional and national journals and has been broadcast on several radio programs. She currently lives in the Bear River Range, in a cabin without electricity or running water, while she works on a collection of nature essays.

KEN BREWER, an award-winning poet and essayist, lives in Thatcher. He teaches creative writing and serves as the director of graduate studies in the English Department at Utah State University. He has had six books of poetry published and has conducted over a hundred readings, workshops, and seminars throughout the western states.

MARILYN BROWN won the 1991 Utah State Fine Arts Novel Prize for the story about her youth in Provo, *Road to Covered Bridge*, a chapter of which is excerpted in this anthology. Her publications include three books of poetry and four novels, and she is under contract with Aspen Books for a children's book, *The Queen's Lettuce*, to be illustrated by her daughter, Simeen.

KATHARINE COLES's second book of poems, *A History of the Garden*, will be published in 1995. Her poetry and fiction have appeared in *The Paris Review, Poetry, North American Review, The New Republic,* and elsewhere. She has received both a fellowship and a project grant from the National Endowment for the Arts, and in 1994 she was awarded Salt Lake City's Mayor's Award for the Arts.

DAVID LEE "lives quietly in St. George, Utah, with Jan, Jon, and Jodee, where he hikes and/or runs the country roads and trails and scribbles, all at about the same rate and pace. The poems are from a new ms., *My Town*, which is scheduled for 1995 publication by Copper Canyon Press."

PATRICIA MCCONNEL is the author of *Sing Soft, Sing Loud* (Atheneum, 1989), and numerous short stories and essays. She is the winner of two creative writing fellowships from the National Endowment for the Arts and other awards. She is presently working on a novel about a woman travelling alone and on foot in the desert of southeastern Utah in the mid-thirties. She lives in Blanding.

WYOMING

LAURIE ANN IHM is a storyteller who lives in Lander. She holds a B.A. in geography, with French and English minors, and is completing a master's degree concerning the Northern Arapaho language movement. She is an artist-in-residence for the Wyoming Arts Council and a speaker sponsored by the Wyoming Council for the Humanities.

RICK KEMPA is a poet and essayist living in Rock Springs. His work has appeared in *New Letters, High Plains Literary Review, Denver Quarterly*, and elsewhere. He teaches at Western Wyoming College.

PAGE LAMBERT, a Colorado native, lives on a small ranch in the Black Hills of Wyoming. She received a 1993 literary fellowship from the Wyoming Arts Council and has an excerpt from her nonfiction book, *In Search of Kinship*, in the anthology *The Stories That Shape Us: Contemporary Women Write about the West* (edited by Theresa Jordan and Jim Hepworth, W. W. Norton, 1995). Her first novel of the West, *Shifting Stars*, an 1850 historical story set in Wyoming, is forthcoming from Fulcrum Publishing.

VICKI LINDNER teaches writing and directs the Visiting Writers Program for the English Department at the University of Wyoming. She is author of a novel, *Outlaw Games* (Dial Press, 1982), and has published numerous short stories, essays, and articles in magazines ranging from *Omni* to *Paris Review*. She has received grants from the National Endowment for the Arts, the New York Foundation for the Arts, and the Wyoming Council on the Arts.

JOHN D. NESBITT teaches English and Spanish at Eastern Wyoming College in Torrington. His short stories, works of nonfiction, and poetry have appeared in numerous magazines and anthologies, and a western novel, *One-Eyed Cowboy Wild*, has been published by Walker and Co. He has received a Wyoming Arts Council literary fellowship.

JOAN PUMA, a novelist, poet, and playwright, spent her first twenty years in Texas and the next twenty in New York, where for fourteen years she was "Night Life" reporter for *The New Yorker*. She has published fiction in *Grand Street*, has a story forthcoming in *Weber Studies*, and had two plays produced; she has also taught creative writing at the University of Virginia Writers Workshop and Sheridan College, and been an artist-in-residence in numerous locations. She moved to Buffalo, Wyoming, in 1990.

JANE ELKINGTON WOHL lives in Sheridan and is a Ph.D. candidate in creative writing at the Union Institute. She is codirector of the Young Writers Camp sponsored by the Sheridan YMCA, has read in Billings as part of The Writer's Voice Series, and has been published in numerous small journals.

Credits

Index of Authors and Titles

Western Literature Series

Shoshone Mike
Frank Bergon

Condor Dreams and Other Fictions
Gerald W. Haslam

A Lean Year and Other Stories
Robert Laxalt

Cruising State: Growing Up in Southern California
Christopher Buckley

Kinsella's Man
Richard Stookey

The Big Silence
Bernard Schopen

Winterchill
Ernest J. Finney

The Desert Look
Bernard Schopen

Wild Game
Frank Bergon

Lucky 13: Short Plays about Arizona, Nevada, and Utah
edited by Red Shuttleworth

The Measurable World
Katharine Coles

The Still Empty Grave: Collected Poems
A. Wilber Stevens

TumbleWords: Writers Reading the West
edited by William L. Fox

About the Editor

William L. Fox was born in San Diego, lived in Reno for thirty-three years, and currently resides in Santa Fe, New Mexico. He edited the *West Coast Poetry Review* and Press, was executive director of the Nevada State Council on the Arts, and has had thirteen collections of poetry published in three countries. He is literary consultant for the University of Nevada Press, writes frequently about the visual arts, and gives readings and lectures throughout the West.